Spinner Magazine Worldwide

Copyright © Dave Henderson
All Rights Reserved

Combo Issue 1/March-April 2019

Vol 1, 2 & 3 revised

IN THIS ISSUE

Dave Henderson

Editor's Note: Well I had elected to transfer the first three issues of the Spinner Magazine Worldwide into one issue filled with great information.

I think the articles in combination found in this issue should give a lot of insight to many. I would hope that I will hear from some of the readers so they can give me some direction on articles by submitting questions to me or requesting things you want to read about.

If you are interested in sending in ideas for articles you would like to read about please let me know.

The next volume of Spinner Magazine #7 will be coming out not long after this combination issues is released.

Hope you enjoy as I have added some new photos and revised the content.
davesrollerpigeons@gmail.com if you have questions or requests

Spinner Magazine Worldwide
Volume 1   May – June 2015

Bird bred/owned by Nerm Hebib of North Carolina

Kit Competition Needs a Fix

By
Dave Henderson

Kit competition as we all know started in the UK in the 1920's and here in Northern California, where I live, we started flying kit competition around 1979 with the Northern California Roller Club. I started flying kit competition myself in 1980 and have pretty much been doing it ever since then. I find it very challenging and gives us that extra incentive to continue to progress our programs. I also greatly enjoy the association (brotherhood) to other fanciers and sharing our ideas and knowledge. I think this is what makes flying the Birmingham Roller far superior in comparison to our racing pigeon counterparts. The best part is we get to enjoy our birds in our own back yards above all else and see them at their best.

Norm Reed and I around 1995 when he judged our WC regional event

The biggest kit competition contest when I was coming into this sport was the Northwest International Fly that was a contest the put Canada Flyers vs. American Flyers in the Great Northwest; Oregon, Washington vs. Canada. This contest had started in 1969 and unfortunately it ended around 2005 with the onset of a huge BOP issue and the death of Monty Neible in that region of the US/Canada. This contest started in part by the late Monty Neible and Joe Houghton just to name a few. There have always been a nice hot bed of fanciers in the Northwest but things are changing that way in part to the heavy falcon problems that are not getting any better. This is just part of the sport/hobby now.

The Northwest International is the father of our very own World Cup Fly that has been going on since 1991. Norm Reed won the Northwest International the year before it became the World Cup. The World Cup brought on a huge influx of participation and excitement around the world in regards to the flying Birmingham Roller. The inaugural World Cup event was in fact won by Monty Neible in 1991, one of the founders of the Northwest International. The rules were also new and brought to us by Doc Reimann of Idaho which had us counting the birds in groups of 5 or more and even rewarded better kits with bonus multipliers that was also a new thing. These rules are still with us today after 24 years.

The World Cup "grew up" in the world of the internet and this had everything booming to new highs and now with all the exchange of information worldwide via the world wide web we have seen a huge drop in printed material like the; American Pigeon Journal, the Roller Journal and several large clubs that put out fantastic bulletin. The Purebred Pigeon magazine is the only worldwide magazine in existence today.

Just like most hobbies or leisure past times, they have their ups and downs in terms of participation and popularity. Yes we have more regions but the participation in the US has fallen greatly on the East Coast of the US. Some regions of the US are nearly impossible to keep a good kit together with yearlong BOP issues. I know many will say that we have perpetuated this problem by not locking down our birds enough which has kept these predators well fed. The World Cup has really not grown since the 2004 (possibly longer) season and I fear it could be stemming from more than the BOP issues.

Where the World Cup has faltered here in the US, the National Birmingham Roller Club has found a nitch with their 11 bird individual contest that seems to be gaining popularity here in the US. This contest in certain parts of the country is dominating but places like where I am from it has still not taken off at all. This individual contest that is part of the National Championship Fly (NCF) series is filling that void where the World Cup once did. It's a shame but this is how things are moving in many parts of the US today.

I think part of this has to do with the fact that the US has lost its dominance in this event and some are grasping at straws, trying to figure out why, when the US largely helped to get this event off the ground for the most part. I think there are some out there that feel we are not getting a fair shake in this contest any longer. It's hard to really pin it down but the US has not won the event since 2008 season.

The biggest issue I see in the results is that we are getting too much wasted action in our kits, or in other words too much waterfall breaking. Most of the best US teams are only averaging around 5-6 bird breaks when the UK and Euro kits are averaging 7-8 bird breaks and it does not even matter where the judge is form. We are on par with the quality and depth but not in pure breaking ability. I am sure this is a selection process issue and maybe even a cultural thing amongst the US kits at times. I am confident that the US kits will eventually catch up, but with all that is going on we may not have enough time, before the entire event comes apart. I would truly hate to see this happen and this is in part why I am writing this article to wake people up.

In 2004 the World Cup had 26 regions and 679 participants (902 total kits entered 24% had 2 kits) and 68 finalists and in 2014 we had 720 participants (1140 total kits 37% entered 2 kits), 52 regions and 72 finalists. As you can see it's been pretty stagnant for growth for the past 10 years at least, but what you don't see is that the US lost no less than 98 flyers that participated back in in 2004 and we have not got them back. If we had not lost these flyers we would be up to around 859-900 participants at this point. The growth in the World Cup has been for the most part - international, which is not a bad thing. I just anticipate we will continue to see a decline in the WC here in the US for various reasons unless we are able to reverse this trend. In 2014 there were 8 of the 53 regions listed did not fly due to lack of participation and there are already 5 regions (8 with the loss of 3 regions after 2 years of no flights) that did not get enough participation to fly for 2015, plus 3 regions were lost this year as well. If a region does not have a fly after 2 years then the World Cup drops the region from the schedule and the region will have to reapply to participate later down the road once it picks up, if it picks up?

I think there should possibly be some research done to find out why participation is dropping in regions that have flown in the World Cup for many years and even why other regions are not competing to their full potential. This could possibly get to the bottom of why things are changing for the worse. I don't think things will die off over night but I think we should do all we can to prevent this early, "head it off at the pass". The World Cup General Coordinator, Adrian Gasparini, also feels the same and you will see this statement in the upcoming World Cup Year Book that will release very soon. Pretty much the World Cup has peaked and now it's going downhill. Now how fast it goes downhill is up to us and the regions involved.

I see several things going on that could be influencing the World Cup here in the US. I know the ever increasing birds of prey is a big issue but I don't think this is the biggest issue for the most part. I think there's a combination of things all at play at the same time. We have many that don't think the US is getting a fair shake by always flying last in the World Cup finals, we have rumors of said cheating in some regions that is giving guys an unfair advantage over the rest of the field at the regional level. I think the rumors of cheating will greatly hurt things in the long run especially when the WC EC is not addressing these issues long term. As noted it appears that up to 15 regions could possibly be flying the same kit twice. I will address more of these issues later in this article.

In 2004 we averaged 26 flyers and per region and 34 kits entered per region. In 2014 we averaged 13.8 flyers per region and 22 kits entered per region, you can obviously see more manipulating by regions flying a 2nd kit (many I consider ghost kits) in 2014. Out of the 420 2nd kits entered; 124 (30%) were either DQ or zeros, 156 (37%) were DNF and actually 10 (2.3%) #2 kits won their regions. The remaining 130 (31%) 2nd kits got on the score sheets at various spots, and in several regions more #2 kits finished in the top 50% then #1 kits. That is 57% of the 2nd kits entered are not doing anything but bring in extra money to the WC. The entries of a 2nd kits amount to 58% of the fly revenue also and this is why they are allowed, but we can make allowances to fix this issue quite easily.

I counted a total of 8 regions in 2014 that did not yield enough flyers to hold a regional contest and another 4 regions that are very weak having 10 or less participants. Should we lose these 12 regions in the next few years this would take us down to 40 regions? If you look at it from a financial angle the world cup stands to lose a lot of money if we can't get ahead of these issues that is plaguing the participation here in the US. We all know that in the US there is the NCF and the Euro Fly overseas already in place that would continue to go on should the World Cup fail.

WC Cheating Exposed...

I know that for the first time, to my knowledge, a region in Northern Ireland entered the World Cup and it was discovered later on that the entire region completely made up and never held a fly. This region is host to a fantastic flyer named Kevin McKinney. Over the last 8 or more years Kevin has been probably one of the most consistent flyers in the World Cup. However due to fanciers dropping out in Northern Ireland, for whatever reason, the region has now gotten to the point where it could no longer support a WC region. Instead of Kevin and their RD informing the WC about this problem they went ahead and made up scores and turned in moneys for a region that didn't even hold a fly. The RD was the official judge and this was how they got away with for as long as they did. Kevin simply paid the $300 fee simply put, bought his way into the World Cup Finals. At the time of the investigation of this, Kevin was actually leading in the 2014 contest. I was told by another UK fancier that Kevin had been caught cheating before and this was why he was no longer flying with the UK region. This just does not shine a good light on Kevin, who also did not step up to defend himself in this situation either. One thing is a fact however that even if Kevin cheated to get in his birds still put up the scores he earned in the finals, how bad is this in comparison to others things? (2018) The World Cup recently changed the rules so that they don't care how many kits are entered only that you have at least 7 flyers to have a region. Is the World Cup maybe missing out on some of the best kits in the World only because they don't have enough to have a REAL region? Are their better kits out there we are not even seeing in competition?

Again many what are participating in the World Cup may not even know this event even transpired...

Admitted Cheating....

When I first got back into the rollers, about 18 months ago now, I started roaming the internet for my roller information fix and got involved with many website discussions. I started noticing some things about specific regions in the World Cup and NCF having individuals state that some flyers were entering 2 kits and simply flying the same kit twice. There was no way to track this as it's an honor system and many regions that had split up over the last 10 years are now smaller geographically and this means they are easier to judge thus allowing these regions to fly all the "A" teams one week and then a week or 2 later fly everyone's "B" teams. This is where the cheating started to happen. I think some want to win so badly they started mixing in a few birds here and there and when no one said anything they said screw it and simply started flying the same kit twice. These contests are only one once per year, so if you kit bombs you have to wait a full year to try again.

I thought to myself I had never heard of this type of cheating last I flew in 2004. The most I had heard of was the entering of "ghost kits" and counting out birds from the original tally, these were really not cheating just the rules were open to allow for it. These were loop holes, you could release 20 birds and if a bird rolled down on release and would not go up to the kit within your first 5 minutes you could call it out of the kit and only score 19. Ghost kits were happening after the fact and there were no rules to stop it from happening. They got hard lined on the total you entered and if you said there so 19 in the kit and you only released 18 you were DQ'd in the new guidelines. Ghost kits are still allowed but you have to enter them in advance as opposed to after the competition had completed now. Basically the RD's now have to plan ahead for ghost kits. *(New WC guidelines don't care if there are extra kits flown, the fees are all the same and based on how many REAL flyers enter)*

As an example; the rules allow for regions to enter 8 flyers and then allows for them to enter up to 8 extra kits that Do Not Fly (DNF), you only need 7 more kits to get an a qualifier for your own region. This is termed "Ghost kits" in the fly circuit. There are also rules in place that state if the birds get a DQ or a zero score, flyers in that region can still get Master Flyer points and DNF kits do not give you Master Flyer points, at least this is how I think it explained to me? This is in my view just manipulating the rules to benefit the region and its flyers. These are minor manipulations that I am sure go on all the time and some may not even realize these details, but Kevin in Northern Ireland took it to the next level and got caught.

Recently, back in December of 2014, there was an individual that actually came forward and said that his entire region was flying the same kit twice and they had been doing this since 2007. This occurred on an online forum and even the NBRC President, Cliff Ball, questioned this individual about his statement which started an entire flurry of issues involving this region, this poster simply sees nothing wrong with doing all they can to push thru the best kits to the finals. I am certain this is and has happened but an entire region doing it seems uncertain to me.

Due to various forms of "cheating under the rules", or manipulating the system, guys started learning other ways to gain an advantage. There are always those that look at the rules and try to figure out a way to get an advantage in the competition where there is no clear written rule. It does not take long to do this when if the RD says its ok they do it even if they are not advertising it. The rules state specifically that not even 1 bird can be flown twice but it has not been enforced over the years so in a way it's a "loop hole". The guys in certain regions know who is doing this and it could very well be that specific regions are ALL doing it, and due to everyone being allowed to do it in their region they think it's ok. So part of our "lack of participation" could very well be coming from the regions that know that specific flyers are in fact flying the same kit twice and know that it will be hard to beat a kit that gets 2 chances to advance when you are playing the rules and they are not. I have heard that some have questioned this over the years but were told if they reported it that they would risk physical harm if they told anyone outside of their region filing an official complaint. The one that complains tend to always be exposed at some point and then they suffer from this.

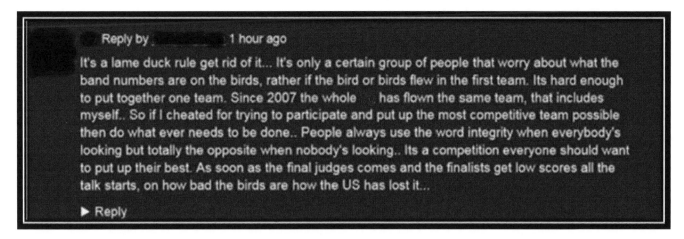

Here is the initial post that occurred on chat blog, it is only shown here as proof this incident really happened. I have the original unaltered one saved as this one is altered slightly

We really have no choice but to eliminate allowing a 2nd kit flown, unless it's flown directly after the 1st one lands. There is really no sure way to eliminate the cheating without dropping this 2nd kit. This is plenty doable so long as we drop the qualifiers to 1 in 10 instead of 1 in 15 like it is now. **(New WC rules is 1 per 7 flyers)** There will be slightly less qualifiers at first but with the splitting of larger regions it will equalize in a few short years. We will also need a waiver system in place to allow smaller regions of say 7 or 8 (or less) to fly but they will be forced to pay a penalty as a way to encourage them to stir up more flyers. I will discuss more of this below.

I sat down and begin to brain storm about how a region could get away with flying the same kit twice and started to comb the archives. It did not take long before I saw the signs of this going on. What surprised me the most was that it is even possible that up to 15 regions could be doing it, and these 15 regions are only from the 2014 season. I had heard that some guys had been doing it going back to the 2004 season and now after seeing how easy it is to do I can believe it.

There are obvious signs that this is going on in some regions, especially in the regions that are known to have a very high BOP issues for the majority of the year. What you see is more #2 kits beating out #1 kits, due to the obvious - they are the same kit. The vast majority of 2nd kits are in fact just entered to help get either a single qualifier or a 2nd qualifier, rarely is this kit as competitive as the A team. It has always been like this since the BOP issues have continued to worsen year after year.

What seems very hard to believe is that a region would have 6 out of the top 7 kits in a region be #2 kits like with Southern California, Region 2 South Africa where we have the top 3 spots are #2 kits or like Melbourne Australia where 7 out of top 8 spots were #2 kits? The region of the individual that has admitted this guilt (see above), he himself finished 2nd place with his #2 kit and 4th place with his #1 team in the Southern California region. This does not add up to me and I am not saying they are for sure cheating but the signs of it are sure there for others to assume such things. Activity like this will do more harm long term than anything else.

I recently asked a few that were RD's what type of discussions were going on with the EC in the World Cup and NCF after seeing this admission first hand online. I feel lucky that I copied this posting from this individual so that we can all see proof this occurred. Many out there many not even know this has gone on or is going on. Comes to find out that a few individuals have filed a complaint about this incident and with their complaint form they were told they must have proof of it happening for it to be brought to the table, I say this is a real bs comment. It is obvious this could happen and in fact is happing and all should be done to secure the integrity of these flies. Ignoring the issue like it does not exist is not going to fix it and we will continue to see a drop in participation from it, with the NBRC fly we are really seeing this happening. The NBRC president as I said participated in this discussion and should have stepped to plate on his own to fix it right away. *(The new rule the 2nd kit must fly within 2 hours of the 1st kit)*

Time to Clean up this Mess...

The reason we can't police this is that when a region is doing this sort of cheating, it matters very little to them if they continue to follow the rules or not. I mean they have been getting away with it this for a long time and nothing has happened to them, so there is no incentive to play by the rules after the fact. The only insurance we would have is if the WC was appointing judges to each region and not a region selecting its own judge(s). Also you will be forced to fly your #2 team immediately after your first team (definitely on the same day), which will also cause a great deal of scheduling issues in many regions that are now doing the flies on separate days, the rules clearly state that if a 2nd kit interferes with the guys flying just 1 kit then they cannot fly a 2nd kit. We will also be having to record down every kit bird flown in each kit, which is a great burdon on the RD and the judge and this will also slow down the entire process which in turn will cause a record keeping process at the same time. Not to mention that some fanciers don't even band all their birds with seamless bands, and I don't think banning the flying of unbanded birds is the answer, so this gets me back to the only way to stop the cheating and also speed up the process is to eliminate the entering of a 2nd kit altogether. We will simply have to raise the entry fee for the World Cup to $32 per kit and then drop the qualifiers to 1 in 10 kits flown qualify for the finals. This is very fair and will cover the expenses that the WC was getting from the 2nd kit.

Example; The WC currently gets $20 per kit to fly at the regional level, this affords the finals judge to make the trip to your region. In 2014 there were 1140 kits entered from 720 flyers. 720 flyers times $20 each is $14,400 and there were 420 2nd kits entered for $8400 giving us a grand total of $22,800. If we simply raised the entry fee to $32 per kit this would have brought in $23,040 and if we really wanted we could simply raise this fee to $35 which would generate $25,200. This would really be a minor change as 420 of the 720 flyers are already paying at least $40 to the World Cup on average, it still stay relatively affordable for most. Granted local clubs will possibly have to have fund raisers to help support the judging of the region as we could lose many flyers if the fee goes to $60-70 for a single kit each season, I think if regions can keep with a $45-50 entry fee it can work no doubt about it. RD's just need to delegate more of their work out to helpers/assistants or Local Area Directors like there used to be many years ago. At some point the RD wanted to carry the finals judge around on his own and wanted everyone else to pay for this privilege when organizing a region is a joint effort.

The only real issue would be that we presently have several regions in the World Cup that only have 8 or 9 flyers and this would be a handicap to them, but I think with the use of a waiver system in place we could allow such regions to compete in the future. I mean one of the smallest regions in the US has been yielding one of the most competitive flyers the last 2 seasons in Adrian Taylor of Virginia. We also have Denmark which could get some kits but just not enough with current needs. These changes might help them also.

The waiver system would have a program in it to assist regions is getting more participation. The EC would outline in steps they would need to do each year to keep flying in a region with less than 10, a waiver application would be filled out by the RD and would have to attach proof that they are taking steps to lure more flyers in to their region. Part of this would be making this region advertise rollers in the local or regional newspapers and posting flyers at various feed stores or even pigeon shows within the region they fly in with the hopes of attracting perspective flyers. I think there would even be interest in some racing homer flyers to participate in a "REAL World Wide Competition". The World Cup could even furnish a pamphlets and flyers that could be handed out or posted so that it is something that is uniform from region to region. We know this waiver program might take more than a few years to work in some regions but it can work for the long term health of our World Cup Fly. If we invest in this program now it will pay off big in the future and for many years to come.

These smaller than minimum size regions would also not get any Master Flyer points at the regional level until they get up to the minimum of 10 flyers. A region with less than 10 would also be forced to pay the same $320 or $350 fees as a 10 flyer region does plus another penalty of $70 or more which would cost them for a waiver package to promote rollers in their region. So just the extra fees alone would encourage the region to stir up flyers even if they had to pay part of their entry fee just to get them active as with an 8 flyer region the minimum fees paid to the WC would be between $48 and $52.50 per flyer. If is region can only get 6 flyers one year then the fees would be between $64/$70 per flyers in that specific region. It's not a huge issue allowing these smaller regions in to the World Cup, it is a worldwide event right, as they will be getting their minimum fees to send the World Cup finals judge to that region in the end. My point is by disallowing these small region to enter we might be discarding some of the best birds that have maybe never been seen. I think that under the circumstances the WC EC might want to implement guidelines to operate this type of waiver program and I know at the local regions they could easily have fund raising events to help pay for this event and keep it the best fly in the world.

Regions should really get creative at pigeon shows or club BBQ events to get people active in competition. Many already share their birds and many help all they can all the time. Many new flyers don't feel paying a fee of $40 or more is worth it to them to fly in the event they know they are not ready for. They automatically feel they have no chance in winning against veteran flyers, but also don't realize all the obstacles that many regions are subjected to just to hold a fly, so getting them in and assisting can at times get them on the same page as everyone else when you show them you are there to support them. I know many regions are now doing bird auctions, raffle BBQ events and even lawn shows to draw out people to show up to the events.

Each flyer of the region should be made to donate items of worth to attract out of the area participation. I have heard some regions are making as much as $5,000 a year just making each flyer donate birds to online bird auctions. So there are ways to raise the money needed to help a region reach their full potential.

Current rules of our World Cup Fly (2015)

World Cup Rules Adopted in the fall of 1995, revised Nov 2006, Oct 2011 and spring 2012

I. A region must enter a minimum of 15 paid kits to qualify as an independent entity. At the discretion of the particular region, a flyer may enter a maximum of 2 kits composed of completely different birds as long as other flyers are not disadvantaged by the schedule. Each flyer is allowed to pay and fly 2 kits but each flyer must fly at least one kit out of the 2 entered. If a flyer has paid for a kit(s) but due to circumstances is unable to fly he must notify the judge as to the reason, or his paid kit or kits cannot be used for the number of kits for a fly-off representative. Each region must fly a minimum of 50 percent of the kits entered for each flyoff representative, (an example is: 8 flyers paying for 2 kits each equals 16 kits which equal one fly-off representative, 15 flyers paying 2 kits equals 2 fly-off representatives, etc.) no region may pay for any ghost flyers, and each region must turn in a fly report for that region signed by the judge to the GC prior to their finals, in order to maintain the integrity of the WC on this issue. The only variance to the minimum of one kit flown for two kits paid by each flyer shall be for the new and or the smaller regions which cannot meet the required number of kits required for the first qualifier so that we can promote growth, with the approval of the GC these regions must have a minimum of 6 actual flyers entering 12 kits and buying 3 kits for a maximum of 2 years, any regions not obeying this shall face possible expulsion from future flys. Any region that does not submit entries for two consecutive World Cup Flys will be removed from the WCRF list of current regions and will have to reapply as a new region under section III. A. of the Constitution. One fly-off representative is granted for the first 15 kits entered plus another for additional 15 kits and so forth. The Regional Director also gets one World Cup Committee vote for each 15 kits entered, up to a maximum of 5 votes per region. The number of votes a RD is entitled to, is determined from the entries received at the most recent April 1st deadline and when entry money has been received for that year. The RD may distribute the votes as he wishes within his region. This policy encourages growth of a region until it becomes so large to manage, that it should split. A region that splits will divide its existing votes in proportion to the number of previous years' participants in each new region. **This highlighted area is very key and if it's a hinder or disadvantage for a competitor to fly a 2nd kit then they have to firstly take in account the flyers only entering 1 kit.

II. Funding for the fly-off is provided by sponsors, individual contributions, promotional sales, and an entry fee of $20 in U.S. funds for each kit entered in the regional competitions. Regional Directors must forward these fees, including a list of flyers and addresses, to their Continental Coordinator, who must forward these lists to the GC and entry fees to the Treasurer by April 1st. Late entries and lists are allowed only for new participants, and all entries must be received by the WC Treasurer before the regional fly begins. Additional regional entry fees are the responsibility of the particular regions. All regions and Continents (regardless of previous arrangements with the WC) must pay the proper amount of entry fees to the WC Treasurer or GC before the entry deadline in order to be granted representatives in the fly-off.

III. The fly-off judge shall be the winner of the previous World Cup Fly unless that individual declines by November 1. In that case, the judge and an alternate shall be elected by a majority vote of the World Cup Committee from a list of qualified and, willing nominees. Past World Cup winners who have not previously judged the fly-off may nominate themselves, but all other candidates must be nominated by members of the World Cup Committee. All nominations are due by November 1, and at least the alternate must be elected. If majority consensus is not reached on the first attempt, a second ballot between the top two choices shall determine the judge with the runner-up serving as alternate. The deadline for final determination is December 1. In case of an emergency where neither the judge nor the alternate can complete the duties, the General Coordinator may appoint a qualified replacement. In the event a judge cannot complete a fly-off schedule for any reason the General Coordinator will: * Secure transportation for the departing judge and his replacement if any. * Inform all finalists of the problem. * Secure a majority consensus by polling all finalists before continuing the fly-off with a replacement judge. If the majority is in favor of continuing the fly-off, those in the negative will be eliminated as finalistsand be automatically qualified with entry fee waived for the next World Cup. * If the vote does not support finishing the judging with a replacement judge the Executive Committee will make the final determination on the course of action to be taken.

IV. The fly-off Schedule is determined by the GC and usually runs for a period from May through July. Each Regional Director must report preliminary results to their Continental Coordinator at least two weeks prior to the regions scheduled fly-off so that the Continental Coordinator can arrange cost-effective transportation for the judge. **This means that the GC has sole control on how the finals are completed and flown. He does not seem to have to answer to anyone of where the finals judge starts and finishes and there needs to be NO vote in this matter...

V. Fly-off rules. All regions must have a regional fly by World Cup Fly-off rules to select the regional fly-off representative(s) for the region.

   1) Kit size. The kit size may range from 15 to 20 birds, but at least 5 must ROLL together in order to score.

   2) Time-in. The flyer shall announce to the judge the number of birds that are being flown prior to release of the birds. No additions or subtractions are allowed after release, but the flyer is allowed to chase up any birds that lands or may hit before time is called in. If the number of birds released is different from the number of birds declared to the judge the kit shall be disqualified. The flyer has up to 5 minutes after release in which to declare time-in. If the flyer does not call start or time-in earlier, scoring begins automatically five minutes after release. Any interference with the kit after time-in may lead to a disqualification. Attempts to ward off birds of prey are allowed, but any directly related kit activity shall not be scored.

   3) Fly time. The kit is in judgement for 20 minutes after time-in or until the second bird lands, whichever occurs first. However, the kit shall be disqualified if more than one bird fails to fly for at least 15 minutes after time-in unless driven down by a bird of prey or extreme weather. A bird down that spontaneously crashes (after one bird has landed) shall be given up to 10 seconds to resurrect and resume flight or else it shall be considered the second bird down.

4) Time-out. The judge may call a single discretionary time-out for up to 5 minutes in case of an attack by a bird of prey , blow-away, or other whim of nature or act of God, the flyer must ask for the "time-out" and ask the judge to put them back on the clock if he deems necessary before the 5 minute deadline. Although the 20-minute time for judgment shall be extended by such a time-out, the 15 minute minimum qualification time is not affected.

5) Bird-out. Except for a 15 bird kit, scoring shall continue if one bird leaves the kit. Scoring is suspended but timing continues if 2 or more birds are out. A bird is not considered out if it is returning directly from a roll or it has been separated by extreme weather or chased off by a bird of prey - even if the pigeon lands or is captured.

6) Extra birds. If additional Rollers join the kit, a simple discount for the extra birds shall be made for each turn involved. For example, if 2 extra indistinguishable birds are in the kit and 7 roll together, the judge would record 5.

7) Scoring. It is mandatory for the region to furnish a timekeeper/scribe for the fly-off judge for each finalist. The judge shall simply estimate and record the number of birds rolling adequately in unison for each break involving 5 or more. The suggested minimum depth for scoring is 10 feet. Afterwards, the judge shall multiply those numbers by 1 for 5-9, 2 for 10-14, 3 for 15-19 and 5 for 20. Those results shall be added together to produce a raw score. Next the raw score shall be multiplied by a quality factor of 1.0 for "adequate" to 2.0 for "truly phenomenal" based upon the judges overall impression of the average quality exhibited in all the turns scored. Likewise, a depth or duration factor of 1.0 to 2.0 shall be multiplied to produce a final score. The judge shall announce the final score before leaving.

8) Integrity. The judge shall NOT score anything that does not meet his standard for adequate quality and depth or duration of performance. This competition is for ROLLERS and not tumblers! Roller flying is a subjective sport and the judge may have to make allowances for extraordinary circumstances. In any case, the judge's decision is final and anyone verbally or physically attacking the judge will be disqualified from the fly and may be banned from future WC events by the WC committee.

I highlighted areas are key points to the rules. Rule 8 I feel has always needed rewording so that judge should judge the birds as closely to the rules as he can and utilize the multipliers more.

I wrote this article not to take down this prestigious event but instead to open the eyes of participants so that we can continue to keep the World Cup going for many years to come. There are some issue that could be hindering the participation of the World Cup and it should be the goal to make this event of the highest integrity of any fly out there.

Best of luck to everyone in the coming season.

Dr. Spintight

Question and Answer Column

This column will be for questions and answers. It will be based solely on what answers are sent in or asked of by the Doctor. If you would like to participate please send your questions to davesrollerpigeons@gmail.com

Q: I am having a lot of problems getting my young birds to fly and kit. Can you give me instructions that will help me with this?

A: Hi, well getting your young birds to fly and kit starts when the birds are pretty young, not after the baby molt. I like to remove my babies before they are fully feathered and approximately 30-35 days old. After I pull them from their parents they are placed in a weaning kit box so that they can begin to learn how to eat, drink and trap train. I leave them in this weaning box from 4-7 days before I move them to a regular kit box.

If you leave your babies in too long and they begin to fly and get adapted to the pen they were raised in the likelihood of them not doing well and getting flying is more than doubled I feel. This is mostly due to the fact that the birds get lazy and overfed and fat and getting them in shape to fly and stay focused about flying is for the most part going to be harder to achieve. Many birds that get lazy and "fat" and are not flown until 3-4 months of age tend to want to pair up and breed and not fly. So it is very important that you get your young birds out early to fly and mingle with other young birds that are in a similar situation. They will bond to each other and this will cause them to become a "team" and kit much faster.

There are distinct ways to train babies to fly and it goes from the weaning cage, to the kit box, to the roof top and then releasing from a training carrying cage out in your yard. The entire process can take 2-4 weeks depending on how young they are when they leave the nest. I like to take them just as the feather under their wings are about to be filled in. Normally the flights and tails are still not grown out at this point. I think they need to be self-sufficient and depend you for food and water. Don't be afraid to talk to them while feeding them and I like to whistle. Always handle the birds so they can get used to you and will not be scared of you. You have become their "Dad".

Don't waste a lot of time on problem birds or birds that are lazy to go up. They might need another week or so in the weaning pen to mature just a little more before they go up, its part mental and part physical.

I also like to use around 2-4 already good flying pigeons to help get them up. So after a few days of caging them and releasing them from the yard and seeing them fly up if they just simply start to land on your house or loft after only a few minutes then it's time to put in some good flying kit birds with them and then box them up and take them as far as you can in your yard and open the cage so when they come out they cannot see the loft. A vast majority of the time this is the last time you will have to worry about them not flying as the older birds will take them up to a good height in no time.

If for some reason some still are not going up and pulling down birds to land then it's time to box them up and take them up the street as far as a few hundred yards even. Open the box and release them and they will be forced to go up and fly before they are able to see where their loft is. The birds will be "lost" and in the process start flying.   You might have to do this a few times but once they start to fly for at least 15-20 minutes you are own you are own your way to having a kit.

Remember to keep the feed tight and don't over feed them. Over fed birds will not go in to the kit box quickly and can also have a tendency to become a problem too. I like to use the 1 tablespoon per bird ratio and work with it. If it's too much and the birds are not doing what you like just cut the feed about 4-5 scoops and they will snap out of it real quickly.   You also never want to fly after you feed the birds and this could also be an issue for some. Keep with a steady flying schedule and don't deviate. Pigeons are habitual creatures of habit and will want to be fed and flown the same everyday if possible.

Q: How can I feed my A team so they will perform well on competition day?

A: well again it's not over feeding or under feeding them. It's also a combination of resting them as well. So it's a system you have to develop with your own birds but you can use ideas from most guys that you will be able to get results. The issue is consistent results.

Most guys will discover that an A team of rollers will only need to be flown about 3-4 days a week tops to keep in good condition and active. Much of the issue is that if you fly them too much they can get weak and start to roll down or they might also stop rolling as much. It's hard to say but I know that I like to give my A team about 2 days off between flights. This way they are able to rebuild their bodies and heal up and hard spinning birds use a lot of energy and also get sore muscles like any other athlete.   You need to treat them like an athlete and not a pigeon.   Part of this is having discipline to not fly them daily and this is part of the problem for most, just flying too much.

The basic feed for me is a 15% no popcorn mix cut 50% in half with pure milo. This is the perfect feed if you ask me. The birds get all well rounded diet and can stay strong and healthy.

You also want your young birds to fly for around an hour so they can build up real endurance before they learn to roll. I think this works great for my own birds. I know many train their birds to fly for 30-40 minutes but I think 1 hour is the magic number based on my own experience. There is little chance of your birds DQing on you if you do this. Yes you might have a problem flying all your birds effectively in one day but I can assure you that it's the best approach.

You also want your bird to fly a good figure 8 pattern where they are changing directions all the time. This will also keep them frequent. You have to start this when the birds are young as it does not take long for a kit to start flying circles which is a bad habit to break them of.

If you have any questions about what I wrote please make sure to drop me an email anytime. Best of luck.

Q: How many pairs should I be using each year if I want to create a solid family of birds in the future?

A: Well it all depends on what your overall plan is for the birds. Do you want to compete? Do you want to create your own family or maintain someone else's family? Do you just want to have the very best in performance rollers no regard to color? Or maybe even become a World Cup contender? These are important questions you need to ask yourself. If you are in it for the long term that I would say your best option is to try and develop your own family of rollers, whether they came from just one loft or not. If you want to be competitive in events like the World Cup or NBRC National Fly then you might want to obtain some birds that can get you there as quickly as possible.

Remember that just because you are going to obtain some very high caliber competition type birds does not mean you need to purchase 10 or even 20 pairs of them. Most competitive flyers have a fairly small gene pool they are working with and this gives them the ability to produce birds that are very much the same. You will however need at least twice as many foster pairs as real pairs if you want to be able to produce enough babies to be competitive.

You also need to be ready for a lot more let downs then good performance for at least a handful of years, maybe longer. Good things rarely happen overnight and a lot of this would have to do with how experienced you are flying and breeding rollers. These birds are not easy and you can't expect to be winning the World Cup in 2-3 years, it can take maybe even decades. So your first priority should be that you enjoy just having rollers to fly for yourself, not to please others.

If you want to do it right I would suggest getting between 4-8 pairs of good quality spinners that you have at least seen the fanciers birds fly. Be prepared to pay at least $50 or more for each. Get referrals from others who are in the know if possible, but beware of pedigree chasing. Pedigree do not make the bird roll better, just select if possible high velocity quality spinners even if they are only 10-15 footers, you need to emphasis on the highest quality spin you can get that are good kitting competition type birds. Many guys will not be willing to open their loft to just anyone that calls them up. You might need to find an individual to introduce you. It might be better to get acquainted to this perspective fancier on line at places like Facebook.

 Make sure you have your lofts set up the right way so I would do my research on lofts and kit boxes before I even considered purchasing any birds. The way your loft is set up will greatly assist you for many years to come more than anything else.

Q: How can I get my birds into the kit box quickly, mine stay out most of the day.

A: Quick answer is you are feeding them too much. I would suggest try feeding just 1 tablespoon per day, if that is too much slightly decrease until you get control. You are not alone as many over feed their birds.

**I started this section to honor my old friend Carl Schoelkopf who is now passed away that had a few segments like this in the old Roller Journal Magazine that used to be done by Dave Gehrke in Minnesota

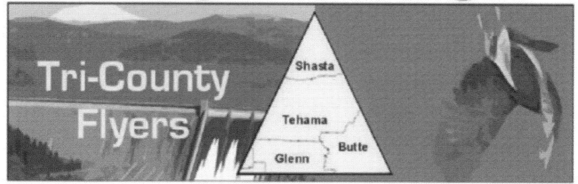

Home of the Modoc High Mountain Futurity Fly

Medicine Cabinet

This section on the Spinner Magazine will be geared towards the health and maintaining healthy rollers. If you have any good information for this section please forward them to me at davesrollerpigeons@gmail.com

Thanks to Jose Martinez for sending this in.

Virkon S

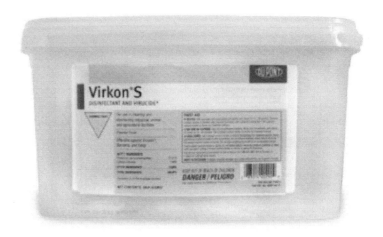

Virkon S is a disinfectant sold on amazon.com and manufactured by Dupont. I was told of this product several years ago and I know it is expensive, but it does a fantastic job. Keep illnesses in check.

Here's what the manufacturer says about it on their website Virkon S is the breakthrough disinfectant formulation that defines on farm biosecurity. With powerful, proven performance against over 500 strains of viruses, bacteria and fungi including Foot and Mouth Disease (FMD), Avian Influenza, Salmonella and Campylobacter, Virkon S is selected by governments worldwide for Emergency Disease Control.

Leading the way forward in best practice biosecurity programs, Virkon® S provides a wide range of applications to commercial livestock producers, veterinary hospitals and farmers.

The famous "pink powder formulation" offers the flexible, fast-acting, convenient, one-stop disinfection package for: Surfaces, Vehicles, equipment, aerial disinfectant or water delivery systems…

I have seen the best prices on Ebay for buckets of this but Amazon has a great deal also, especially if you have prime and need it fast.

I use this product to clean and sanitize all my waterers by simply dipping them in a bucket and pull them back out, it kills any bad bacteria on them. I don't even rinse these waterers off, I simply fill them and use them. The Virkon S is also doubles as a preventative product against birds getting sick or coming out of a sickness after leaving the nest during stress. I can't really say much more about this product it's amazing.

The Virkon S is just an all-around good health product to give to our rollers, you can give it to them in the water about ½ to 1 teaspoon per gallon for several days a week and the birds really perk up, their eyes seem to be brighter and they have more vigor after use. It is very amazing to see the transformation.   A little bit goes a long ways.

I would suggest using it as a vitamin supplement when breeding your pigeons at the later stages of baby development. This will prevent the babies from developing any kind of illness as they are weaned.   When giving as treatment probiotics will need to be given when done treating.

You can also use in bath water it assists on the plumage as well and will also work in sanitizing the pigeon loft and perches via a spray bottle.   Truly incredible product!!

Dupont is promoting another item, a similar product, but is being marketed for internal uses. I have not seen this product yet but it is out there I have heard.

This product is only promoted for external uses and should you try it in other methods this is on the fancier at hand.

My friends Tim Paustian and Joe Martinez during NBRC Convention

Featured Article

Birmingham Rollers
An Uncertain History
By
Dave Henderson

Where did the Birmingham Roller come from and who was involved in creating this very fascinating breed of pigeon? I know that some out there may not really care much about this topic or the history of the Birmingham Roller and or who developed this breed, but I find this to be very interesting after having breed and raised the Birmingham Roller for more than 30 years now. The very first rollers date back to the United Kingdom in the Birmingham England region, also known as the Black Country going back to around the 1870's, or was it much sooner?

Much of this most recent interest in this topic came from reading a small 2010 PRC pamphlet written by LaRon Doucet, Pensom roller historian, about the Old English Imports by Bill Pensom from the Black Country. This very small book was written and published in 2010 for the Pensom Roller Club members here in the US. Although this small book does not state a lot of details on this topic of Birmingham Roller history, it did however stoke my interest greatly that put me on this journey to learn more.

Although I don't fully agree with some of what LaRon is saying about this "Pensom Strain" this topic has greatly got me thinking about old literature that discusses the history of this breed, how it was developed and where the Birmingham Roller "sprouted" from in the UK. One will soon find as even the UK Pigeon Project discovered that there is so much word to mouth stuff and not a lot of actually written documentation about the Birmingham Roller and it's development as most of the population going back to the late 1800's in the Black Country were filled with fanciers that were not able to read and write.

There is no shortage of Roller history after 1930 but before this date, especially before 1920, the information is hard to come by. I am sure there is some lost literature out there that could pin down more of this past and the Birmingham Roller but where it is I have no idea. Will it ever come to the light of day? I don't know and if it did would it be factual even?

The very first comment that is recorded in a book that describes tumblers doing acrobats was recorded in 1676 by Francis Willughby (Francis died in 1672) in the book Ornithologiae Libri Tres, completed by John Ray in 1676. He noted in his writings after his death that was published in latin, "These are small and of diverse colors, they have strange motions, turning themselves backwards over their heads and show like footballs in the air". Obviously this does not coin the phrase "roller" but it tells of them flying and performing like rollers or tumblers. These dates coincide with old literature stating Flying Tumblers in the UK are dated going back to the late 1600's.

http://en.wikipedia.org/wiki/Francis_Willughby

Wendell Levi, author of the well know book The Pigeon, mentions that he first discovered written literature about Birmingham Rollers in 1876 with a single line by Robert Fulton in The Illustrated Book of Pigeons. This was a very high tech book for the day with 50 full color hand painted illustrations which might have easily taken 4-5 years or more to complete I would imagine and were all painted by JW Ludlow. So the information from this book could have easily be written around 1870.

http://www.pigeoncote.com/books/antique/antique2.html

James Lydell also mentions the Birmingham Roller in his book published in 1887 called Fancy Pigeons, this also noted in Wendell Levi's book The Pigeon.

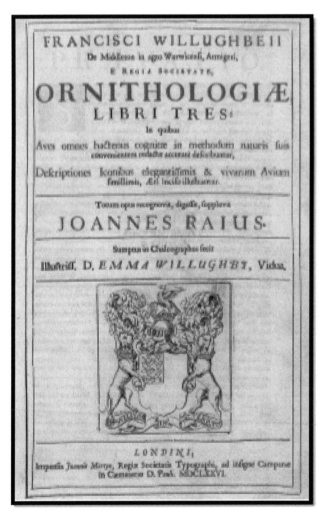

Here's the cover page on this book from 1676

Sample Tumbler print by JW Ludlow for example of work

Some of the best written text describing the performance of the rollers that would eventually became the Birmingham Roller was published in 1879 by George Smith in his book How to Breed the Macclesfield Tippler and the Tumbler pigeon. George was a breeder and flyer of High Flying English Tumblers as in 1870 when working on this book, Tipplers were unknown where George lived in Nottingham, England. Tipplers did not appear in Midlands until around 1875. George stated in his book page 11 that the tumblers many years before would not fly as long as they did today. He stated 5-6 hours was a good fly time due to all the tumbling and rolling these pigeons did. He also noted that some were seen rolling 5-6 yards and at times would even be seen rolling all the way to the ground and killing themselves. So as noted by George we see the Old English Tumblers split off and would become the Birmingham Roller and also the Flying Tippler. It's just not certain if there were more breeds involved with the birds that eventually would become the Birmingham Rollers. George does mention in this same paragraph that these tumblers were crossed with non-performance tumblers to create birds that would perform less and fly more in the creation of the Tippler, he mentions 7-8 hour fly times in 1870.

It's hard to say how many years before George is thinking when he says MANY YEARS BEFORE, this could very well be 20 years or more but he didn't not make an exact note of a date. I think it is similar to what we find today where it's all word to mouth and that no one still alive could confirm the date he is talking about. I think it is very obvious that the birds he was talking about were in fact rollers that would go on to become the Birmingham Roller.

http://vliegtippler.tipplers.com/informatie/artikelen-interviews/its-origin-and-development-job-ofield-1932/

I think some have noted that there were Tumblers (rollers) flying around the Midlands going back to around 1860's by Bill Richards who passed away in 1938 after having bred and flown Rollers for 70 years. This is documented by Bill Pensom. It is also believed that Bill Richards could very well be the source for most of today's modern Birmingham Rollers. It is also believed that Bill Richards might have been the only family of rollers known before 1920. I think that LaRon Doucet could be mentioning this "Pensom strain" due to the idea that all modern day rollers could be from Bill Richard's birds? To me why didn't Richard keep the name attached to them then?

The interesting thing is that there is also documents showing that the Roller was also being developed in the US about the same time as in England as there are records of guys showing birds around 1870 and them being called Birmingham Rollers. Charles Lienhard of Ohio, Pennsylvania had rollers in 1870 and ERB Chapman noted in his own book Rollers and All About Them (1934) that he obtained his birds from Mr. Lienhard in 1883. The Early rollers in the US were believed to come thru Canada also originating from England as well.

Just like Wendell Levi states in his book The Pigeon, that probably no exact origin of the Birmingham Roller will be found as there is insufficient literature to discover this and what breed(s) were behind the current Birmingham Roller developed in the Black Country that all of the birds today originate from. There were many fanciers in those days, many worked in the coal mines or steel producing plants and the pigeons were their past time, similar to many us even today. There could very well have been an immigrant that contributed to the current rollers behind many rollers in the early days.

The competitions started pretty basic really and were judged as an individual roller with depth and quality being the main concern of the birds being judged. What those standards were in comparison to today we can only guess. This started in part to find out who had the best individual bird on a particular day. I suspect when someone had a top quality spinner he won plenty of contests before it was sold or lost in those days. They did not cherish birds individually like many of us do today. In fact I have discovered that here in the US that many fanciers have "favorite" birds but many overseas don't have favorites like we do and look at the birds slightly different then we do. They also don't take many pictures of their birds like the USA fanciers do on average.

The breeders of these rollers, in the early days, did not use any scientific approach to developing them and raising pigeons. They kept the birds in very basic shelters (lofts or sheds) and there were literally hundreds of fanciers in the Midlands region back in those days. Bill Richards was amongst one of the earliest to practice scientific breeding to create his family of rollers in those days.

It is said that Harry Young, a well to do individual, saw the advantage to just going around the Black Country and buy up all the best quality rollers he could, this is estimated in the mid to late 1800's but data is hard to find on Harry Young. I am still awaiting a new book by LaRon Doucet to be released in the hopes of showing a better connection to all of this, but in reality we might never know what really transpired in his day. LaRon tells that both Harry Bellefield and Bill Richards both got their rollers from Harry Young. Many of the fanciers back in the early 1800's did not hold a huge "prize" on their pigeons and would prefer to sell them to support their families like any other livestock at their disposal. It was hard times back in the Black Country, in those days, and money are very scarce. The vast majority obtained good rollers by pure luck mating's.

There is incredible DNA research going on about pigeons and their origins today. Much of this data is being conducted by Michael Shapiro at the University of Utah in Salt Lake City. I know that in humans they have actually been able to tell when the genetic material that made us was created and wondered if this would be able to happen with our Birmingham Rollers. Unfortunately the DNA research is more about the mutations in general and at this point in developing other breeds and not so much of this is directed at specific breeds and when they were created.

There are some that pay a great deal of attention to this DNA research and what is shown in the research. They do however know which breeds played roles in developing other breeds. We know by this research that specific breeds are directly related to rollers in a specific order of development but not sure of the dates so to speak. We see the Oriental Roller was directly involved in the creation of the Birmingham Roller but this is estimated to have been more than 1000 years by some. The Oriental Roller is amongst one of the oldest breeds of performance tumblers/rollers and is said to have literature stating this back as far as 4000 years when pigeons had first become domesticated.

Here is what Dr Richard Cryberg said when analyzing this data from Shapiro.

"What Shapiro's data shows is the Oriental Rollers and Birmingham Rollers shared a common ancestor quite a long time ago. Just judging by the tree Shapiro draws based on the Bayesian Statistical Analysis of his data a long time ago is probably at least 1000 years and perhaps more. It is definitely not a 100 years. Several other breeds split off both the Oriental Roller and Birmingham Roller branches of the tree after the original split. For instance the Parlor Rollers split off the Birmingham branch perhaps half way, time wise, between the original split and today's birds. That would suggest that Parlors are several hundred years old as a breed unlike the speculation in the book "The Pigeon" by Levi that the split was in the mid to late 1800s and in the US no less. When you look at the divergence, particularly in color mutants, in the Birmingham's and Parlor's that recent a split never made any sense".

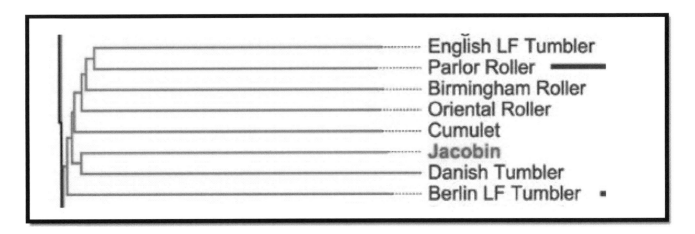

http://www.bbc.com/news/science-environment-21279422

More on the DNA by Dick Cryberg…

What Shapiro's data shows is Oriental Rollers and Birmingham Rollers shared a common ancestor quite a long time ago. Just judging by the tree Shapiro draws and based on the Bayesian statistical analysis of his data a long time ago and is probably at least 1000 years and perhaps more. The data says that for sure it was not in the past 100 years.

Several other breeds split off both the Oriental Roller and Birmingham Roller branches of the tree after the original split. For instance Parlor Rollers split off the Birmingham branch perhaps at the half way mark in development wise between the original split and today. That would suggest that Parlors are several hundred years old as a breed unlike the speculation in "The Pigeon" by Levi that the split was in the mid to late 1800s and in the USA no less. When you look at the divergence, particularly in color mutants, in Birmingham's and Parlors having a real recent split never made any sense to me.

Actually, in the whole tree that Shapiro derived from his microsatellite data the only breed that looks suspect to me is the English Pouters. Rather than being grouped with other pouters it is grouped with the Roller family and the split is rather old. I suspect this placement may be subject to change when we learn more. Other than this one case the rest of the tree makes reasonable sense to me based on all that I know. With more knowledge the timing of branches would be expected to change a bit, but I would expect the overall tree would remain pretty much intact.

Bill Richards' was a long term roller guy in the Uk and here's what Bill Pensom wrote this about Richards.

"The real breeders from the beginning of the century could be counted on one hand, and the greatest of them all was the late Bill Richards of Harborne, Birmingham. He was regarded in the highest esteem by all the breeders of Rollers. His birds could be recognized anywhere, and he could tell by looking at another fancier's birds whether or not there was any of his blood in the other's birds. His birds were small and tight and compact.

Their predominant color was red check, dun, and the various shades of blue and blue check. The few odd self or two, were but throwbacks. He had a remarkable eye for a pigeon. He could readily sum up the quality of any bird he saw including physical defects which would have escaped the eye of any other fancier. He was a regular visitor to the Black Country, where he was a household word. Bill Richards never sold or gave away any of his birds. The only blood of his Rollers which got into other hands was obtained by the noble art of catching. Catching strays was always considered a sporting event in Flying Tumbler circles in those far off days. His family of Rollers was the only one in existence up to the twenties which portrayed a well thought out process of breeding skill. The facet of the limited variety of color proved his belief in inbreeding, which everybody else was frightened of. Bill Richards died in 1938, after 70 years of keeping Rollers, and never a day without them."

(by Paul Gomez)

I wonder if based on what Bill Pensom said of Richard's and what many have said about Pensom if Richards taught Pensom the secrets of being able to spot a good stock bird by characteristics of the pigeon in your' hand. This paragraph above seems to state as such about Richards and many have stated the same about Pensom over the years here in the US.

Another, well-known name, in Uk Birmingham Roller history, was Jim Skidmore what was born in 1875 and died around 1949. Jim was a well know flyer living in Blackheath, part of the the Black Country, and was a very popular flyer dating back to the 1920's and 1930's. Skidmore was said to have gotten his birds from Bill Richards, but guessing they were caught as Richard didn't give birds to anyone as well. I was able to dig up some good stuff about Jim thru various sources including ancestry.com and the interview with Ollie Harris in 1987. OD Harris mentioned that Jim Skidmore also did not sell any birds and most had to get them from the old art of catching them, however a fancier named Joe Barnsley had a unique ability to catch Skidmore's pigeons and would sell them to the locals whomever desired them.

I find it kind of convenient that the top flyers in those times didn't sell or give birds away but others ended up with them. How did they know where the birds came from when they would catch a stray? I know many were not banded. There had to be others that shared their ideas with and were befriended in those days? If this is not the case then this was a very unfriendly environment don't think? I would guess that there were some friendships built in those days even if there was talk of this not happening. Example: If I was a top flyer and was always getting others offering to buy my bird and didn't want a lot of people bugging me I would tell people I don't sell birds or give them away, but we all have friends to share our ideas with that were also share birds with.

Through some online digging it turns out Barnsley and Skidmore were neighbors and as a matter of fact Barnsley was Skidmore's father in law. I was thinking about it logically and why would Barnsley have to catch rollers from his own son in law? I know if I was Skidmore this would just piss me off so I think it was most likely the opposite of what Ollie Harris mentions in his interview and that Skidmore was actually just allowing Barnsley too sell his birds in part to help support him in his old age. To me this makes as much sense as anything does.

George Mason with Bill Barrett in the early 1980's, photo from the MRPC

Said to be Jim Skidmore, from the Midland Roller Pigeon Club

It was said that Pensom was very good friends with Skidmore and that Pensom got his birds from Skidmore and Richards. Here's a short paragraph about what Pensom says of Harry Young.

"Harry Young - A businessman who travelled the country buying birds at any price. A true fancier and clever breeder. Birds from his stud were reputed for starting many a loft with deep spinning top quality rollers. Pensom himself never met him but he was known to

Pensom's father. Both Bellfield and Richards obtained birds from him." Thanks to Steve Atkinson for sharing this paragraph with me.

In the above paragraph it does also appear that Bill Pensom's father was also a roller breeder/flyer, so much of the UK history that Pensom knew about might have very well come through Pensom's father and his knowledge of the old days, much like OD Harris knew about the rollers of the past by being a 3rd generation roller breeder. OD Harris has stated in his interview that the Birmingham Roller was being flow in the Black Country at around 1800.

To me it appears that Harry Young was a real breeder and flyer of the Birmingham Roller even though there is really only limited information about Harry. I would also assume if he continued to buy birds throughout his career with the rollers that he might have had his "OWN" family of rollers but was still not afraid to bring in unrelated birds at times. Again we look at the luck of pairing up rollers and if you had many good ones it makes sense they would produce some of the like right? It does say that he was probably generous with his birds and helping guys out with high caliber pigeons. So he "shared the wealth" with the rollers he paid money for so why would there not be a "group" that knew Harry that also did the same?

I was able to speak recently with an Irishmen named Donny Cook, Donny is one of the few that is still living that knew all the more recent greats; OD Harris, Barry Schackleton, Ernie Stratford, Ken White, Bob Brown and was very good friends of the legendary Bill Barrett for more than 30 years. Bill Barrett's family of pigeons were very popular from 1960 thru the 1990's in the UK, maybe still even amongst some of the most popular stuff as in the case of Heine Bijker, 4 time World Cup Champion who is said to have developed his own family from Barrett related birds.

Donny went on to tell me that Bill Barrett got his birds around 1950 shortly after Jim Skidmore died from a Scotsman named Tom Brown, who obtained many of Skidmore's birds after he died in around 1948 or 1949.

However in a 1987 video interview with Bill Barrett, he states that Bill Pensom got Barrett in to rollers in a 1943, during the war. Barrett mentions in this video that his family of birds were from Skidmore, Pensom (1943), Bloomer (1947) and another fancier named Bismore (1951). He also stated that in 1966 he went to visit Bill Pensom in California and brought back 14 pigeons with him that he went on to incorporate a few of these back into his family as well. Barrett also says in 1943 that Pensom was seen quite often seen with Skidmore and that they were very good friends; at this time in 1943 Bill Pensom was approximately 39 years old and Skidmore 68. This tells us that Skidmore died at around 73 based on these time frames.

The thing that really sticks out to me about the past and the roller culture in the Black Country from the 1930's to the 1950's was that many seemed more than willing to trap in stray rollers and use them in their stock lofts without any knowledge at times of who's birds they were at times. I am sure many of these birds were not even banded. This was how "raw" most of the programs were in those days and just getting good rollers was just pure luck for many fanciers. To me this seems way out of place and something that seasoned fanciers just would not do, but in fact it happened all the time even going into the 1970's even after birds were banded regularly. There is a well-documented case where OD Harris strayed in a Bill Barrett bird that ended their friendship for remainder of their lives.

So really how often did these UK fanciers do this practice of trapping in strays? I am not certain but from reading and seeing interviews most were content with this practice, I am assuming that the birds were good rollers that they did use?   I think in terms of what I know today I would not be apt to just stray in a roller and put it in my stock loft? I know that many others would not do this today either. To me when you have a REAL family of rollers doing well for you this is not the kind of thing that fanciers, that know what they are doing, will practice. However I think many of the prominent UK fanciers had a standing agreement that should they stray in their bird(s) from a specific fancier they will be contacted and their roller given back to them.

After watching the interview made by McCrae of Barrett, Ollie Harris, and Bob Brown just to name a few I think I can relate most with Barrett and his practices and methods, even though I have never followed what he said and nor do I ever recall reading any literature by Barrett and his methods. It's just plan ole learning by experience kind of stuff to me, just mostly common sense. Many just don't see this until they gain enough experience in this hobby and then you can relate to what some will talk about.

Donny again confirmed to me that Bob Brown was a top flyer in the UK for many years, possibly even the most decorated roller flyer in UK history, but he was not as good at breeding and selecting birds for the stock loft. He had the unique luxury to have any bird at his disposal from Barrett's loft whenever he thought his program was faltering, so he never had to do it completely on his own. This does not surprise me as after watching Brown's interview he claims that he outcrosses every 5 years with a single hen and pairs her to all of his top 4 cocks and moves forward with these crosses. As we all know whenever a cross is made the birds can become very different, however in Brown's case most were probably just coming from Barrett anyway so it's not a REAL outcross situation, but he does not go into details about this in the interview. I don't really quite understand his philosophy myself but this is what Brown states in his interview.

I just could not imagine going ALL IN with a single hen every 5 years, no wonder he was a competition guy through and through. I have seen many here in the US do similar things but maybe not to a "schedule" like Brown used and maybe Bob was just estimating this behavior. Many who go with the "law of averages" for competition basically breed a huge amount of birds to go through in the hopes of getting an elite team from the large number of birds produced. It is always when these types try to line or inbreed that they run in to problems down the road as they were not selective enough in their process, or they simply had no real knowledge of their birds in the first place.   I think the main reason Pensom had so many pairs was to cover all his angles, lot of variety in his rollers, for potential customers. No one in those days would ever be seen raising the same number of birds he did in the Roller hobby in the 1950 and 1960's.

If you are in the rollers for the long term it's always best in my opinion to create your own line of rollers to your own liking, based around a few select pigeons you have.   Crossing is just a project people with a family of rollers and if you can get something better out of your rollers go for it, but you have to fully evaluate these crosses or it can easily back fire on you over time.

Barrett with his fly Trophy's in 1987, MRPC archives

The Pensom Legend...

Bill Pensom was born in 1904 and passed away in 1968 and resided in the USA for his last 18 years of his life. Pensom was a 3rd generation roller fanciers same as Ollie Harris, which appears to have been fairly common in the Black Country with a great following in the pigeon hobby in those days.

I of course never got to meet Bill Pensom, he died when I as around 2 years old, but none the less here on the West Coast of the United States he was legendary for his birds and knowledge, and after 50 years since he has passed there are many that still make reference to the Pensom Rollers out here, especially from the Kiser/Borges birds which are very prevalent in my own region here in Northern California. If you look at things closer in fact most of the birds on the West Coast go back to the "Pensom" Imports and I would go out on a limb and say that every family of rollers that developed since Pensom's death here in California somehow go back to Pensom or Pensom Imports if they trace back to local rollers and no recent imports. If you look at the birds that we used and what the fanciers in the UK used they all have a similar back ground to them, just were developed independently, which makes them different. Whether this has to due in part to the climate in comparison to the UK or specific characteristics that differ from the UK and the USA birds as are selected by fanciers, it's really hard to pin down why there are differences from both sides coming from very similar genetics.

Pensom came to the USA with a lifetime of knowledge and experience to a region that was eager to learn and he became our teacher and mentor for many in this hobby. Southern California has been a very rich roller hot bed of history for the flying Birmingham Roller, in a large part due to Bill Pensom relocating there. Quality spinners have remained consistent in Southern California over the years and this has spread Worldwide now, there is and has always been a specific style of spinners that is standard on the west coast and this is no doubt due to the Pensom influence here. This is not because Pensom was the inventor or creator of the Birmingham Roller but because he brought a degree of awareness to those that listened and read his "how to" articles about the True Birmingham Roller. Pensom was an educator to the fanciers in the Southern California as well as many others location throughout the USA. Just like breeding the Birmingham Roller today it will not come easy, but to those that will benefit the most will pay a great deal of attention to the qualities and characteristics of our best spinners.

I think the fanciers of modern times tend to be more educated then fanciers of the past and this level of knowledge is what continues to drive the birds to higher standards, even though many might tend to disagree with this scenario. Better means a lot of things to a lot of different fanciers and this is why it's very hard to gauge the amount of success that has gone on. The standards we follow today were not the same as the ones they used 60 years ago and this can seem different to many of the past and present times.

After talking to some that knew Bill Pensom and also reading about Pensom's influence in the UK, he appears to have been a pretty well respected roller fancier in the UK, but nowhere near the Legend that he became here in the USA. I know many might disagree to some point or another on what transpired in Pensom's tenure, but his efforts in writing alone has left long lasting impressions for all that pay attention. It was well documented that he started to "preach" his ideals in the UK as a young man in his early 20's and is more known for his no non sense articles over there. He was all about educating those that would listen to his methods in order to improve the OVERALL quality of the rollers WORLDWIDE, even if he really did not achieve the most as a flyer of the Birmingham Roller. There is no difference with many fanciers today that have not yet seen the ways to progress the birds, but if they continue to hone their skills they will eventually get there to some degree or another. I think it might be entirely possible that Pensom was not able to communicate as well until he fell into a full time gig here in the USA as an educator to many that wanted to learn more about these amazing pigeons. It's interesting how much you can gain about rollers just sharing your ideals with others, brain storming your idea amongst fanciers that think like you do.

I have been very fascinated with the Birmingham Roller from a very early age, same as Pensom was until his death in 1968. I often would think about things I might ask him if he was still living today, more technical aspects of this sport/hobby. There are slight communication issues with Pensom I suspect coming from the UK and this is expected. I wish he was alive so that I could pick his brain about what he really meant with specific things he wrote about.

I think it was very obvious that Bill Pensom was at a level of awareness with the Rollers like no other in his era, but did he really have the best rollers? Sometimes the smartest guy doesn't have the best birds. Pensom talked very highly of LeRoy Smith and it seems pretty obvious that Pensom could not touch Smith and his ability to breed and fly rollers, and I can't recall ever reading an article by LeRoy Smith. Pensom often said he would take Smith's culls over many others best birds, so this might give you an idea of what I am talking about here.

I have read where Pensom bred from 50 or 60 pairs and usually around 500 birds per year while living in California, so maybe this hindered Pensom as well. We all know that the more bird you have the more time it takes to manage what you have. There is always a point where you are just pissing in the wind because you just don't have enough time in the day to fly birds and have a life away from the Rollers. Like everything we need to balance everything in our lives that is important to us. I would assume that Pensom had a little experience with pigeon thieves and if this was not the case why park birds at various lofts when you kept 50 or 60 pairs at your own loft?

Bill Pensom and Lester Lemyer compliments of Dave Sanchez (mid 1950's)

It seems very obvious that Pensom did fly competition, at least in the UK. I would have to assume this because the All England Roller Club created a competition called the "Pensom Shield" that started in 1966. Now if Pensom had no real impact on the hobby they surely would not have created a competition in his name would they? I think not. The egos are just not an American thing either, because these same jealousy issues took place in the UK as well and still do.

I now know that Pensom actually was part of a local club in Los Angeles affiliated to the National Birmingham Roller Club in the mid to late 1960's where he in fact participated in kit competition.

The late great Bill Barrett had a lot of good things to say about Pensom and he claims he promoted the rollers in the UK and educated fanciers on how to breed better rollers and manage them better. He did this in part with articles he wrote as well as speaking to fanciers that had little knowledge of how to breed and get the most performance out of their rollers and it appears he did the same thing here in the USA. He started writing these helpful article from an early age to. Maybe an issue in the UK was that many in the Black Country could not read or write well and this might have been part of what held down his influences more there, just not able to comprehend what Pensom was trying to say in those days.

To my recollection Bill Pensom was brought to the USA by a handful of well to do roller fanciers with the goal of further educating themselves on how to breed and fly the True Birmingham Roller first hand, which in turn got everyone familiar with what a high quality Roller looked like here in California. This tends to be always happens when someone as influential Pensom relocates to an area. We saw this many years ago (1990s) with the best Ping Pong player in the World living in Ohio. This drew in many other top players to Ohio so they could learn first-hand and to be more influenced by this player named Tim Boggan if I recall correctly.

By the time Pensom came to the USA kit competition was a big thing in the UK and Pensom was more in the mindset of the Individual high quality spinners still and had foresaw kit competition ruining the True Birmingham Rollers as he saw it at this time. I read where Pensom eventually did start to breed "competition rollers" that he obtained from his close friend Ken Payne and this consequently pushed him out of the club that had his name. He did go on to resign from the Pensom Roller Club and this brought on the creation of the National Birmingham Roller Club (formed in 1961) that is still in existence today. This was fully exposed to the roller community in 1968 before Pensom died.

Pensom had been a carpenter for many years, he knew how to build lofts and I have heard he was working for Andrew's Hardware in Southern California after arriving to the USA in or around 1950. Pensom was essentially Don Andrew's loft manager and also build wooden loft equipment that was sold in Andrew's stores. Andrew's was very instrumental in creating the Pageant of Pigeons in Southern California that still continues even today. Pensom would go onto publish his roller book in 1958 titled The Birmingham Roller Pigeon, so this tells me that Pensom had a bit of time on his hands.

I had not picked up this book since the late 1980's and as I recall back then many were preaching this book as the "Holy Bible" of the Birmingham Roller. I actually preferred the True Spinners book published by David Kowalski more at the time but I was really not in the "Pensom Generation". True Spinners appeared much easier to read and there really was not a lot of "know how" books back then that were readily available except for Pensom's book. Do I feel that the DK book is a better book, not really it's just different? You get another point of view. I grew up and would borrow the American Pigeon Journals from some old timers in our local club and I found there were plenty of Pensom articles in them back in those days. However as I look back now, with 25+ years of experience under my belt, I can see much of the insight in the Pensom book that I did not see many years ago. Yes some things are very vague and does not explain as clearly as I might want it to but I can get a good idea of what he was really trying to say in this articles.

I could honestly tell that high quality spin was a real passion for Bill Pensom. Pensom spent many hours researching characteristics of the True Birmingham Roller to find out what made these birds what they were. He paid attention to very small details and was even said to have the ability to select top quality breeders on the ground thru physical characteristics seen in the bird in hand. They talk about Bill Richards having this same ability so I would assume that Richards passed down his ideas to Pensom's dad or to Pensom in his youth of what characteristics Richard's might have looked for, Pensom was only young man when Richards died. We all know this is in no way something that works 100% of the time and many times do we even know what are best birds are in our stock loft? It takes several years of success to discover these things and no one could ever convince me that Pensom could select your best birds on the ground with 100% accuracy. Different strains carry on different characteristics it's as simple as that even if they roll equally as well.

I suspect that much of the characteristics he paid attention to was the eye of the roller and other subtle physical qualities that the bird may have had that he liked. It could've been the "eye clusters" some pay attention to, but I cannot recall every reading anything about Pensom describing these clusters in the pupil of the eye, but I can assume it was passed along by some, because if not where did this characteristic of our rollers come from?

One specific quality of the spin that I recall many commenting of over the years and this was the "H" style spinners when I was first getting my feet wet, at least many were telling me that this was his preferred style that many have stated over the years and showing a small hole from the side. To me the ones that I was shown seemed a bit on the slow side for my taste. It's hard to describe this in writing because you really can't get descriptive enough without seeing this in person and reacting to it.

Here is probably the most famous bird Pensom owned, #514 PRC 1953 hen. Pensom did not discover her worth until she was about 5 years old, which tells me what I thought that he just had way too many pigeons where Howard McCully said Pensom had 50-60 pairs. Both parents as I recall were bred by JL Smith and not Pensom.

I am really uncertain to how good Pensom's eye sight was, he did wear glasses but perhaps there were reading glasses only just like many over 40 wear everyday. I know moving into the 1970's that many were realizing that "H" style was so preferred and that most were looking for the small spinning ball type of spinners, many not even paying attention to style or even a hole in the bird for the most part. I personally like the style that appears to look for like an "A" in my opinion, it tends to be more smooth and fast in combination. You can have fast "ball" rollers and also the slow ball sloppy rollers too, which look like crap in my opinion. I reference these at the "X" style and a slow "X" style looks the worst. If you breed for the "A" style I find the over quality will be better on average across the board.

I think many will simply say they like the wings to be in an upward position while spinning and I would agree with this, but in reality the wings are however in a downward position we know now, it's just the bird is upside down when we see the "H" or "A" style. I discuss more of this in my own book, The Birmingham Roller; A Performance Pigeon.

LaRon Doucet, Pensom Roller historian, talks about a "Pensom Strain" of the Birmingham Roller that goes back to the UK days that many today were not aware of. I really can't say he didn't have a Pensom Strain here in the USA or even in the UK but after speaking to several in the UK region it seemed that Pensom was continually picking up good quality birds all the time in the Black Country from various sources. There is writing of him as a city bus driver and would make not of good kits in certain locations so he could come back and visit them later on and see their birds. Chan Grover I know told me this was true.

What I have seen however is that he was not just content with the birds in his loft and was still continuing to get birds from Smith and Plona even while in the USA as well as many others over here from time to time, 514 is proof of this. Pensom is quoted saying from several firsthand accounts that Smith's culls were better than many of others best birds.

Pensom also did a last import from Ollie Harris for himself in 1965, I assume some of these had to have gone to Herb Sparkes (via Howard McCully) as some of these are behind the birds that Joe Kiser and Joe Borges have had for many years now. Technically these were not "Pensom Rollers" but instead Harris birds that Pensom imported. I would have to say from what I have seen writing and heard was that Pensom was somewhat of a collector here in the USA and as well as in the UK, old habits are hard to break. Chan Grover was also a collector for as long as I knew him, so this could be a generational thing? But I can't confirm this obviously. This does not mean that Pensom did not possess top quality rollers but it puts a big question mark (?) on this "Pensom Strain" that LaRon speaks about. I mean if you want to go with the basic premise that if Pensom bred babies from any rollers he picked up and then these babies are now Pensom Rollers we can do that here, but is this how we develop strains of rollers, I think not. Pensom can't have it both ways and neither can anyone else. It literally takes years to developing specific genetics into a tight gene pool before we can call them a strain and when you "out cross" then we have many more years just testing the outcome of these type of pairs. If you have 50-60 pairs there is NO WAY in hell you can keep up with this type of thing, especially when you are selling the vast majority of the birds you produce each season.

There is no secret that people that are successful with performance rollers tend to keep to a small gene pool and seldom bring in stray birds from other lofts, in the UK we saw this with both

Skidmore and Richards. So with the tendency to do what Pensom was doing leads me to believe that there really was not a "TRUE" Pensom Strain like is talked about but more of a collection of "Pensom" birds that were worthy of what he deemed a True Birmingham Roller.

Even in the article in this issue of Spinner Magazine there is an article by Bill Pensom called **"The Breeding the Birmingham Roller Pigeon"** he himself makes note of the different strains and families he imported to the USA, noting they were NOT the same pigeons, even though they all became known here in the USA as "Pensom Rollers".   I think it just goes on to tell you that you can get good spinners as long as you select for it no matter what the blood lines are, so long as the birds mix well together, this is found out through good ole "trial and error". So Pensom was obviously playing the NUMBERS game that many still do today.

What really made a Pensom Roller the Pensom Rollers people have been talking about all these years? To me it appears obvious that they were called Pensom Roller due to him importing rollers to the USA from the UK. This is because everyone knows that all the birds that were imported to the USA were not bred by Pensom, in fact the majority were not. Had they all been bred by Pensom I think I would be more adapt to calling these Pensom's, but this is not the case. Pensom imported literally hundreds of rollers to the USA from the UK. He sent 44 birds to the USA in the mid 1930's.

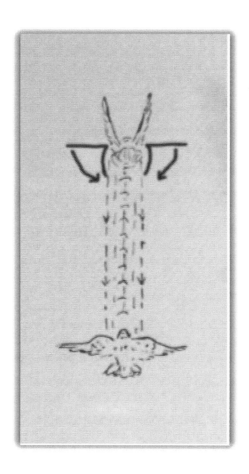

Diagram from Pensom in 1958

The Kiser/Borges birds that are also called "Pensom's" were in part from OD Harris imports and also Hugo Blass. I was told this by many out there to include the late Chan Grover, who was friends with Pensom. This was why Kiser/Borges did their own importation from Ollie Harris in 1981. So why do people still call these birds in the Pensom Rollers if the genetic background is from Ollie Harris? This really does not compute to me. Even Ollie himself stated in his 1987 interview that if he were to get any birds to bring back into his family it would be birds from Sparks here in the USA. So Ollie obviously felt very strongly about the birds he had sent in 1965 to the USA, that were intended for Bill Pensom himself up until he died in 1968.

I suppose it all goes back to marketing the birds? Pensom was a name or brand and this gave fanciers a better ability to market the birds for sale maybe? This could be why there were many colors in there as well? Everyone spoke highly of Pensom's dark checkers but if they were much better than the others why yellow, grizzle and other weaker colors? We can talk about these things later on, he was ultimately breeding the True Birmingham Roller right? We all know how hard it is to get good birds in various colors, because we are normally looking for the color first and roll second when this is going on. It's easy to breed for color but when you add high quality spin to the equation it gets much harder to get high quality (equal to your best) when you are also looking for specific colors.

Pensom talks about not wanting to give out pedigrees on his birds (only parents), for the fear that some that are dishonest could manufacture a pedigree and sell it as a "Pensom Roller" no matter what kind of bird it really was. Homer Coderre told me a story of a guy that came by to visit during the 1960's. This individual told Homer it was one of the best birds he'd ever seen in the air and Homer offered it to him as a gift after it landed. The guy asked if he had the pedigree of the bird and Homer told him only on the dad's side and the guy said that it had no value without a full pedigree and turned down the offer. Pensom tried to make fanciers focus on the birds in question and not the background of the bird by only giving out the parents of the birds they had, but this is hard from some to grasp when they are looking for some sort of special link to other "famous" birds in their birds. This makes sense to most everyone and should the said fancier have success with specific birds he could maybe come back later on and get cousins or other relations to this particular bird to give him more depth in the breeding loft, but to discount high quality spinners just because they don't have a "fancy" pedigree is pure stupidity.

Since the 1980's I have seen some slight changes in what some are calling these to this in recent years where some are calling these old Kiser/Borges birds now Harris birds, which might be more acceptable, but all the same they have been in the USA no less than 33 years now these should not have any mention to Pensom or Harris attached to these right? The only mention would come if anyone asked on the background of them. They should have taken on their own strain by whomever is working with them at this point. I think this again is a marketing ploy as we see a lot of popularity in the UK birds here in the USA in recent years mostly from George Mason birds, but the list also includes Stratford, McKinney (Ireland), Bijker (Holland) and even South Africa birds from Hannes Rassouw down from the late Ron Swart. Again I see this more as a marketing scheme as since 2009 the USA has been getting beat by many of the other countries to include the; UK, Ireland, South Africa, Australia just to name a few. Ted Mann was recently crowned the

2015 World Cup Champion flying also birds from Ron Swart, which are mostly South African birds, but also a blend with George Mason birds from Jim Sherwood.

In the UK, Pensom knew there was a huge market in the USA for the Birmingham Roller and they had CASH to burn on quality birds, and many of the UK fanciers breeding these birds were more than willing to sell their top birds for cash to help support their own family and Pensom started importations to the USA starting in 1932 when Pensom was only 28 years old. I would suspect that the early shipments in 1932 and 1936 where many of the birds were actually bred by Pensom but there is no written record to tell of all the imports past 1940 if I recall correctly, I am not aware of the exact numbers from these shipments. The later shipments to Smith and Plona were the birds Pensom was more interested I have heard, prior to him moving here.

I am not sure what a good roller was worth in the 1930 thru 1960's in the USA but they might have been worth more to US fanciers than to the UK counterparts and this was why the importations continued I am sure.   Lester Lemyer was said to be picking birds from the air from Pensom for $30+ back in the 1950's, so he obviously had more money than most in that time.

Bill Barrett said he had 1 pigeon (the best bird from a particular fanciers' loft) in his foundation stock which cost him 12 Shillings he has stated in his 1987 video interview, which in today's prices would be approximately $12 USD in today's money, he said that this $12 was nearly a week's wages in 1947 in the Black Country when he purchased this bird. By today's standards you are not going to get the best bird from a guy's loft for $12, it's just not going to happen. This is no comparison to the $50 or more that fanciers will pay in today's market, in fact many will pay hundreds of dollars for specific pigeons today. So I think this was the main driving force for the UK fanciers to sell off their prized rollers to the Americans to make high profits, but it didn't last long I was told.

**In today's market it is even more expensive to import pigeons as there are many rules and regulations to get through. The average bird that is now imported into the USA from the UK region will cost no less than $275 PER BIRD just to import them and this is not even taking into consideration the cost of purchasing said birds.

After personally speaking to Donny Cook of Ireland he confirms that over time as Pensom continued to ask for more and more birds to ship to America, the guys started holding back their prized stock for themselves, noting that high quality roller pigeons are hard to come by, even in the homeland. So what he told me was that the first couple of shipments were top rate but as the shipments continued over time the overall quality of the birds in these shipments continued to worsen on average, he even noted that some were making fun of what some were paying for 2nd rate birds that were shipped by some. These serious UK fanciers were now no longer going to part with their best pigeons but Pensom still had orders that he needed to fill going to America. I think you can get the jest of the story here.

The Pensom imports worked two fold for Pensom. Firstly he was making good money, traveling back to his homeland, for the fanciers who would normally get very little money for their top pigeons and secondly he was getting access to these birds for his own personal use as well if need be. Many of the birds that he had access too, he might not have had the money to purchase them for himself even, but by becoming a "Roller Broker" this would give him access to these fine pigeons prior to shipping them to the USA. I call him a broker as he imported Birmingham Rollers from the top lofts in the Black Country, somewhere between 10-20 strains of rollers. Noted in the book "A Roller Digest" from 1967 for the Pensom Roller Club and also noted in The Birmingham Roller Pigeon by WH Pensom and others tells of the "Pensom" imports that first started in 1932. Many of these imports that are not even all documented as they did so many of them over the years. I wonder if there were others that started doing it also knowing what Pensom had going for himself. I guess this is a topic for another article.

Here are the original "Pensom Imports" from 1932, Bill Pensom was only 28 years old at the time, to Father Schlattmann of St Louis.

HRC 32.18 Blue Self Hen

HRC 32.5 Clay Hen

HRC 32.195 Blue Check Oddity Hen

HRC 32.166 Black Badge Cock

HRC 31.1Blue Badge Cock

HRC 30.464 White Black Neck Cock

HRC 30.885 Blue Saddle Cock

HRC 27.1007 Black Bald Cock

Other importers followed to include; J. Leroy Smith of New York; Raymond Perkins of Connecticut, Chandler Grover of New Jersey, Ciro Valenti of Missouri, Al Walker of Michigan and Francis Buckley also of New York. The majority of the birds came from Pensom or Jim Skidmore, however there were up to as many as twenty different lofts in these imports, many strains of families. These all would go on to become "Pensom Rollers". Bill Pensom imported in his last pigeons in 1965 and all 14 of them came from Ollie Harris.

In the first shipment of 1932, it does appear that 4 of these birds were young birds when Pensom shipped them (3 of them young hens) and one was no doubt right out of Pensom stock loft being a 1927 bird. What does this tell us? Well it doesn't tell us much really, but what Father Schlattmann did with them is the real story he did share his pigeons with others and helped start the craze of Pensom Imports as the velocity in which these "Pensom" rollers performed were a drastic improvement over the Whittingham Rollers during the same time. It is said that Father Schlattmann was killed in the 1940's in an automobile accident and where the birds ended up I am not sure. I would hope that they ended up in a loft so that they could continue to be improved upon. It would be interesting if someone had pedigrees going back to this original imports in their lofts, but then again how could you insure this over several generations of roller breeders even? This is the kind of stuff that Pensom was warning us of.

As Barrett openly admits his family of pigeons had a great deal of Pensom birds behind them, more than any other breeder, but they did not continue to be called "Pensom's" they became

Barrett Birds, Pensom didn't bring in birds from Barrett in 1965. This might be something to consider huh?

I also know that it's documented that before Pensom died Barrett made a trip to California to Pensom and ended up bringing back birds from Pensom's loft. I wonder how these birds were incorporated into Barrett's birds moving forward. I wonder how many of these 14 birds actually made the cut in his stock loft as of that interview, I assume Barrett felt these were something he needed, but maybe Pensom felt these birds are something they need to take back to the UK to help them? Maybe Barrett gave them to others and he didn't take them all for himself? There is more questions created in this single transaction.

I was led to believe in the interview with Barrett that kept a small gene pool and this is how many family of bids are started. So I would assume that Barrett probably didn't need all these birds he got from Pensom. Barrett seemed to be a solid breeder so I can't assume any different here.

We all know there reaches a point where the person breeding and flying them needs to take credit for what they have done, good or bad. If your aim is to sell birds for top dollar then your only option is to join the mainstream and compete with the best of them. This is really the only way you will be able to get $100 or more per bird if that is your intention, at least long term. The roller hobby is a friendly one for the most part and money is generally not a main concern for most, it's bettering the hobby as a whole that gives longevity to our hobby. Granted giving all your birds away will not help either, you must make guys feel like your birds are valuable or worth something, giving birds away many will not show any worth to them.

I think ultimately Pensom greatly enjoyed and wanted to help other fanciers become successful like many others in the hobby even today. Bill Pensom was a brand created and pushed by the Pensom Roller Club members in those days until the falling out in the early 1960s. Pensom bred around 500 birds every year in California as stated by McCully and this was in a time where the birds of prey were a non-issue. Bill Pensom was just a normal guy like any of us are but he took it upon himself to create more for this hobby. He wanted to promote and educate fanciers to get the most out of their own pigeons and to better the hobby in general, this type of thing takes a lot of volunteer work in writing articles as well as giving the advice to get there. So even though Pensom was making a lot of money selling birds that is not all that he did for the hobby.

There may never be the number of fanciers there once was back in the Black Country during the 1920's and 1930's but the fanciers that are still doing it today are far better educated and able to do more with them. Competition never did ruin the Birmingham Roller like many have stated and I think Pensom would be very proud to see what kit competition has evolved to with our modern World Cup Fly, there is always the ones that might disagree but I will have to just say put your kit up of Champions and see how they fair?

Thanks to the many sources that were made available to me on this topic, more than I can name here. Please support the NBRC NCF and World Cup Fly

Where Did Rollers Come From
By
Dr. Richard Cryberg

Many people develop an interest in discovering who their ancestors were and where they lived. This can become quite a passion. A passion that has never caught my fancy I guess. Although, it would be interesting to know if I had some cousin x times removed that was a horse thief. We often ask these same types of questions about our pigeons. How were all the different breeds developed? Specifically, the big question is, what the ancestors to the Birmingham Roller were. This ancestor question is of interest, but I do not think anyone believes it will tell us how to breed a true spinner. Just like my horse thief ancestor does not make me a horse thief.

Until quite recently about all we had to go on in determining where Rollers came from is spoken and written history that really only goes back accurately maybe 150 years. Before that it was pretty much pure guess work. But, with the modern developments in learning what DNA sequences can tell us we can now put some real science behind such a question. Mike Shapiro and his team of scientists have done exactly that[1,2]. I am going to try and explain in English part of the kind of data they needed to perform their work. But first, Figure 1 shows the results they discovered. This chart is a sort of development tree going back in time. At the far left is the wild C livia. As you move to the right you see the lines split and eventually end in a breed name for some variety of pigeon on the right. If you look at the way the breeds are arranged many breeds are very close to other breeds that you would logically expect to be closely related. There are also some surprises. For instance Iranian Tumblers are quite far from the other acrobatic breeds.

In order to construct a family tree like this from DNA data what you need to do is find some elements in the DNA that will have changed somewhat, but not a lot, over the time frame of interest. The time frame in the case of pigeons is more or less 5000 years. You have probably read about work in humans using mitochondrial DNA. Mitochondrial DNA is genetic material carried exclusively in the cell organelles called mitochondria. This DNA is separate from the DNA that makes up chromosomes. It is quite stable stuff as most changes tend to be lethal and eliminated. So, change is very slow. In constructing a family tree for humans we know that humans left Africa at least 50,000 or more years ago. So, you need to look at DNA that is pretty stable, but not perfectly stable over that time period. Using such data in humans allows us to trace back the pathways that lead to modern Europeans and Asians and Pacific Islanders for instance. We can get a pretty good idea of the geographical routes those humans took to get to their present locations by examination of the mitochondrial data. But, mitochondria are too stable to look at relationships among pigeon breeds, so Shaprio and crew needed some other type of DNA probe. They picked a structure that is called a microsatellite for their first attempts.

Microsatellites are simply DNA repeat structures. As you probably know DNA is composed of structures called bases that carry the DNA information. There are four bases A, G, C and T. It is not important to know exactly what A, G, C and T stand for. They are simply the first letter of the chemical names of the four bases. DNA consists of long stretches of these four bases arranged into the chromosomes. You could describe a chromosome perfectly simply by listing these bases in the order they occur on each chromosome. For instance a sample hunk of a chromosome might read ATCCGTTAGCTA. A typical chromosome is many millions of bases long. Only a small amount of any chromosome is actually a gene. Most of the chromosome, more or less 99%, is made of what are called non coding bases. None coding simply means this part of the chromosome does not get transcribed into any useful protein. Microsatellites are simply short lengths of such non coding bases where there is a regular repeated sequence of bases. For instance CACACACACACACACACACA. Or AGTAGTAGTAGTAGTAGTAGTAGTAGTAGT. In each of these cases the repeat length is ten but in the first case only two bases are repeated while in the second three bases are repeated. Definitions are somewhat arbitrary but in general the number of repeats in a microsatellite ranges from 10 to 100. The number of bases per repeat unit can range from 1 to 6.

Microsatellites are ideal to study how breeds evolved from each other over a 5000 year time period. What makes them useful is the number of repeats can change occasionally, but not often. So, let's just take a simple example of one microsatellite and see how it can be useful. Take a bunch of breeds of pigeons and determine the microsatellite length in each breed. Maybe our data shows we have three groups of pigeons. One group has this microsatellite 15 repeats long, the second group is 16 repeats long and the third group is 17 repeats long. It would be reasonable to think that for each of these three groups an individual breed within the group is likely closely related to the other breeds within the group. And, at the same time that breed would be much more distantly related to breeds within the other two groups. Well, that is sure a start. But, when microsatellites mutate they can either grow longer or shorter with pretty much equal probability. So, one microsatellite is not enough to draw solid conclusions.

What Shapiro did was look at 32 microsatellites in each of the breeds of pigeons he examined. He then took this data and subjected it to a particular kind of statistical analysis. This statistical analysis generated the first pass relationships between 70 different breeds of pigeons and is the data reported in paper 1. He was able to establish fairly solid relationships between 40 breeds and grouped them more or less into five families which shared common ancestors after divergence from the wild rock dove. The branch of the tree that leads to the Birmingham Roller traces back to a split with a common ancestor where the twig that split off formed the Budapest Short Faced Tumbler. At a later date the line split off the Tippler and then the West of England Tumbler. Sometime later the Birmingham Roller split off and after that split the Portuguese Tumbler and finally the Parlor Roller split off into distinct breeds. This family tree says that the Birmingham Rollers closest relatives are the West of England Tumbler and Portuguese Tumbler.

In a later paper2 these relationships were further refined. In this second paper other DNA probes were used to refine the microsatellite data using 1.48 million DNA loci followed by a similar statistical analysis of the data and led to modestly different conclusions. In this refined approach the Birmingham Roller split from a common ancestor that it shared with the Oriental Roller. Later the English Long Faced Tumbler and Parlor Roller split from a common ancestor they shared with the Birmingham Roller. Only 40 breeds were involved in this second study so elimination of the

West of England Tumbler and Portuguese Tumbler from the tree is not meaningful as they were not included.

One of the very interesting findings to me was that Iranian Tumblers are not at all closely related to all the other air performing breeds. The Iranian Tumbler is most closely related to the Shakhsharli and Lahore. Both the Iranian Tumbler and Shakhsharli are only occasional single flippers. It would appear based on this data that a tumble mutant may have happened at least twice independently to lead to this division. Or, an alternative explanation is that breed crosses were done to move the performance trait into these Iranian breeds followed by enough back crosses to pure Iranian birds to destroy genetic evidence of the cross. The only real way to tell which happened would be to learn the exact DNA nature of the performance mutants and see if Rollers and Iranian birds share exactly the same mutation in one of their performance genes. If they did this would show breed crossing happened.

What does all this tell us about the genetics behind rolling? The implication is there was a long time ago some pigeon that was an air performer. This original bird likely did nothing much besides single flips. With breeding time other mutants happened that impacted air performance. These mutants resulted in a variety of different types of performance ranging from single frequent flips to coop tumblers to birds that rolled horizontally, etc. The whole variety of performances we see in today's breeds. Very often mutants that impact some particular aspect of a pigeon act in far more than simply an additive fashion. To take a fairly well understood example consider muffed feet. Muffed feet are simply a combination of the mutant that causes grouse legs plus the mutant that causes slipper. Neither of those mutants by themselves produce spectacular leg feathering. A grouse legged bird might have toe feathers an inch long and slipper about the same. Yet, the combination produces feathers as long as six inches on the toes. Shapiro has also shown that all crested breeds contain as one essential element the peak crest mutant. Yet combinations of peak crest plus other mutants produce the head feathering found on a Jacobin. Likely the same is true of air performance. That is combinations of two mutants that each by themselves may not produce a great deal of performance can result in birds much better than simply additive effects.

We know from many peoples experience that if you cross a Birmingham Roller to a non performing breed it takes many back crosses to recover a half decent roll. A modern Birmingham Roller likely consists of the original tumble mutant plus several mutants that have happened since then that all contribute to today's outstanding performance. A reasonable guess, based on the difficulty of recovering roll after an outcross, would be someplace around three or six mutants in addition to that original tumble mutant. Add one or two more and you have a Parlor Roller.

1. Sydney A. Stringham, Elisabeth E. Mulroy, Jinchuan Xing, David Record, Michael W. Guernsey, Jaclyn T. Aldenhoven, Edward J. Osborne, and Michael D. Shapiro; Current Biology 22, 302–308, February 21, 2012

2. Michael D. Shpiro, Zev Kronenberg, Cai Li, Eric T. Domyan, Hailin Pan, Michael Campbell, Hao Tan, Chad D. Huff, Haofu Hu, Anna I. Vickrey, Samdra C. A. Nielsen, Sydney A. Stingham,

Hao Hu, Eske Willerslev, M, Thomas P. Gilbert, Mark Yandell, Guojie Zhang, Jun Wang; Science 1 March 2013: Vol. 339 no. 6123 pp. 1063-1067.

Dr Richard Cryberg is working scientist with his own pigeon genetics projects' and I thank him for his time giving us his view of the genetics behind the Birmingham Roller.

George Mason, Deano Forester and Dave Moseley

Meet David Moseley

Name, age, where do you live; describe your location in UK

David Moseley, Over the last few years I've moved a number of times and we just moved in to a cottage with a nice outlook, so will have to wait and see

When did you first start raising the Birmingham Roller?

When I was about 10 years old I sent to Scotland for some birds from a man named Tom Brown. He sent me 2 pairs that bred me a lot of roll downs, LOL. Had lots of birds I did not let out because they would bump

Who have you looked to for advice and guidance over the years?

No one really, observation I have found is always the best way to go. I flew Tipplers for about 18 years and I worked with a man named Arthur Newton. It just so happens that he held the World Record for flying Tipplers. He taught me a little about feeding pigeons and gave me the basics of management advice.

How long were you flying in competition in UK before UK joined the World Cup?

I started flying in competition when I was about 18 years old. I started flying in the World Cup in the 1990's but can't recall the exact year that I first participated.

How was/is kit competition ran in the UK before the World Cup and how are they ran now? Do they have an All UK champion fly there?

They were run here in the UK way before the World Cup ever started and they are still run very similar even today. We have a National Fly that promotes the winners from each club. We don't have an All Champions Fly as there is really no need for it really. The competition can be tricky because of the differences we get in weather conditions and the fly can change hands easily because of these issues.

How did you get started in your current family of the BR and how many pigeons are behind this family you have? Do you have a partner behind the scenes that you work with in conjunction with your breeding program? Who or whom would you say has contributed the most to the current competitions going on in UK today in your opinion?

I was first introduced to real Rollers when I met Ollie Harris in the early 1970's via Eric Scott who has now passed away, god rest his soul. I got 2 pair of Rollers from Ollie and that's what I have worked with every sense. It has been somewhere around 40 years or so with these birds. I think the fanciers here that might have contributed the most to our sport today would be; Ollie Harris, Bob Brown and Bill Barrett. I personally think that Ollie's birds are the most popular here in the UK now and may be the strongest strain in the UK and is standing the test of time.

How did the Anglo Fly come into play I see these days and what rules does it fly by?

The Anglo Fly came about when me, Graham Dexter, Bill O Callahan and several South African flyers got together and sorted out the guidelines for this fly. As normal rules can change all the time, I asked for a copy of them. I find it to be a very interesting fly and there are no individual winner only the Country with the highest score wins and it's nice to see the camaraderie with all the guys that participate in this great event on both sides.

How many stock birds do you breed from on average each season? How many babies do you produce on average?

I don't use a lot of stock bird, maybe 6 or 7 pairs each season. I don't breed that many young birds as I don't really like flying young birds much. I am very selective on all of my stock birds.

I have heard your family comes down from some birds from OD Harris? How did this come about?

Look for the answer above because I have already answered this question

What have you done with your family since you first got them?

The birds from Ollie were very good fast spinner and strong flyers, but they also carried some bad traits of wanting to fly too high at times. This took me about 10 years to get them to stop flying like this. You can spot the birds that fly in the front of the kit and take them up, when I see a bird like this I would immediately cull it. Now the birds are flying much slower and at a good height for watching, but you also have to learn how the handle these birds because they are not easy to fly.

What is the best Bird you have every flown? Describe it

How to answer this… When I put a team of good solid rollers together you don't often find an individual bird that stands out because if you do your job correctly there are none I feel. Most individuals normally come from bad traits in comparison to good kits. So it's really hard for me to really saying anything about this because I am not really into these individual type birds. There are some events where they look for individuals but I don't participate in these.

What has been your best stock bird in your family?

Well I would have to say that what I put in the stock loft always works. Lots of them I would consider my best pair but when you are striving to create a stock loft of birds that are compatible to each other they are all my best. Believe me this sort of stock loft can take you a lifetime to identify and create. Just when you think you have cracked it you start looking for better ways of doing things.

What kind of schedule do you have to fly your rollers? Many of us are working "stiffs" and are limited to how many birds we can keep and train due to working and or family constraints.

Well if you are doing your job right you won't need big numbers of birds and just a good pair of eyes and a stable family of rollers to work with. If you are having to breed from big numbers and have a large stock loft of say 20 or more pairs you are doing something wrong I would say.

What advice would you give to any new flyers out there wanting to fly in competition?

I would have to say be very selective and only pick the very best birds. Keep your stock loft small and create y our own family of birds from these. Never think the grass is greener somewhere else, it's not! Most birds are the same wherever you go, but it's the man behind them that makes them look good. You can never buy success so keep your cash in your pocket

Yours in the Sport, Dave Mosely

All England Roller Club

The All England Roller Club was formed in 1964 after talks between some of the top fliers of the time. The aim of the club is to promote through friendly competition the breeding and cultivation of high quality performing roller pigeons based on ideas developed by the founder members.

Fly Secretary Donna Chantry 01274 770668
aerc@blueyonder.co.uk
www.allenglandrollerclub.co.uk/

1976 at Barry Shackleton's loft (MRPC archives)

1976 during show in UK; Mick Kelham, Ernie Stratford, Bill Barrett, Ron Adams, Barry Shackleton, George Mason and John Thompson (MRPC archives)

Meet George Ruiz

Name, age, where do you live; describe your location in USA

George Ruiz I'm 49 years old and live in Henderson Nevada which is next door to Las Vegas

When did you first start raising the Birmingham Roller?

I started with roller pigeons when I was about 12 years old but I also had other breeds at that age

Who have you looked to for advice and guidance over the years?

Several friends have helped me over the year, but too many to really list. I have listened and learned something from nearly everyone I have encountered in this hobby. You just need to keep an open mind.

How long were you flying in competition before joined the World Cup?

My first competition fly was in the World Cup and I flew a kit of squeakers and got no score but I learned from it and have continued to improve my management

How is the World Cup ran in your region there? How does this region participate and pull off its fly?

Judges, time frames etc I'm in the southern Nevada world cup region. We usually fly in May and they sometimes bring a judge from out of the area or we go with a panel judging system

How did you get started in your current family of the BR and how many pigeons are behind this family you have?

Do you have a partner behind the scene that you work with in conjunction with your breeding program? I have the Higgins family of pigeons at this time and I have a good friend that helps me at times named Danny Guerrero from Norwalk California

Who or whom would you say has contributed the most to the current competitions going on in your region today in your opinion? Are things changing do you think?

Don Macauley without a doubt. He puts in a lot of time and effort to keep these region active, without Don we would not be able to maintain a fly here each year. I don't take competition super serious and there is nothing wrong with. You have to like them for what they are pigeons

Give us some insight on what is behind the Las Vegas group where you are from.

The Las Vegas group has the annual William Pensom show in spring of every year. We have a nice group of flyers in this region but most don't fly in kit competition

How many stock birds do you breed from on average each season? How many babies do you produce on average?

I breed from 12 pair in individuals to ensure who the parents are and I try to breed at least 80 birds a year.

I have heard your family comes down from some birds from Jerry Higgins related pigeons? How did this come about? Do you have other birds besides these?

At this time I only have the Higgins family but in the past I have flown and bred several different families of birds but the best I have ever seen is the Higgins birds so that is why I picked them as my choice to fly and breed

What are your goals with your current family of birds? Do you plan to incorporate any other families of rollers into your loft in the future?

My main goals are to fly a nice kit for myself I don't take competition too serious like other folks but when I do, I fly the best that I can.

What is the best Bird you have every flown?

Describe it It's a cock and he was a 30 foot blur and his kids are just like him I have 2 sons and 2 daughters and a grandson and granddaughter in breeding loft

What would you say is hindering the USA from winning the WC in recent years and we appear to be slipping farther behind our foreign counterparts, what is your opinion of this?

I will not mix anything into my family of pigeons, as I said I don't care if I win the big one or not. The time of the year the WC is flown needs to be rotated in the USA, our birds are at their best in the early fall, not the summer. The English or South African birds are no better then what we have here in the states now that is my opinion on that subject.

What has been your best stock birds in your family thus far? The best Bird I ever bred and flown is a bird named Q ball a red check cock that was a 5 to 40 foot spinner with amazing blur out speed.

What kind of schedule do you have to fly your rollers? Many of us are working "stiffs" and are limited to how many birds we can keep and train due to working and or family constraints.

Due to work I can only fly 1 kit per day. I am just happy I have a job

What advice would you give to any new flyers out there wanting to fly in competition?

Don't get into this hobby to for the sole purpose of competition, you will only end up disappointed. There are so many obstacles in this sport; BOP, bad weather, the time of year we fly. I just want to enjoy my birds in my own back yard, enjoying your birds is worth more than winning and competition in my opinion.

Not the best picture, but Rick Mee, Dave Henderson with my son Alex (now 25)

Sport Roller Club
Croatia East

More information Contact
Anton Matjanec anton.matjanec@gmail.com
Tomislav Grubanovic tomislavotok@gmail.com

Fans of Birmingham Roller pigeons, Anton Matjanec, Mario Filipovic and Miroslav Bunic established the club named *Sport Roller Club Croatia* in 2007, at first time in independent Croatia. The intent of establishing was a membership of all breeders who loves sport way of holding and competing with Birmingham Rollers. First club competition was organized in 2008 and there was a world judge champion Ferid Catak from Denmark. After that, our friends and world famous and renowned breeders Eric Laider from Denmark, Hejne Bijker from Netherland and Cedo Luburic from Serbia visited our *Sport Roller Club Croatia* and take us in secrets of holding and competing with Birmingham Rollers. Our biggest success was in 2010 when we won in voting to obtain right for competing in *World Cup Fly*, which was in South Africa. Ever since then, our club was visited by our friends Adrijan Gasparini from Australia, Joe Emberton from California, USA, Kevin McKinney from Northern Ireland and others. Our best ranked member in World Cup Fly was Mario Filipovic who was managed to take high fifth, ninth and twelfth position on world rang list, despite of problems and losses by birds of prey. Tomislav Grubanovic took twenty-ninth position at his first competing in 2013. Because of big number of members, World Cup Fly decided to enable Croatia for creation of other region, so Croatia is now representing by two regions in *World Cup Fly – Croatia East* and *Croatia West*.

Please visit us online at http://rollerklubhr.forumotion.com

Young birds of Marko Uzunovic

Tomislav Grubanovic, Marko Kutlic, Erik Leidler, Mario Filipovic in 2009

Tomislav Grubanovic old hens

This article was taken from the Feb, April and of May 1968 American Pigeon Journals. This is the last APJ article that Bill Pensom wrote before he passed. This is a very important article and I think anyone that is interested in Bill Pensom needs to read this one, many of the younger generation has not seen it. I think like many others that have had these birds for their whole lives is that you fine tune your knowledge over the years, and we also preach the basic fundamentals over and over. Pensom was always writing on the same topics over and over so this makes sense to me.

Breeding the Birmingham Roller Pigeon
By
William H Pensom

The breeding season will soon be upon us, and the fanciers who have not already done so will be giving serious thought to the mating of their birds. There are numerous kinds of performers of many varying types. The fancier has to decide for himself which class of performance and type appeal to him the most. Ones' own evaluation of the stock at hand depends upon the knowledge gained by previous experience. Each year fanciers add to their store of knowledge by the education derived, not only from their own birds and practices, but also from those of others. Whatever the choice of the fancier, he must use his wits to not only maintain existing qualities, but to try and improve upon them.

It must not be forgotten that there is always room for improvement in any branch of domestic livestock breeding. While I am conscious of the fact that many fanciers hold their own interpretation of what constitutes quality Birmingham Rollers, I am also conscious of the fact that there are many fanciers who have yet to see the ultimate quality expressed by the true Birmingham Roller. It is for their edification that I pen these lines.

First of all, we have to be able to recognize the champion Birmingham Roller. Such a pigeon is one of small dimensions, six to eight ounces in weight when in proper flying condition; round of body, which is not deep or shallow; not too pronounced in chest, and rather long cast; nicely refined in head shape, which may well vary in contour between long, curved, or flat; pinched in face. There is generally a space between the end of the keel bone and the vent bones. They are short of leg and are to be found both clean and muffed legged. The most important feature is the eye, which should be bright and expressive of high intelligence and character. The eye can be of any color: pearl, yellow, orange, bull or brown and multicolored.

Many fanciers discard birds, which are possessed of bull eyes, odd eyes, and mixed-colored eyes, mostly to satisfy a fad. In so doing, they very often throw away the very birds they should keep. In any case, the eye indicates the temperament and the potential of the pigeon as a progenitor of good stock. There may be exceptions to this description, but they should be treated as such, since they would not be capable of contributing much towards the goal we seek.

The true Birmingham Roller has no equal or peer. It stands out above every other known performer. In performance it rotates with lightning rapidity, and of such violence as to portray a small ball with a hole in the center, the size of a dollar piece, spinning downwards for a considerable distance. The presence of the hole indicates perfect spinning; without it, the pigeon is either rolling too slowly or the roll is shapeless. Such birds never attain championship class. The mature Champion Roller is also better equipped to control the depth of the spin when coming to drop, and barring accidents, will fly and perform to a ripe old age. There is no other class of performer which gives so much satisfaction as the true Birmingham Roller, both in the air and in the breeding pen; anything else are just rollers.

It is obvious that there has to be more understanding of the breed, for without the right kind of stock, such high quality cannot be produced. It must also be understood that the Birmingham Roller is one of the most difficult of breeds to cultivate, and only real fanciers possessed of patience and determination to own the best should consider breeding them.

Very little can be accomplished in a few years, although in the process a fancier will always have at his command birds of no less quality than other fanciers seeking the same goal, which is most satisfactory.

Each year he will recognize quality in performance and any outstanding bird should be used in the stock pen. Depth of performance is secondary to correct spinning, and while the champion is generally set between twenty-five to thirty feet in depth, it is important to keep in mind that those birds which rotate the most revolutions in the shortest space regardless of depth are the ones to value most.

It is common among some fanciers to exaggerate the depth a bird will roll; for example, 15 feet becomes 30 feet or more, 25 feet often being estimated as a hundred or more. A true spinner very seldom exceeds 30 feet and very often this depth spells disaster.

Mating In mating these pigeons for the best results, we have to consider the efforts of the bird during the processes of developing into a first class spinner, and the effects on its development of the physical and nervous system. Birds, which begin their performances at an early age generally, go through a most exhausting process, which often inflicts in the mind of the owner some doubt as to the value of such a bird. In consequence of such development the pigeon does not enjoy a complete moult in its first year. No pigeon is mature until it has completed two full molting periods, although this does not deny the use of young pigeons in the stock pen. A suitable mate for the above example must be chosen from those which did not begin to develop until a much later date, or until after the first moult. This is the only method to guarantee aerial and spinning stability. When a fancier has established a stud of stable, high-velocity spinning pigeons, his best plan in the future will be to choose mates as they look on the ground rather than by selecting them out of the air. Mates should possess similar qualities, especially as regards expression of character, the only compromise coming from bodily make-up. Since color or shades of color are closely allied to character, it is to our advantage to give much consideration in this direction.

The basic colors are blue check, red check, and dun. Mixtures of these will give the best results.

When aerial performance, both collectively and individually, is of no primary importance, the art of mating becomes of little or no concern. This appears to be the most popular category for fanciers: to exercise their skill in producing birds to certain physical and colorful standards, at the same time maintaining a decent standard of performance.

It is from this area we can hope to breed with some regularity birds specifically for the show pen. It should be understood that it is impossible to cultivate the highest quality spinning rollers, maintaining these true qualities, and to try and produce show pen winners at the same time. It cannot be done. In order to breed show birds, a fancier needs two breeding lofts; one for show and one for high class Rollers.

Competition Flying The Roller fancy is notorious for its confusion. This is caused, I believe, by a lack of knowledgeable fanciers capable of teaching the novice. A cure for this confusion is an indulgence in flying contests. In this connection local clubs should be formed to foster and encourage members to fly their kits against each other. The use of the British system or rules for flying completions will give the most satisfactory results. No contests should be made with kits of less than 20 young birds and 25 old birds. Kits of lesser numbers have no incentive to give of their best if judged on collective or simultaneous performance. If fanciers are so isolated that they cannot enjoy competition, there is nothing to stop them from introducing this order of things to themselves; it will still pay dividends.

In striving to produce the ideal spinning Birmingham Roller, many breeders are apt to confine their choice of breeding material to those individuals, which conform to the desired standard of performance during flight. Insufficient attention is paid to such things as constitution, temperament, and even to the reproductive background. Genes for qualities which are ignored or considered to be of little immediate importance may be lost or dissipated, not through the workings of a mysterious or malign force, but because no effort has been made to retain or cultivate them.

Any hereditary character, which is ignored or taken for granted, instead of being watched and consistently bred for, may quickly be lost in a breed or strain, possibly beyond recall. The careful consideration of all desired qualities is essential if they are to be preserved or enhanced. This applies equally to structure, constitution, temperament or ability. Any idea that inbreeding can by itself be the cause of any form of deterioration or degeneration is totally unjustified. High flying and true rolling ability may certainly be stabilized and improved by inbreeding if sufficient care is given to the choice of Rollers used for breeding in each generation, and is accompanied by sensible selection. If a weakness appears in inbred stock, it is because the parents or other ancestors carry the genetic factors responsible. Inbreeding may be said to be a device by means of which all qualities, good and bad, which lie latent or hidden in a strain may be brought to light. To accuse inbreeding of creating faulty conditions of any kind is ridiculous. The importance of selection has already been mentioned, but it is not a creative force and its effects are limited by the nature of the material to which it is applies. The conception of a breed as possessing an unlimited degree of plasticity, and capable of being modified in any direction by selection is mistaken; so is the assumption that by selection we can ensure that each generation will show a progressive development of the attribute selection is based upon.

Selection can never cause the emergence of a quality, either physical or mental, that is not already represented genetically in the stock used for breeding. The only way to effect improvement in any direction is to make sure that the appropriate genes are present in the pigeons mated, and to endeavor to fix them in duplicate in the strain or in a goodly proportion of the birds bred in that strain. Whether that end can be achieved through a program of inbreeding and selection, or may necessitate some out crossing in the preliminary stages will depend entirely on the nature of the foundation stock.

Pedigree Breeding

One essential of scientific breeding is the keeping of accurate records. Many breeders have very complete memories of outstanding pigeons of past fame, but very few of us could remember the characteristics of birds that go into even a three-generation pedigree. It is essential to have a complete picture of ones breeding stock before commencing breeding. The building of a strain depends on the breeder creating his own pedigrees. A strain is something, which is established; therefore, it cannot come except by inbreeding. The breeder alone, from the start, is entirely responsible for what goes down on paper. Pedigrees can only be molded and established in accordance with ones own practical experience. I possess information and pedigrees on some of the birds used in the manufacture of my strain from 1914. These were birds I kept and some, which I was closely associated with in the lofts of the old timers among whom I lived. Like all livestock breeders who sell their stock, I am frequently asked for pedigrees, and in nearly every case this request is carried out. Beyond giving the parents, the rest is given very reluctantly.

I fail to see what useful purpose can be served by supplying information on Birmingham Rollers which I have bred in the past and which in no sense would benefit anybody but myself. I firmly believe that pedigrees of the unknown can and do create a condition of degeneracy, since pedigrees for Rollers depend entirely upon the observations of the breeder himself. How can one portray on paper the true characteristics of rolling pigeons such as temperament, reaction to mental instability, and relation of mental instability to organized training and environment? It simply cannot be done. Therefore, when a fancier mates his stock according to pedigree, he becomes victim to wishful thinking with the hope that something good will come of it. The correct procedure to pursue in the creation of a successful stud of rolling pigeons is to purchase the right kind of stock from the right kind of fancier. It is important that the beginner either sees the quality of the vendors birds in flight or takes the work of some reliable fancier who has seen them in flight, and who knows the breeder well.

If the purchased stock is of any value the beginner, after a period of three years, should be able to own a flock of rolling pigeons to be proud of. Only dissatisfaction can accrue from less that the best. There is no formula available which can establish a Birmingham Roller as a product noteworthy among pigeons except the evaluation and praise of qualified authorities on the breed who are able to frequently witness outstanding birds in flight. The only guarantee another breeder can have of the birds he has acquired other than the integrity of their breeder is that the birds stated in the pedigree have met with the full approval of other qualified breeders who are better informed in the intricacies of cultivating real rolling pigeons. It is generally known that there is a society in this country, which bears my name. It is a society consisting of some ardent fanciers each with a desire to cultivate and perpetuate the Pensom strain of Birmingham Roller. In fairness to them and to myself I feel I should be allowed to pass a few comments about the situation. The club was inspired by the late Ray Perkins of Connecticut, and in cooperation with the late Bob Evans of San Mateo, was fostered and instituted in 1945. I was asked if I had any objections to this; my answer was "Not at all."

For a number of years the club existed for the sole purpose of cultivating highflying, deep spinning Rollers of the highest quality. This condition did not last however, as a craze for breeding Rollers to a special pattern for the show pen soon overtook the principles on which the club was founded. Many practical Flying Roller breeders dropped out because of friction and confusion brought about by this turnabout in thinking. Large quantities of pigeons were broadcaster free to anyone who would join the club. The result was that the offspring of these pigeons, which had been bred under the illusion of the being dual purpose Rollers, were further distributed, meeting with the approval of the show man and the lesser-informed beginner, and the disapproval of those who knew better. This was anything but a savory reflection on my strain of Rollers. I am frequently reminded that this condition still exists. I had always expressed disapproval to the club rule that "anyone who kept other than Pensom Rollers would not be eligible as a member of the club". I felt, and still feel, that such a rule is a denial of fanciers to think for themselves, is against the better principles of cultivating true spinning pigeons, and is a restriction on the endeavors of true flying fanciers to improve their stock from other sources.

Where is the fancier who would refuse a better pigeon than his own from any source? I have often imported different strains of Rollers from Birmingham, not in any way to cross with my strain, but as a means of educating those who are anxious to extend their knowledge in the field of flying Tumblers and Rollers. Many fanciers have benefited by these ventures. In view of these importations I resigned on my own accord from the club. I am not blind to the fact that some may think otherwise. This event gave rise to persecution of my birds and myself; I don't think I was the loser.

While pedigreed birds are an essential for membership, I have to say that I know of many longstanding instances of birds being pedigreed which can claim no right to this distinction. The Rollers represented by this society are not representative of my strain of Birmingham Rollers; moreover, the erasure of my name from the register would better serve the fancy and myself in particular. Over the years there has been opposition to other fanciers besides myself by the jealous fantasies of others who supposedly breed and produce better birds than anyone else. They apparently are constantly in the running for the number one position in the fancy at any cost.

Words are the price. These attributes contribute nothing to their pigeons, to themselves, or the fancy except suspicion.

We have heard plenty about what is called the Whittingham strain from time to time, and of Mr. Whittingham being the world's greatest Roller breeder. I feel it is incumbent upon me to try and clarify this belief, which I do entirely without any personal prejudice, in view of the fact that there were so many others of that day who were, without any possible doubt, masters of the game far above any claims of the former. To some this may seem antiquated to talk about, but is extremely important that a true record of the history of the fanciers and the breed be recorded. I am familiar with what went on in the flying Tumbler fancy in and around Birmingham since 1900, and with the exception of Bert Goode of Harborne, who is the last of the old Roller men to be alive, I am the last one left who can authenticate the situation.

Whoever imported Flying Tumblers from England prior to the First World War from any source must have got all they wanted for three pence a piece; this is all they were worth. The real breeders from the beginning of the century could be counted on one hand, and the greatest of them all was the late Bill Richards of Harborne, Birmingham. He was regarded in the highest esteem by all the breeders of Rollers. His birds could be recognized anywhere, and he could tell by looking at another fancier's birds whether or not there was any of his blood in the others birds. His birds were small and tight and compact. Their predominant color was red check, dun, and the various shades of blue and blue check. The few odd self or two, were but throwbacks. He had a remarkable eye for a pigeon. He could readily sum up the quality of any bird he saw including physical defects, which would have escaped the eye of any other fancier. He was a regular visitor to the Backcountry, where he was a household word. Bill Richards never sold or gave away any of his birds. The only blood of his Rollers, which got into other hands, was obtained by the noble art of catching. Catching strays was always considered a sporting event in Flying Tumbler circles in those far off days. His family of Rollers was the only one in existence up to the twenties, which portrayed a well thought out process of breeding skill. The facet of the limited variety of color proved his belief in inbreeding, which everybody else was frightened of. Bill Richards died in 1938, after 70 years of keeping Rollers, and never a day without them. I was fortunate to acquire 25 of his birds at this time from his brother Ard, who was a famous breeder and exhibitor of the badge marked exhibition Long Faced Tumbler.

Next on the list is Harry Bellfield of Cradley Heath, Staff's. He was a most unassuming man, and as successful with his pigeons as he was with his business. He liked a Roller, and nothing but the swiftest and straightest spinners pleased him. His birds were varied in color and pattern, both clean legged and muffed. He did not keep as many as did Bill Richards because for one thing he was victim to the wiles of his many admirers who constantly contrived to get pigeons from him at any price. There are few who are proof against such acute agitation. H. Bellfield was noted for an outstanding grizzle cock, which was a wizard in the air. It was one of the most reliable pigeons that ever flew. As a stock bird this cock was responsible for most of the good pigeons flown at any loft, which had been fortunate enough to acquire offspring of this bird. I purchased many birds from Harry Bellfield during the twenties. After seventy years and, like Bill Richards, never a day without them, he was compelled to give up his birds on the advice of his doctor. I was sent for and advised to take all of them. There is no more distressing moment than when acquiring a man's pigeons on such terms. On retirement H. Bellfield purchased a home especially suited to flying his birds. His loft was situated on the peak of a knoll, and on occasions, due to wind direction, you could look down on his birds and watch them roll. His birds were deep and extremely regular, and it was seldom they could fly for more than twenty minutes. He flew several times each day, weather permitting, and each time they would fly and roll to their utmost. He also had in mind when he chose this situation the existence of extremely long grass which grew all around the knoll, and which varied very little in growth all the year round. The idea was to lessen the possibility of any of his birds destroying themselves should they make a mistake and roll all the way. All outstanding Rollers are subject to mishaps, especially when the wind is blowing in a certain direction. Harry Bellfield was a great Roller fancier.

Another fancier of note, and whose name was also a household word, was Elija Tomkins of the Lye, Stourbridge. He was an old fancier with experience from the cradle. He was especially noted for his patched breed. These birds were mostly red checks with uneven white patches distributed on various parts of the body, or whites with an uneven distribution of red check patches over various parts of the body. They were very attractive birds and as good as they come as spinning Rollers. A fifteen-year-old cock from E. Tomkins played a prominent part in my family of Rollers; in fact, it was the sire of my dun hen 1613. E. Tomkins was also a great old fancier, a description any words of mine could do little justice to.

Ben Homer of Cradley Heath was also very prominent in the fancy, and any bird acquired from him was a treasure for anybody. On retirement, he spent all his daylight hours down in the garden with his birds, a small house having been built for this purpose and his convenience. His main Old Un was a white cock, a son out of H. Bellfields old blue grizzle cock, or Silver, which is the term used for a light blue grizzle in Flying Tumblers.

When Ben Homer passed on I acquired the white cock together with three more of his favorites, a wish he expressed before his death. These birds also helped me along. Another outstanding fancier was J. Thompson of Harborne. A lifelong fancier, and noted for his two old pairs, a dun bald cock, a blue chec badge hen, a creamy badge hen and a magnificent red spangled saddle cock. It was a pair out of these famous pigeons that produced my old Spangled Cock. This cock was a champion spinner for fifteen yards, and produced the bulk of my strain. He was also a big winner at the shows in his day. He lived until he was eighteen. It may be interesting to note that Byron Wedgwood of Show Tippler fame offered me a good price for this cock on behalf of J. E. Graham who was in England at the time. There was not enough money to buy him. Old Jack Taylor of Rowley Regis was another unique figure in the fancy. He was a hard man to deal with, but if you did obtain a bird from him, so long as he had bred it, it was a great asset to the loft. I did not know him intimately as he was about 80 when I first met him. I often saw from a distance his two bull terriers, which would have killed anybody attempting to set foot within 20 feet of the pigeon pen.

Of great interest to me was a stuffed specimen of a blue saddle hen, which Jack Taylor said was over 100 years old, and was supposed to have broken her neck during flight. This hen was typical also of the best rolling pigeons known to me through my experience and typical also of the best Rollers at the present time.

Jim Skidmore of Blackheath was also an outstanding fancier and his collection of Rollers was always the envy of all who saw them. In his later years he established a family of 90 per cent red checks, since by the knowledge he had gained, he had begun to interbreed. His stud consisted of birds from Bellfield, Richards, and myself.

A fancier of high repute was Harry Young, a businessman. He had the reputation of traveling the country and buying, at any price, every good bird he could find. He was also a true fancier and clever breeder. Birds from his stud were often given credit for establishing many lofts with the highest quality deep spinning birds. I never met Harry Young, but he was well known to my father and his associates and from this source I gained a good picture of him. Both Bellfield and Richards obtained birds from him.

There were scores of other good fanciers, outstanding in their different ways, but lacking the skill of the others. They were the follow-the-leader type of fancier, so to speak. There is no one alive today who can tell me anything new about Rollers or the Roller fancy, or about its existence from 1900 to the present time. I am familiar with all the best fanciers in Britain today and they still keep descendants of my strain, a strain molded from the best of the stock of the foregoing fanciers. These are also the Rollers which I sent to the United States and which are to be found in many lofts throughout the world today, particularly in the United States.

Corroboration of this will be found in the lofts of Leroy Smith, Patchogue, Long Island, who has kept this strain of Rollers since 1934. What of Roy Smith? A fancier of 60 years or more, and one who has tried every known domestic breed of Rollers up to the time he received his first imports. His reason for keeping them is obvious. Roy Smith has made a name in the Roller world as an outstanding breeder of first class spinning Rollers and he has kept the family as pure as it is possible to keep it. He would not even use a pigeon from anybody even though such a bird was produced from a pair he had either sold or loaned out. Roy Smith has been of great service to the fancy and if any man deserves a Master Breeders Certificate, it is he. It may not be generally known that Roy Smith is acclaimed as one of the greatest breeders of Brown Leghorns in the world, if not the greatest, which testifies to his genius as a breeder of livestock.

Another fancier deserving of praise in this connection is Stanley Plona of Connecticut. He also is a close friend of Leroy Smith, from whom he obtained his stock and he also is as particular in his choice of birds, and a stickler for the one family. Visiting Connecticut last year, I was able to witness one of the best kits of stable, deep spinning Rollers I have ever seen. It is by the generosity of these fanciers that the Roller fancy is able to sustain and enjoy the pleasure only Roller pigeons can give. Incidentally, these are the only fanciers from whom I will obtain a bird to use in my loft. There is no doubt that by this time I am already condemned for blowing by own trumpet; certainly I am, and I could and ought to blow it much louder. It is not personalities that are important. It is the facts, and these I set myself out to put before the fancy, not only for the benefit of the fancy, but in consideration for those who like the facts. When I read the hysterical convulsions of those unqualified experts who dare to opine the non-existence of those pillars of the fancy in favor of the unknown, I am duty bound to state the true facts, as they have existed before and since the turn of this century. No wonder the fancy is in a state of confusion.

There are large numbers of Birmingham Roller lovers who are constantly being misled by nit-picking bigots who know no more about Rollers than those they hope to educate. Fanciers are better advised to use their own common sense and try to evaluate their own efforts. They should travel as much as they can and obtain first hand, the lessons available from the most successful breeders known. I am in the happy position of being able to substantiate anything I say about Rollers, should there be any doubt about it. When I say anything of importance I am dogmatic about it. I use the definition "I" and not "we" which is nothing but a defensive expression and one of doubt. Who is "we" in a debate of this kind? Is it etiquette or what? When a man writes any treatise, he alone is entirely responsible for it. This responsibility cannot be shared by anybody else, and he should expect to take the consequences. It is a sorry state of affairs for anyone who has to become a false authority.

2015 European Cup Fly results

Place	Name, Country	Breaks	Total
1	Ferid Catak, Bosnia	6,5,9,7,7,8,6,5//8,7,5//5,9,5//6,5,5 = 105 x Q1.5 x D1.4	228.9
2	Nikola Vukasinovic, Serbia	5,6,8,6,5,6,5,6,6//5,8,5,5,7,6//5,5,5//6,5,6,5,5 = 131 x Q1.2 x D1.2	188.64
3	Dusan Popovic, Serbia	5,6,6,6,5/5,5//6/5,6,5,6,7,6 = 79 x Q1.3 x D1.4	143.78
4	Radnic Goran, Croatia	6,5,6,5,5//5,5,5,5//6,6//6,5,6,5 = 81 x Q1.2 x D1.2	116.64
5	Colin Bailey, England	5,6,5,7,7,5,7,6,7 = 55 x Q1.4 x D1.3	101,1
6	Mark Croady, R.Ireland	5,5,7,6/7,5/7,5 = 47 x Q1.3 x D1.2	73.32
7	Robbie McNally, R.Ireland	5/6,5,5,6/6/5,5 = 43 x Q1.2 x D1.2	61.92
8	Henri Smit, Holland	6/6,7/5,6/7 = 37 x Q1.3 x D1.3	61.53
9	Eric Laidler, Denmark	5,5,7,5 = 22 x Q1.3 x D1.3	37.18
10	André Gergely, Hungary	5//5//-//5,6 = 21 x Q1.2 x D1.2	30.24
11	Alan Milne, England	5,5,5 = 15 x Q1.2 x D1.2	21.6
12	Henk Nijman, Holland	5,6 = 11 x Q1.2 x D1.2	15.84
13	Mark McCory, England	5,5 = 10 x Q1.2 x D1.2	14.4
14	Dom Butterworth, England	5,5 = 10 x Q1.1 x D1.2	13.2
15	Boric Recek, Slovenia	//-//5//5 = 10 x Q1.1 x D1.1	12.1
15	Milos Tubic, Serbia	/5//5// = 10 x Q1.1 x D1.1	12.1
15	Paul Green, England	5,5 = 10 x Q1.1 x D1.1	12.1
18	Charlie Grout, England	5 = 5 x Q1.2 x D1.2	7.2
19	Helmut Ungar, Germany	5 = 5 x Q1.1 x D1.1	6.5
20	Darren Deacon, England	5 = 5 x Q1.0 x D1.0	5
20	Mick Gater, R.Ireland	5 = 5 x Q1.0 x D1.0	5
22	Andrew Cara, England	withdrew	0
22	Davy Bird, England		0
22	Dom Carton, R.Ireland		0
22	Hans Van Rossum, Holland		0
22	Heine Bijker, Holland		0
22	Kevin Bowden, England		0
22	Mark O Neal, England		0
22	Peter Ritz, Germany		0
22	Raj Das, England		0
22	Shaun Overfield, England		0

Spinner Magazine Worldwide
Volume 2   Sept – October 2015

Ted Mann Stock cock bred by Ron Swart

Roller Eye Sign

By

Dave Henderson

Well there are many qualities of a top quality performance Birmingham Roller. There is the Body, the wings, the back/tail reflex, the keel, the vents, feather qualities and let's not forget the eye. Many key physical properties of a top quality performance roller will also be unique to the specific genetics (gene pool) behind the individual family of birds in question and you have to remember this.

My #1 Henderson cock bird shown with the "clusters" here (A)

Like with many athletic creatures on our planet, in this case our roller pigeons, the physical abilities within a creature or animal can insure its survival, this could be related to size, strength, and even the ability to adapt to the surroundings. Wild animals have to be able to survive or they will quickly die, it is survival of the fittest type of environment in the wild.

Now with domesticated animals, like the Racing pigeon and the Birmingham Roller, physical properties can be identified that may or may not make your pigeons better as noted above (for survival) which can and will also relate to the eye and qualities of the eye at times. These physical and even mental characteristics can make these pigeons a "champion" or even a cull and many times it's not a physical characteristic that makes them as such but more a mental quality within specific pigeons. It's your job to be able to identify these subtle qualities in our best and worst pigeons to better move our breeding programs along in a positive direction each season and this is really the most important ability a pigeon breeder should have.

You will get many varied opinions about eye sign and what constitutes a "good" or "bad" eye in our pigeons'. The Racing Pigeon hobby really has discussed specific eye sign qualities of their breed that many look at, but unfortunately these qualities are not the same in each breed or even the same from the various families of pigeons within the same breed. In the Racing hobby they have various qualities that tell them about specific birds; like if they will be a good breeder to being a good racer and everything in the middle. I know much of this is very confusing and even contradictory as we are looking for the best all-around pigeons that have the performance and the ability breed more birds like itself. I mean what good is a good spinner if it has no ability to reproduce itself right?

Well this is where it gets technical as in performance pigeons many will perform a concept called Hybrid Vigor to create exceptional performance within 2 good families of pigeons which may not be good at producing good birds like itself. You might ask why we would want such a pigeon. Well it is everything to do with winning contests. This involves the blending of 2 line bred families of pigeons together to create the ultimate performance pigeon and many do this in the performance pigeon world, but this is another topic of performance pigeons altogether.

Now getting back to eye sign, some fanciers have shown us specific qualities of the eye and will even assess the qualities of some pigeons with no direct knowledge to the performance of a specific pigeon. This is the key to the entire equation when it comes to the eye sign of our rollers in my opinion and one that many will overlook, but for most that want to show off their best pigeons the guy assessing the eyes, for the most part, will assume that you are showing him one of your good pigeons which may not may not be the case and this is where the "bs" can get really thick at times and only you can assess if it's a good birds or not by watching it fly and perform.

I know for most the whole eye sign theory reeks something that you might leave in the toilet daily, but I think it's really something you should also try to pay attention to as well. At the very least eye sign is similar to color balancing so at to create well balanced birds. This whole eye sign thing only works when you have a "family" of pigeons to work with I think and are not from the kind of guy that is constantly picking up birds all the time from various sources often. There will be no continuity in just continually crossing birds generation after generation and your loft will be built only on the pure luck method or working on the law of averages primarily. Fanciers that resort to this type of loft will be breeding a lot of birds and hoping on making the laws of average work in their favor and many will do this. There is nothing wrong with this method however there is a much easier way to do it and also by breeding and handling less birds in the process.

Like anything with our Birmingham Rollers they firstly have to perform to a high standard in the air to be considered for stock, at least you should be doing this 99% of the time. There are circumstances at times that can make us stock up birds out of the nest to further evaluate them in the stock loft and are simply securing the bloodline that can be lost at times. Sometimes a special breeder might die on you and you want to secure the specific genetics in a bird for future breeding, but many times you panic in these situations even though if you are doing things right you will have backups to these great birds that can suddenly die on us even if you have to borrow birds back that you might have shared over the years.

Problems can really occur when guys are blindly stocking up bird's generation after generation like this for evaluating in the stock loft without ever flying them, many pedigree breeders will do this. This type of thing can happen when people are trying to keep specific genetics for various reasons and it is possible that unflown birds can be very good producers and it's all done thru the evaluation process and you fully evaluating birds in your stock loft. All of us should be evaluating our stock loft every year to prove to ourselves the birds in there are doing what they are there to do which is produce good quality spinners and if they are not doing this simple thing they are not deserving of the title "stock bird".

The eye sign on our pigeons is only a tool to help us to better evaluate our pigeons and rank them within your own lofts. What if you discovered that many of your best birds all share a specific characteristic of the eye that you never paid attention to before? I think that if you were able to find a common characteristic of all your best breeders why would you not pay attention to it? I know for me it's about efficiency and the quicker you can identify prepotent breeders the more it will benefit you in the long run. I mean what really does make some birds better at producing good birds compared to other birds of similar genetics? It could very well end up being some sort of genetic trait that a simple blood test can find but what if it is a simple characteristic of the eye like Pensom thought? If we can identify these small traits that you have never noticed before it will help you to better evaluate your stock loft. These are all things we should be doing all the time to make us better pigeons. The eye sign of a specific pigeon can be amazing but if it is not producing you good pigeons there is no reason to keep it in your stock loft unless you are just looking to make pigeons with pretty eyes.

HMONG BIRMINGHAM ROLLER CLUB

See Lor aka Yuri (President) (916) 58-0281

Members

Sor Lor - Koua Vang - Teng Lor - Pao Vue - CJ Vang - Johnny Her

FOLLOW US ON FACEBOOK

SPEED - DEPTH - VELOCITY - RESPECT - FAMILY - SACRAMENTO

Roller Eye Sign

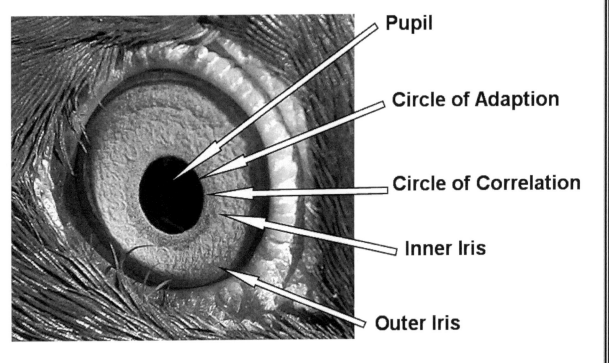

- Pupil
- Circle of Adaption
- Circle of Correlation
- Inner Iris
- Outer Iris

Here's a diagram showing the various parts in the roller eye

Let me toss out a few eyes from my best birds so you can look them over. They will not all be the same and I think at times their eyes can almost be like a finger print and unique to each bird as well as each eye being slightly different. They obviously share similarities here but are rarely identical from what I have seen. The 3D patterns in the Iris that give it depth and even the other features listed here will be all slightly different from bird to bird. Nothing is easy but if you continue to want to educate yourself with your specific rollers and how to breed better birds, being progressive, you will be much more aware of things later on and many of these things you will take for granted.

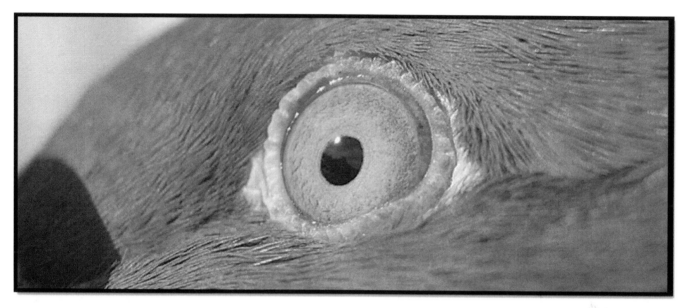

1

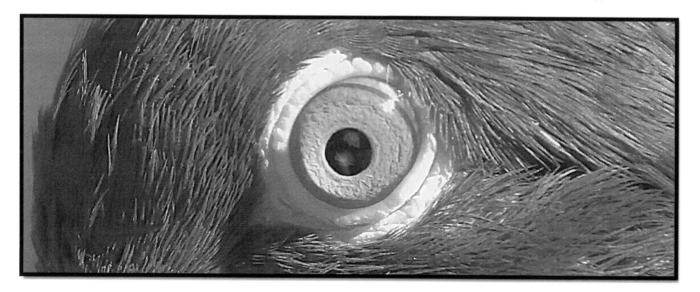

2

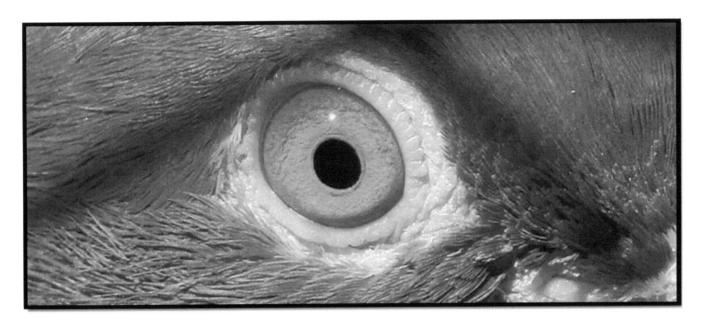

3

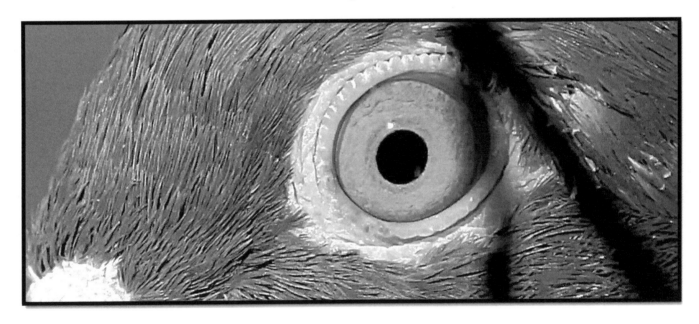

4

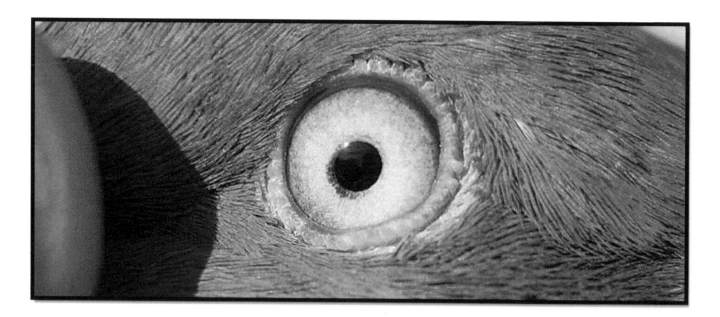

5

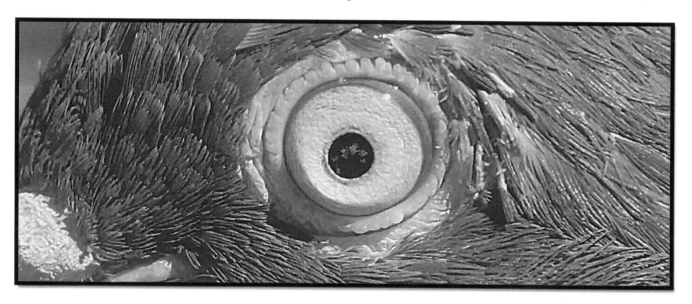

A pearl eyed bird with heavy clusters (6)

Well here you can get a look at some of the eyes of my best producing birds. The pearl eye on the bottom (5) is the only aerial champion I have currently in my loft **(now deceased). The #1 eye is the bird behind all my best birds in 2019.** Although you can see some similarities to the orange eyes listed and in fact they are very closely related. The two orange eyes in the middle together (2 & 3) are a pair of full siblings off a very prepotent stock pair I had for many years and both of these birds are good producing as well **(#2 is now deceased).**

You will also notice in the first orange eye (2) that it has 2 large gold flakes in the eye, this is called an eye cluster. These are larger than most of them you might see and this bird currently is probably my #1 producing cock bird and it might be over the next several years that all his babies start to dominate my loft, but that is still being evaluated at this point, but certainly he will probably become his own side to my current gene pool. This cocks two son are good breeders for me as well. One thing that is consistent is that orange eyed birds have **gold** colored clusters and pearl eyed birds have **silver** colored clusters.

Some might say that the clusters are formed with these "lose" particles from the Iris forming in the pupil due to the Iris being too full. I can't really say what it is that causes this but the consensus seems to be that birds that develop this feature tend to have a natural ability to reproduce better than your average pigeon. Again for me this is still not a proven fact, so far 2 of my cocks that show it are giving me good birds and I notice it more common in my cocks. I think that this was a key feature the Bill Pensom looked for in birds for many years and one that he really didn't advertise about it either. He mentions characteristics of the eye but never made notion to "eye clusters" in his writings to my knowledge. Yes many have stated that when Bill Pensom would pick up and handle a good bird the eye was one of the first features he would look at when evaluating a pigeon in the hand. I think it is obvious that even for Bill Pensom this was not 100% true as if it was more of today's fanciers would have loads a fantastic good producing pigeons and this is simply not the case. I think, like several I know, that it's the balancing of the birds like with color that makes the best birds and the eye is just part of that balance.

The diagram shown above that outlines specific parts of the eye and what they are called and display specific features that you look for in the eye with a magnifying jewelers' loupe. You can see that not one of the posted eyes are identical and all are slightly different. I wish they were all equally good pictures but they are not. It can be difficult to get a good clear photo of the eye, but it can be done.

I think the 12x - 15x version is about the right strength and can be found online at many places from ebay to amazon for $10 or less. I also have a 20x version that works well too but can zoom in maybe a little too close at times to see the action within the eye that is also very important.

Here is common eye loupe you can get, on the left a 13x by Carson

Another product to consider a Carson MagniLoupe available online

What I normally look for is an alert eye that appears to moves a lot seeing where it is at all times even when you are holding the bird in your hand, it's kind of like a nervous look but still keeping alert and being able focus on its surroundings. Some are stated as calling this eye movement "bounce" as in some cases the eye is moving and reflexing as you hold the bird to look more closely at the eye. I think again that the amount of bounce you see can be at trait of specific families of birds just like other qualities you will see. The traits like everything come down to specific families of birds that have been line bred for many years.

When you see birds that have the ability to produce good spinners with multiple mates some have said the eye clusters is a common trait for this ability no matter what kind of pigeon, however it's obviously not 100% or breeding good rollers would be easy and everyone would have them. You have to track these things and over a period of time come to a conclusion that it works or does not work with your specific family but you will never know unless you dive in and try to figure it out.

Guest writers will be given a free ¼ -½ page ad for each issue they contribute in. You could use this for yourself, your club or any other pigeon related topic

Southern Gauteng Region
consists of five clubs in South Africa

V.R.K - Vanderbijlpark Roller Club	G.B.R.C - Gold Reef Birmingham Roller Club
Albert Wallis, Wynand Deyzel, Charles Puth, Hennie De Bruyn, Hennie Phal, Hannes Rossouw	Niekie Deysel, Jan Deysel, Rob Lombaard, Jan Lubbe, Johan Venter
S.A.B.R.C - South African Birmingham Roller Club	H.P.S - Hyper Paints Spinners
Poen Sahabodien, Willem Potgieter, Mark Sacks, Walter Benfield, Riaan Naude	Dominic Peter, John Paul Peter, Mark Peter, Jade Peter, Gesham Thebe, John Chauke

W.R.K - WestRand Roller Club
Sparks Axsel, Dirk Axsel, Tommy Laubscher, Christo Troskie, Theo Troskie, Basie Masiso, Henk van der Westhuizen

Regional Director - Niekie Deysel
Ndeysel@deyco.co.za

It's always nice getting another point of view on things and I really appreciate Milo's view on the eye sign. A lot might think this is just wasted efforts but it can certainly work to some degree with specific families of Rollers. People don't realize that specific families of birds have specific characteristics to look for. One idea does not cover every family or strain of roller out there so it's up to you to find the characteristics of your best birds and see if there are anything obvious that they have in common except for their spinning ability. Much has to do with HOW YOU select birds so this also plays into this.

Eye Sign Voodoo
by
Camillo Paci

Eye sign can be a touchy subject. Some swear by it, taking it into great consideration when selecting pairs for breeding, and others think it to be complete nonsense. What could a roller's eye have anything to do with its performance or breeding abilities? That is a completely rational question. Unfortunately, I do not have a rational answer. I have to base all my statements on the value of eye sign theory using only my observations. For those that take the time to learn what it is, there can be clues in the eye... I am not an ornithologist, so I can't explain the "whys" of the roller, but tell you the observations I have made time and time again that has shown me there are definitely connections.

For example: Why do my web-footed rollers almost always turn out to be good rollers? I have no idea. Why do my dark blue checks with marked white rumps turn out to be great rollers? I have no answer for that either. I believe these are clues in my own family, and worth my attention. So lastly, why do my best producers almost all share the same eye sign traits? I don't know, but it is certainly worth careful examination.

Can eye sign theories be applied to different families of rollers? Perhaps. It is much more likely that eye sign theory can be applied to different families of rollers than the other traits I just mentioned. Although these eye sign traits are most likely family specific, it would not surprise me if there are families of rollers out there that share these eye sign clues, and by observing them, perhaps we could bring about better breeding practices.

I have found many roller fanciers quick to dismiss the eye sign theory, so much so that I no longer share my findings on open forums unless asked. I find that very unusual simply because it is a visible and tangible study.

You just pick the birds up, and observe. I would think expression, or say character to be much more complicated. In fact, it is much harder to put into words for those that ask what to look for on those topics than eye sign, and rather uncommon to find fanciers even having the capacity to identify these traits. It isn't uncommon for me to express to a fancier that a particular roller has a "vacant" look, only to receive a "vacant" look from the fancier. Surprisingly, there is much more literature on character and expression then there has ever been written about the eye traits of the performing roller and how it relates to selection. I think the physical characteristics of the eye, have been lumped into the expression and character descriptors of standout rollers. I believe there is much more to be discovered and only through observation, can we decode the relevance of eye sign in our birds.

I've been asked, if you are so sure about your theories, why don't you just breed those birds together to make more like them? I wish it were that easy. Great eye sign and expression (which is a bi-product of a great eye) can't be easily reproduced simply by breeding two birds together that share the traits. It just doesn't work that way. Often it's just luck of the draw. I've had birds with excellent eye sign throw mediocre eye sign birds, and vice versa. Selecting birds for stock is to be done from the air first and foremost. But that is not the entire process. Great eye sign is a marker for great breeding history, and expresses itself through careful selection. William H Pensom once said, "Always mate best to best regardless of relationship". This again depends on how a fancier interprets best; best does not necessarily mean a bird that excels in the air. It means, more so, a pigeon that possesses in its make-up the right type, the right expression and the right kind of feather." I firmly believe in that, and try to look at more than just what the roller does in the air. Maintaining a top notch breeding program requires much more than just plucking good rollers from the sky. This is why I continuously find myself looking at the eyes of my best and worst performers, among other things.

So in the spirit of sharing some of my theories and observations, I will attempt, as best I can, to describe what I consider to be good eye sign. I have included two pictures of a near-perfect eyes for reference so readers may follow along. As far as eye sign terminology goes, I use technical Racing Homer terms. Although I use racing homer terms, they do not indicate the same things in rollers as they do in homers. After all, as fanciers of two totally different breeds we look for totally different things. If you aren't familiar with Homer eye sign terms I recommend just Googling a chart so some of this makes sense, or look at Dave's above

Starting from the center of the eye there is the pupil. It should be in the center of the eye, not off-set, and should be round. The pupil is black, and at times can contain what is referred to as "clusters." I describe this phenomenon as free floating flakes that look a lot like the gold floating in Goldshlager when it's shaken. They almost appear to be tiny parts of the Iris that have broken off. They are rare in my family of birds. So rare, that I have only seen a handful in all my years with rollers. I have written extensively on the subject of eye clusters, and from what others have shared, it is a sign of prepotency. This however is not ALWAYS the case, as I have come across a few with this trait in a few families where there appears to not be a correlation at all for this characteristic. Although it can't be assumed that all birds showing clusters make superior breeders, from the data I have collected, and the input from other fanciers leads me to believe that clusters are indeed linked to prepotency of the pigeon. If you have one with clusters, it could be a good one. The only catch is that the clusters (as well as many other fully developed eye sign traits) are not visible until their second year, or even later. The eyes go through many changes from juvenile to adult ages.

The next thin ring surrounding the edge of the pupil moving outward is the Circle of Adaptation. In a pearl based eye, I like the Circle of Adaptation to be blue in color. Continuing outward we should see the Circle of Correlation. I like it to start off pearl white, and bleed outward into a faint pink. Then we will see the inner Iris, and the outer Iris. Pearl pink, then blending into a rich dark red (Burgundy) color as it hits the final circle, which is referred to as the Health Circle on the outer edge of the eye. I like this to be almost a dark blue. If you were to take all the pearl and pink colors you see in the rings of the iris, it would be a dark bluish canvas. The more of the blue you see (bleeding) thru the granulation of the red and pearl iris colors, the richer the eye overall, and possibly even the better the breeder it is. My best breeders have what I call "Blue Eyes." They are not entirely blue obviously, they just have that "canvas" showing thru. Now all eyes are different, as you will see different shades of blending, and different colors and shades, but the distinct breaks in the circles should be clear to the eye. The final key I look for is the richness of the Iris granules. The absence of these granules will give the eye a "flat" or "dull" look. The Iris granules are the seemingly free floating masses we see in the inner and outer Iris. Some of you may have heard my "Miso soup" analogy. When you get a bowl of miso soup and it is stirred, it appears to be one solid color. As the soup cools, the egg, oils, and other ingredients begin to separate. That's what I like to see in a pearl based roller's eye. If the eye being observed is orange-based, then instead of color variations, there will be drastic differences in shades, and in some cases, blending of green and yellow. The principles mentioned above however apply in all colored eyes.

I also look for what I refer to as the "Electric" eye movement. I have found this to be an invaluable tool early in a birds training. If you have a bird with such eye movement, you can expect for it to develop quite the rolling impulse. When looking into the birds' eye, and holding it firm, I watch for a vibrating movement of the eye itself. It is not to be confused with the pupil reflex. That's important, as it indicates a highly functional eye, but this is something different. As the bird's eye shifts around in the socket you will see a tremor, or a vibration as it moves. The more aggressive the tremor is, the more sensitive the roller is to synapse response and neurotransmission. What does this mean? Well, I think it means a "control side" roller, being a bird that has a greater control over its rolling impulse, has little to no tremor. A "roll side" roller, being a bird with far less control to resist its rolling impulse, will show a nice electric shake. If you are holding the bird firmly in one hand, and with the other hand placing your index finger on top of the birds head and your thumb under its beak, you can actually feel the tremor. My best performers almost all have a nice electric eye. Birds with a nice electric eye have what I can only refer to as an alert, piercing, gaze. It is the opposite of a blank stare and instead of moving or "panning" slowly to follow your movements much like a still camera on a tripod or a rolling camera does, rotating on a horizontal plane, a quick vibration can be seen instead in the electric eye as it rotates, as if a hand held camera were being moved by an trembling hand. This occurrence very much relates to the overall expression of an individual in my opinion. My best performers have it, and best breeders as well. How it relates to better performance I can't be entirely sure, but it's constantly popping up in my best ones.

So these are nothing more than my observations and theories, but they all point to key traits that I look for. I feel many times the best way of describing my observations is to show on a live roller. To me that has always been the best way to share new discoveries in our hobby. As I have said before, one does not, or rather should not, pick breeders based on eye sign alone. The best performing rollers will catch the handler's attention, and upon closer inspection, may reveal eye sign traits I have described. A lot of what I see gets lost in translation, so hopefully these descriptions have been helpful. I've been raising rollers for a long time, but there isn't a day that goes by that I don't learn something new, no matter how insignificant it may seem. I encourage all my fellow roller men to take a stab at it. Handle your rollers frequently, and see if there are any commonalities in the eyes of your best producers and performers. If not in the eyes, then maybe in something else. For those that believe in eye sign theory, but are afraid to discuss it for fear of being ridiculed, remember that just because someone else doesn't see something in their birds, that doesn't mean it should be dismissed. There could be something to it. Keeping an open mind can open doors for improving our birds.

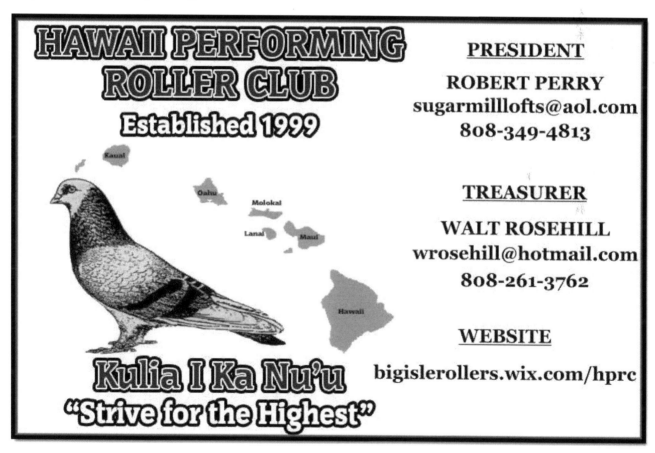

In The Spotlight

Interviews in the hobby

Meet Ted Mann
2015 World Cup Champion

Ted Mann at his loft

Name, age, where do you live; describe your location in Washington and the weather conditions on average; summer and winter

I have retired to Eastern Washington. The summers are warm like California's central valley but short. Winter is also short but can dip to 20 below zero for a week at a time. My lofts and kit boxes are designed to be open with full flow of air through them in the summer, and close up completely in the deep winter when it is coldest.

Incredible open area where Ted Mann is located

My breeding pen is insulated and has heat and lights, allowing me to breed through the winter. There is little to do in the winter so it is a good time to raise babies. This does three things. One, it keeps me entertained. Two, it prevents me from breeding later than May when I am preparing for the world cup, and the flys and wet nests become a problem. Three, my early rounds of youngsters are old enough to compete in the world cup.

I notice that you live between Yakima and the Tri City area in Washington State, how is this area in terms of the predators and do you have to lock down at specific times of the year?

The annual rainfall is eight inches leaving most days compatible with flying. The falcons and Coopers hawks are present particularly in fall and again in spring. I live in a flat open area with clear views in all directions for miles. The coopers hawks have a hard time sneaking up on the loft, but the falcons are difficult to dissuade. I have two red tail nests approximately 100 yards from the lofts. The one red tail is particularly territorial and I have seen three occasions where he has come out of the sky in a full stoop and tried to kill the peregrine. Now when I see a peregrine or a prairie it is passing over on its way home in a straight line. That is not to say I don't lose birds to the birds of prey. I lose two to four a year. Not forty like a lot of folks including some just thirty miles from my location.

I would first like congratulate you on an impressive win in this years' World Cup Finals. It has been 7 seasons since a US flyers has won this event. How does it feel to have won this very prestigious event?

Quite frankly I was absolutely stunned. I had hoped to be in the top twenty out of vanity but to win it didn't really occur to me. I have looked up old scores and there are a number of lofts that flew which have put up larger scores in the past. I can see that the weather and winds created a vacuum where my score being adequate, gives the impression of being remarkable, which it isn't. I was sorry to see so many flyers have bad luck. We all hope for a day the birds can show their best. I was the only person who got that.

2015 World Cup judge John Wanless said this kit was absolutely pleasure to watch

How long have you been raising, flying rollers in Washington? Have you had pigeons for most of your life? (When did you first find the rollers) Please give us a little insight on your "pigeon" related background up to and including your 2015 world cup team.

My pigeon experience started in 1960 with some not very good homers. Actually probably not homers at all. At thirteen I was very interested in the idea of homers and caught a ride from my home in Redding, California to the Bay Area. There I took busses to San Mateo, Oakland,

Richland, Berkley and San Francisco area to addresses of pigeon racers listed in a periodical I had. I met Elio Lumachi, Pete Henry, and several known flyers of the day. They were quite surprised I'm sure, to find me unannounced on their doorstep. But after I explained where I was from and that I had come to meet them, they were very gracious and taught me a little about handling and flying homers and showed me around their beautiful lofts. It was not a time of year anybody had birds, so I tried not to show my disappointment, but I had such a good time and it was so interesting I wasn't really totally let down. Just a little. I joined a racing pigeon club when I got home, and flew some birds I found that were not very good. That fall towards the end of the old bird racing season, one of the club members came to the banding with a crate holding two pair of racers from Elio Lumaci. Elio remembered me and sent the birds for me.

Is there anyone in your area that you have looked at for guidance and fellowship for flying rollers over the years?

I still had pigeons when I went to college and took them with me. I went to Davis (in the Sacramento area) and flew with the Yolo racing pigeon club. Which is part of the Camellia city combine and flew with the Bay Cities combine. From flying in the 200-bird races of Redding I was now flying in races with over 5,000 birds. While flying in this club I met Mr. John Fechko. We became good friends and he was a mentor to me every sense of the word. John was a California state judge for both rollers and racing homers. We spent a great deal of time together handling and training pigeons. About 1973 John invited me to a pot luck dinner. It turns out it was a Roller club pot luck and fund raiser. John bought some raffle tickets and gave them to me. I won a beautiful pair of rollers. They produced good individual spinners and a couple birds which were show-worthy. A good friend of mine from Redding, Professor Richard Dalrymple, loved his clean legged show tumblers. He invited me to go on a couple trips with him to pigeon shows. So I loaded up my best little roller and we went to where he grew up, Salt Lake City. The show was the Great Western. We had dinner with Dick's friend Chandler Grover. I was still focused on racing pigeons but found the conversations with Chan Grover most enjoyable. My little cock won best of show in the roller division and we were back on the road to Sacramento. Our next trip was to Pomona, California, to the Pageant of Pigeons. There we saw beautiful lofts -- much nicer than the house I was living in while going to college. My little cock won- best opposite sex -so I left Pamona with my head held high in spite of living in a house that wouldn't pass for a good pigeon pen. The final show was the Camellia city show in Sacramento. Once again the little cock won a trophy –Best Young Cock, and with that my show career ended.

I flew the racing homers until 1990. In 1990 my occupation changed and I was on the road a great deal, and didn't have time to fly the birds. I eventually let the birds go to my friend Carl Schoelkopf. We had traded birds back and forth since I was in Redding. In the fall of 2011 I called Carl in Redding, California. I told him I was missing the birds and thought I would like to get a couple pair of rollers again. I no longer had the desire to spend the hours driving up and down the road to train racing homers. Or drive an hour and a half to open clocks etc. etc. Carl told me I lived around the corner from Bruce Kuhlman. Bruce is a roller man we had met at a pigeon show in Kennewick, WA, near where I live, which Carl came to visit me to participate in. Bruce lined me up with a couple pair of his fire balls. They did some wonderful deep fast spins for me. This was in the spring of 2012. I met Joe Hanson thru Bruce and we all spent Saturday mornings watching Joe's birds and eating donuts.

Give us a little background on the birds you won the World Cup with and from where did they come from originally? How many cocks/hens in this kit and the average age of them. How did you start off with these birds and move along to 2015

I joined the roller club and listened to the stories of roller competitions. Not a primary interest of mine, but it sounded like fun and these gentlemen gave me some birds. In this club was a flyer by the name of Ron Swart. I met Ron and found him quite likable in a rascally way. He made me laugh and we became good friends. Ron was devoted to his pigeons and in his typically gentle way told me my birds were trash. He invited me over to his house and I became a frequent guest. He told me a collection of stories that sometimes varied in the telling on different days but the one thing that was consistent were his birds. I had never seen birds roll in groups all together before. His birds did this on a regular basis, and over and over. I saw one bird do a spin that was so deep I wouldn't even guess its length.

Some of Ted Mann's stock birds

Finally I told Ron I would like to get a pair of these pigeons someday. He had disposed of quite a few birds and I knew he didn't have a lot of birds. The next time I saw him he said he had a bird for me. Ron was not one to actually give a bird away. You either really wanted it or he wasn't going to waste it on you. He told me an astronomical price, I waited a moment with my poker face to see if he was kidding, and he wasn't. Well, I didn't want to be in a poker game so I figured I would see where this would go. I paid for the bird and we went to get her. There were two cocks side by side in another compartment. He asked me which one I liked the best. I told him, his response was "me too," and he gave me the bird. This was the best money I ever spent on a pigeon. I had my rollers for thirty years, and homers forty-five years. I am no longer a young man, I'm retired and don't have another thirty years to build up a family of birds. If I can buy thirty years of progress. Why not. So I decided to jump in head first.

Ron couldn't have done me a bigger favor. About five months later, Ron called me up one morning and said, "Come over and bring a crate." I went to his house and Ron took ten of his South African babies out of the nests and told me he wanted me to take them. I asked him if he wanted me to fly them and he said no. "You don't know which ones will be the breeders." I was relieved as I didn't want to risk them. I then asked him what was up. Something wasn't quite right and I knew he had been to the doctor. He told me then that he had terminal cancer and only had a very short time left. He was right and Ron was gone in only a few short weeks. We talked a little but I felt funny talking about the birds under the circumstances knowing he had so little time to get done what he needed to do. The birds from Ron including an as a result of this hurried passing of the birds and Ron, I had not gotten any pedigrees on any of the birds. I now had seven pair including an additional pair he had given me after the first pair.

It is now the spring of 2013, and Ron and I were going to fly the famous World Cup Fly together and he would show me how to get the most out of the birds. Ron passed away well before the World Cup even came however. I bred all the birds in rotations for the next two years, assessed the breeding potential, and eliminated four pair. I had met another club member Ed Taylor. Ed had also received several pair from Ron and was working more with his other family. Ed agreed to sell me his four pair from Ron and I was back to a rotation of breeding again. Except Ed had some pedigrees on the birds he had. Norm Brill, who also was a good friend of Rons', and one of our club members as well, helped me with some pedigree information he had. Since then John Farr, Mitch Reed, Clay Palamides and Jim Sherwood have helped me by supplying copies of what pedigrees they have. Tim Paustian, and Scott Reece have also offered to help fill in some of the blank spots as well, so it has become a two part hobby. It has become a bit of detective work for me. The deeper I get into it, the less it is what I thought it was.

The saving grace was the first pair of birds that Ron gave me, bred the best performers I had ever seen. I bred six beautiful little blue check hens out of this pair. At five months old I'm watching the kit and I see six birds breaking together over and over again. I got rid of all the other birds, moved the six hens into the stock loft and breed them all to their half-brothers, their dad, their uncle which I got from Ed Taylor, and anything else I had from Ron that was closely related. I kept enough birds to fly the cup and managed 35 points, and then disposed of all the birds but Rons "South Africans." I wasn't going to wait to start working with what I saw breaking. I was headed to more breaking, I loved it. I bred and disposed of more birds. Four birds (two pair) were added to the stock loft. Of all the Swart birds I acquired I have three pair remaining, and now the two pair I stocked gave me the five pair I currently breed out of.

Here's is Ted's #1 Pair (21 & 02)

One thing the homers taught me in flying the Bay Cities Competition was to cull ferociously. After you have culled, do it again because you are only half way there. Never waste a perch on a bird you wouldn't breed out of.

In the summer of 2015 I had five of the six little blue check hens in the competition loft, the sixth in the stock loft, all 2 and 3 years old. I had additional two year olds out of some of the little hens plus sisters a year younger. Ten yearlings and three young birds finished out the team for the 2015 World Cup competition, this was ten cocks and ten hens. I was looking forward to seeing what these little birds could do. I thought they may be competitive, maybe in the top twenty, but holy smokes. Who other than Bruce Kuhlman thought these little girls would win the World Cup. I still can't believe it.

Winning the World Cup is a major accomplishment and the winner is asked to judge the finals in the upcoming event (2016), will you be able to Judge the WC finals?

In all honesty, one day I think how cool and the next no way. I have been meeting so many people from all over the world, and a chance to meet these people in person and see their lofts would be amazing. Then the next day I think of ten weeks away from my wife and my birds, and how much time I would spend in airports and it doesn't seem quite so exciting. I would like to see John Wanless again and his birds. Not to mention Eric Laidler, Henne Bjiker, and many of the top flyers of the last decade. It is a thought provoking decision.

When I first saw your score pop up in Washington State I recognized your name (just didn't recall from where at the time) and have since realized that you were at one time living in my home town here in Northern California? We both shared a common friend named Carl Schoelkopf and I recall that I had even met you on 2 occasions when I dropped by for a visit to Carl's after work back in the mid to late 1990's. How did your days living here in Northern California develop your senses and ability to handle the birds in this years' World Cup fly?

What makes this question interesting is that I did not develop any knowledge about rollers. I did learn about homers and flew homers from the time I was thirteen until I left for college six years later. Carl and I trained together and talked about our homers and what we were doing constantly. It was after I left Redding and went to Davis, I guess still Northern California, that I acquired the rollers. I never competed with the rollers, and as a result of not competing I treated them the same as my homers. Flew twice a day every day and fed them good rich food at sixteen % protein and lots of safflower. I had the rollers mainly to put under the homer hens for long races. For the five and six hundred mile races I would put roller eggs under the hens. They would give everything they had to get back to their babies, and these tiny little babies were not a physical drain on the homers. Those little babies would be practically pressurized with a crop as big as their body. These little rollers grew up to be incredible slick and gorgeous encouraging me to try showing the one I thought was the best.

It wasn't until I acquired the birds here in Washington that I realized what roller are capable of for performance, rollers are not small homers at all. I had my birds flying 3 and 4 hours or more. Like tipplers, they would sky out and I would see them just before sunset. Bruce Kuhlman had introduced me to Joe Hanson. Joe liked his birds to fly 40 minutes. While we ate donuts and watched Joe's birds fly Saturday mornings. Bruce, Joe and I would talk about feeds and feeding practices and its effects on the birds' behavior. I acquired some birds from Jim Sherwood, who I had met through Ron Swart. Shortly after I received these Masons I began acquiring birds from Ron as well.

Mid 1990's Redding Area Flyers around the first time I met Ted Mann

Jim Sherwood was very generous in his suggestions on how to get the most out of his birds. Ron and Jim both feed their competition teams similarly. Ron had passed away as I was preparing for my first competition and the birds were not performing at all. In desperation I called Jim Sherwood and he said quit feeding those birds so good and give them straight wheat, a half cup for ten birds. The birds changed overnight. I began experimenting with wheat, milo, oats, barley and tried feeds from 9% to 13% with undeniable results. Suddenly I had different birds. I can't say I have come up with the perfect feed, but I have found the range in which the birds do fine and if you don't change it, everything will stay consistent. I will note, when a homer is in condition to fly a race, the roller and homer have the same texture to the body, the corkiness that makes them feel light but maintaining the fullness of the chest and back. The oil spot on the ninth flight, and the bubble on the keel. I am not a believer in flying the birds to hungry, or breaking them down to an emaciated dry feathered skeleton. I want them to hit peak performance and be corky on fly day. Fat birds don't win flys but neither do stressed out thin birds.

Like the homers, the rollers put in a physically demanding performance. For which they need strength and endurance, but just enough endurance they don't sky out. I have found with my birds the last three days before the fly that are the most important. They need just the right amount of rest. Too much and they flatten out, not enough and they don't come out rocking. Same with the feed, to much they are in the clouds and not enough they are back on the loft in ten minutes. No matter what you do, you just hope for the best when you open that kit box door. You can't help but wonder is this too much, not enough, finally you just pay your dime and take your chance.

I notice in the pictures you sent that you are feeding your WC team on the floor and they appear to be eating a regular mixed grain of feed with popcorn, how do you feed your kit to get the most out of them, and is this your normal fly mix? How do you manage them, fly them in a normal week or month? I am referring to your "A Team" and how do you fly and handle the young birds in comparison to your "A Team"?

Ted's molting mix

I have read articles on feeding and controlling the rollers and I have tried a few different things I have read about. I'm afraid I am not going to be much help on technical stuff here in this interview. The young birds I feed them like homers. They are raised on a 17% protein mixed feed and stay on this mix for the first two and a half months. At this time I start thinning them off this with wheat and sometimes milo as well. At three and a half months they are on the same feed as my old birds get. The young birds go into a team as soon as they are doing over twenty foot rolls frequently. I want them stimulated to roll and break as soon as possible. As for the team birds get an 11 ½% protein mix and thing that makes a difference is the volume of feed I give. Changing the feed always knocks the birds off their conditioning, and you have to wait for them to adapt to the new feed before they are performing again. As for flying, every time I give the birds a rest, they go flat on me. I fly almost every day and give them about 1 cup of feed for ten birds. I adjust up and down from that point based on flying time. If I cut their feedback so the birds are flying for only forty minutes they lose too much weight and become washed out.

Here are some of Ted's kit birds

Joe Hanson had his birds fed right with a forty minute flying time. I try to hold mine down to an hour and a half. After an hour and a half I will cut the feedback slightly. I flew two kits in the elimination trial and had a two hour window. The second kit went up with exactly twenty minutes left of the two hour window. I had served a half ration to keep them low and they still flew an hour and forty minutes. If the birds went up and just sailed around I would be more aggressive about controlling their time, but the birds go up and work for the whole hour and a half. This is when they are in good condition and ready for a fly in competition. I really don't mind them flying for one and half hours, but if they are not performing regularly then I start to pay attention. When I don't see breaks like I should I know I have too many birds not rolling in the kit and it is time to separate out the nonperformers. When the birds hit the seventh flight in the molt, I will increase their protein to 16+% and add some safflower until they finish the head molt and tenth flight. This is a time the birds flatten a little and don't feel like hard spins. This is not a good time to cull, nor a good time for a fly. After that tenth flight comes in, I have the best performances of the year. Molt is over, weather has cooled off, and the babies are all now over five months and spinning their little heads off. If not, then it's time for their little heads to come off.

Here's Ted's World Cup kit eating

I see by the Multipliers that your team was awarded some exceptional depth and quality multipliers. Do you have to do anything to get them to perform like this or do they do it on their own when flown with basic feeding principles? Do you follow any breeding methods to develop these birds into your family?

From day one the youngsters from the first pair of birds performed deep spins and frequent brakes. It was only the youngsters from this pair that were braking. The six little BC P/B W/F hens that became the foundation of the loft. The only thing I do is eliminate all the birds that are not as good as those original six. With five pair you can see I have eliminated all the average breeders and am dealing with a subset of the original collection of genes I started with. As noted above my feeding principles stay constant and it's the birds doing all the work at their best.

How would you describe the percentages of good spinners for kit competition in your birds? How you would describe you average culls? Do you get high percentages to sort out or approximately how many good ones do you get say out of 20 or more babies you breed?

The young birds this year have the highest percentage of good spinners I have produced thus far. My first year I kept those six little hens out of 120 birds produced. This year 18 out of my first twenty birds went onto the team by the time they were six months old. The consistency in the youngsters is a dramatic change over the past three years. I bred over 100 birds last year as well. I kept ten yearlings on the team and stocked two. The rest went away. I should note, eighteen of twenty youngsters went in with the team birds to get used to flying together and keying on each other. The eighteen birds will not be there on competition day. The final culling is done preparing the team for the competition. Five weeks before the competition I watch the birds closely and pick out the birds that are missing the breaks. Some birds will roll just before or just after the breaks. The birds that are left up in the air when sixteen or seventeen birds break, or just miss most the breaks get pulled out and put back in with the youngsters until I am down to twenty. Some I may give a little more time, the younger ones that are frequent and deep but need to mature and improve. By the end of November all the youngsters are at least seven months old. What wasn't culled before the Nationals will be assessed and fifteen hens, and fifteen cocks will remain for the next world cup in spring. Now that eighteen percent of good spinners is more like ten percent. For every young bird that stays, an old bird has to go or transition to the stock loft. I still have five of the six little BC hens on the team, but they have all spent time in the stock loft laying a round or two of eggs to go under fosters, and back to the team. These girls have been on the team for three years. It's time to replace these girls with birds with young birds. If not with birds in the young bird loft now, then with birds next spring. The youngsters just keep getting stronger and even the youngest are spinning deep and fast. I'm sure there will be some that break big.

I feel the birds are coming together. The birds are handsome mongrels. There really is no type in these birds.

Nobody would describe these birds as peas in a pod. I have long cast birds, short cast birds, small birds, medium birds, you name it, its' all in there. I am strict about good strong bone structure, this means no weak vents, flat keels, hatchet keels, long humorous, narrow week backs or other extremes. I like a lot of variation as I prefer to breed unlike birds together, not duplicates. The strength of this "non-family" of birds is the robustness that comes from hybrid vigor. These are crosses bred to crosses bred back to crosses. There is not a pure blood in my loft. Heaven forbid. What can I say, I should be embarrassed, but they put on a good show.

Would you like to recognize anybody that may have helped you accomplish this incredible task of winning the World Cup?

I would very much like to acknowledge someone. There is more than one person that helps somebody through shared knowledge, or even just camaraderie and support. But in this case there is one individual that I could not have won the World Cup without. RON SWART. Ron really did something nearly impossible in such a short time. Ron selected birds from Jim Sherwood, Hannes Rossouw, Ellis Mcdonald, Wayne Federer, and a little extra from who knows where else. Ron put together this selection of genes from all of these birds into more than a couple hundred birds. Once Ron created these two-three hundreds birds he selected approximately twenty birds from them to breed from. He continued to breed large numbers so that he could pick those few birds that expressed all the traits he was looking for in one pigeon. He never went back to the original pairs. He bred his new birds strictly to each other. Ron never did get to see the outcome of this program though he predicted it perfectly. When Ron handed me the ten babies he had bred for the next generation of breeders, he said "If I only had a little more time". He told me "These birds can win the world cup". I am so glad they did. I have to give credit to Ron Swart for his vision of these fantastic pigeons. I am truly grateful he entrusted his new family of birds to me. I am also relieved I didn't let my good friend down. Hats off to you Ron.

I know many that have won the WC have been bombarded with inquiries on selling birds. Is this something you are open to or are you going to refrain from doing much of this? How will you handle inquiries like this?

I have never sold birds and I am not comfortable asking for money. Also, you probably noticed that I keep very few birds. I will keep about 15 cocks and 15 hens in separate boxes, and my five pair of breeders. Two kit boxes will be empty by Nov 30th, waiting for next year's young birds. And two kit boxes will have fifteen cocks or hens. The birds I cull are disposed of. I am not doing anybody a big favor by giving them culls. Picking out the thirty best birds should work, but I may not have thirty birds that I consider equal to my best. If that's the case, it may be twenty birds over winter and rely on the young birds I will start breeding November first.

What advice would you give to any new flyers out there wanting to fly in competition that will get them going in the right direction early?

My only advice is get the best birds you can get your hands on. Look at the scores on the world cup competitions since its inception. You will see a limited number of scores over six hundred. This is the level of competition. If you get birds that have never posted that kind of score, you will most likely never see it. From what I see there are only so many lofts in the world posting big scores. And it's the same people over and over. You can't express a trait that isn't present. So make sure you have birds with the traits you want. Then improve upon them. If necessary find a bird that has the traits you want and introduce those traits into your birds. Remember, when out crossing, make sure you are not improving the out cross.

Most importantly my advice is don't think too much about winning competitions. Get some good birds and just have fun with them. If it goes well and the birds respond with stunning performances, enter them in a competition and fly for fun and camaraderie. Don't make winning the competition the main goal as it may take some of the fun out of it. As I have proven this year, there is a great deal of luck required to win a competition, and not necessarily the best flyer wins. It's a horse race and any one could win on a particular day. Let the birds make you feel like a winner with their daily performances just for you.

Ron Swart seen here during the 2011 World Cup Finals

Adrian Gasparini - GC
International 61 3 417989789
Local 0417 989 789
etts@bigpond.net.au

worldcupfly.com

Tim Decker -Treasurer
951-685-5903
tldecke@yahoo.com

# Thinking Outside The Box

Awarding Bonus Multipliers
A More Accurate Way
By
Dave Henderson

Around 12-15 years a back my friend Joe Urbon and I began brain storming various ways that we could come up with a much fairer system to judging and awarding points to our kits using the current 1,2,3 scoring system used by the World Cup, NBRC National Fly and most other clubs today. A system that once the judge hands us our score sheets we will know what transpired up there in the opinion of this judge without having to pick his brain much, so this event can move on to the next competitor quickly. This system would also give the readers of this score sheet an honest assessment of how this kit did on this particular day. As well as making participants feel more at ease getting this score. Many have at times suggested that judges will use the multipliers at the end of the fly to hinder or help specific kits do better/worse after the fact and this will prevent this from happening.

I know there are some who don't watch their kits the entire fly while being judged as they get nervous and uneasy, however there are also many, like me, that watch their kit from beginning to end in the hopes of learning more about what my kit really did in this competition so I can have a mental note to myself once I get my score sheet. We all know that the judges, for the most part, don't always see things exactly like you might see them and this is expected. I know that many when they get their score just see numbers there and have a hard time knowing exactly what the judge saw. Many times they have to pick the judges brain to figure out what he can do to improve your team in the future. I want a more accurate system so that when our judge is done scoring everyone that looks at this score sheet will know what this judge really saw in your kit and it will give you a way to progress your team in the future so that you might get the most out of your rollers for future events.

I remembered the one time that my old friend Rick Mee judged the National Fly and had written up a standard he would follow while judging this event. He explained in his own terminology and descriptions what he would be looking for in your kit. He explained multipliers and what the kit would need to do in order to score in his opinion. I found this to be a very nice approach to know what he would be looking for and what his expectations would be during the competition. I wish more would do what Rick did here when judging these flies for us so as to allow participants to get a feel for his ideals and standards. I would however prefer to get this information and standards well before the competition started so you can better set up your team knowing the things a specific judge would be looking for.

Even with this type of written standard many that are not aware of the antics of this particular judge could still be left wondering what this judge meant without standing underneath him while judging. Sitting underneath the judge while judging is the only real way to know what he is looking at in your kit.

I looked at the current score sheets and when the judging is over you can see the breakdown of each break your team performed but with the quality and depth multipliers you only get an average of what this judge saw and it is pretty hard to know exactly what he saw in your breaks. I figured the only accurate way to award the bonus multipliers and have the flyer understand and know how to improve his kit is to award the multipliers for each break individually. This would do 2 things; 1st you will have a way to know when it's best to call in your birds so as to maximize their potential and 2nd you would know exactly what the judge saw in your team for each break. This is real information that can help you improve your kit for future events.

Here you will see a sample score sheet that I what I am suggesting should be changed on the current system of scoring our kits. After each 5 minute judging period "/" mark is made so you know how many breaks the kit did per 5 minute increment.

As you see the score keeper will score the break and next to the break give the quality and depth multiplier as a fraction so that you will know exactly how your kit started working and how they finished scoring in this competition. I think a lot will be gained by this type of scoring improvement to our current system.

Let's assume that this flyer called in the kit less than a 2 minutes after he released them and if he would've waited several more minutes before he called them in, by the looks of the score sheet, he probably would've gotten a much larger score as this kit began to roll bigger with better average breaks in the last 10 minutes in comparison to the first 10 minutes.

Let's break it down by the first 12 breaks scored compared to the last 9 breaks scored here. In the first 10 minutes the kit had an average birds per break of 6.33, Q 1.39 and D 1.35 and in the last 10 minutes an average birds per break of 8.55 with Q 1.36 and D 1.41. So you can see the significant of the scoring if the flyer would have waited even 3 more minutes to call in this kit to be scored. He might even have landed possibly 2 more ½ turns or better.

Here's the break down for per half of the fly; 142.53 pts in the first half and 192.17 pts for the 2nd half of the fly. This tells us several things that the flyer can learn with this system and also gives the breakdown of quality and depth multipliers.

The first half of the quality multipliers were approximately even with less than 3% difference in quality, the depth gave us around 5% better results in the 2nd half on this scoring which is still not huge but had the flyers had 3 more breaks that were on average 8.55 and an over q/d multiplier of 1.9176 for an average score of 16.39 in comparison to a 6.33 average birds per break at a q/d multiplier of 1.8765 and 11.88 score per break which is about a 38% better average score per average break.

I think that most can see the significant in the scoring and knowing the suggested scoring awards the kit every point it earned. We also keep up the integrity of the scoring better as well as the judge will not be able to manipulate the scoring at the end of the scoring which can give the judge the ability to take a win away from flyer if they choose to. It will have a running tally that the score keeper will use for this and there is no changing these once they are written down.

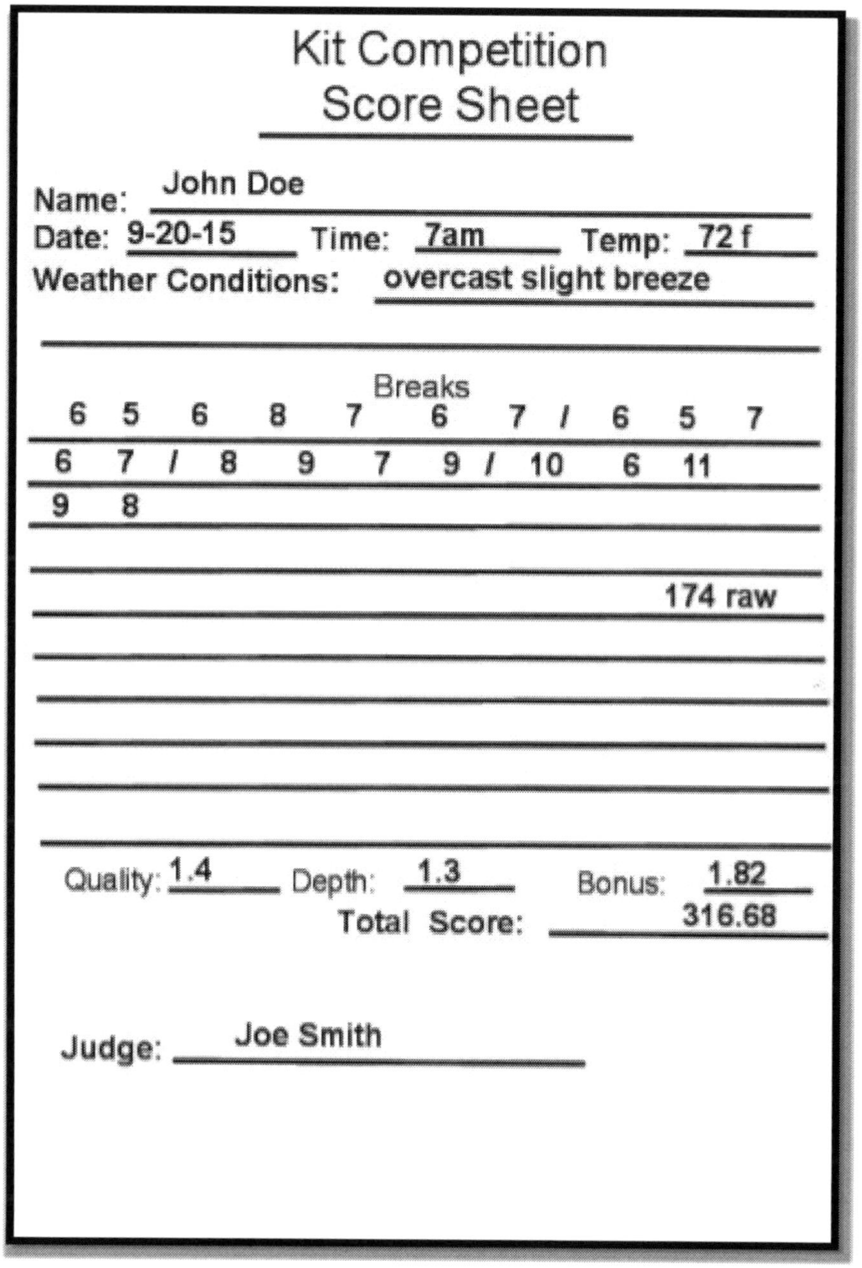

Kit Competition
Score Sheet

Name: __John Doe__

Date: __9-20-15__ Time: __7am__ Temp: __72 f__

Weather Conditions: __overcast slight breeze__

Breaks

6	5	6	8	7	6	7 /	6	5	7
6	7 /	8	9	7	9 /	10	6	11	
9	8								

174 raw

Quality: __1.4__ Depth: __1.3__ Bonus: __1.82__

Total Score: __316.68__

Judge: __Joe Smith__

Shown here with current method of scoring

Kit Competition
Score Sheet

Name: John Doe

Date: 9-20-15   **Time:** 7 am   **Temp:** 72 degrees

Weather Conditions: overcast, slight breeze

Breaks

6 4/3	5 2/2	6 3/2	8 3/4	7 2/4	6 3/4
7 4/4 /	6 5/5	5 5/6	7 6/3	6 6/3	7 4/3 /
8 4/4	9 3/4	7 4/4	9 4/5	/ 10 4/4	
6 3/4	11 4/4	9 3/4	8 4/4		

64.72 + 79 + 103.88 + 87.1

Total Score: 334.7 pts

Judge: Joe Smith

nice active kit, got better as they went along. flew nice pattern, set up well. Flew thru some breaks. Nice kit to watch and judge kit flew 20 minutes

Same breaks scored with suggested method of scoring

So not only will the flyer and readers of the scores be able to gain more by reading such a score sheet but the integrity of the event will be held to a higher standard and this will also lead to happier flyers on average.

I would hope that this short article can better to educate guys on how to continue to improve on our current scoring systems and take a lot of the guess work out of it at the end.

Feel free to contact me about this further at davesrollerpigeons@gmail.com

WORK EXPERIENCE

Living with Predators
BOP news
By
Dave Henderson

The return to raising birds again has been a real eye opening experience for me the last 2 years. It's mostly about learning the hunting habits of these predators and when to fly and when not too fly. The predators are also habitual as are our own rollers, meaning they like to be fed and flown the same daily. Nothing you do is going to be prefect fix against these predators but it will certainly better than to just simply keep raising birds to feed them to the predators at the same time daily. These rollers are like pets to me for the most part, part of the family even, and you have to treat them as such. This means being especially careful when flying them when you know that the predators are around often

Last season I was bombarded by many predators from the very first day I started training babies, I think it was partially due to the babies being easy prey for them and this encouraged them to not forget my address and come back often. I swear at times it seemed that they were just sitting in a nearby tree and just waiting for me to release my birds... This started in late May and continued until I locked down in November. I was unable to breed earlier as my loft was not completed soon enough and boy did this prove to be a frustrating time to train babies. I just could not believe how bad that these predators have gotten in last 6 seasons here in where I live.

I would put out 8-10 babies and 50% of them would be taken in the 1st week of roof training. It was very frustrating and come late July I was being hit by multiple predators every day that I flew them and at various heights as well, meaning Cooper hawks and Falcons. Some might see this as "every day" but it was not every day as in reality once I would be hit whether a bird was taken or not I would lock my rollers down for at least 5-6 days before flying again and then not fly at the same time of day I was hit last, kind of like an attempt to starve them out of my back yard. It really didn't matter what time of day I flew either... I was so frustrated and disheartened by this. I had bred a late round in July that I refused to let out because of this and instead opted to send them to a friend. The birds were just starting to develop some short rolling and would be eaten.

Years ago I had fly my birds only in the evening or late afternoon due to work restraints and I had developed a way to counter the shark induced overflies that can often be caused fly flying in the early evening as many of us know. I basically had to stop flying on the weekdays as when it got dark shortly after getting off work and on the weekends when I flew in the morning the predators seemed to be everywhere. Over time the birds kept getting in poor flying condition from being flown only twice per week and became easy prey to these predators and I would just simply have to lock down or would risk losing everything. You might lose 1 bird when you fly but if the predators would often keep chasing them up until it got dark and in that case you could risk losing more of your kit if they stayed out all night?

If you are flying in an area with thick trees in your back yard the ground attacking predators will be your worst enemy and this is mostly due to how your yard borders on trees and shrubs. This is what I have to deal with too and because of this I erected a 21 foot landing tower to counter the Cooper hawks ground attack. This would allow birds sitting on this tower to see them coming from further away and prevented them from sneaking up on them after they landed from a flight like last season. This landing tower came in very handy as the birds sitting on it could see even on to neighboring streets and in all directions.

I also learned where your loft is positioned can also encourage these predators come back more regularly. So if you have your kit boxes up against an object that would allow the predators to come from behind them and catch they will do this and at times the birds will not even see them coming and nether will you. You will just hear the birds get slightly spooked and then a bird is gone. So take this into consideration as well and place your kit boxes with plenty of open space around them in all directions. You would be better suited placing your kit boxes in the middle of an open area with at least 20-30 feet of space all around them. This will give them a fighting chance to get away and many times they will be able to out fly these predators due to this arrangement.

This year has been a little easier on me but I have come to realize that I have no less than 3 pairs of falcons that hunt me in this area. It can be very frustrating especially when these pairs' rear babies and then they attack your birds in tandem, kind of a like a training mission for them. It's never going to be a positive thing for the rollers when they can get hit from 2 sides at the same time and this can cause them to panic more than usually which can lead to you losing birds. I notice that so long as you can give your bird's daily flying for about 4-6 weeks they can develop enough muscle and smarts to out maneuver these predators 9 out of 10 times. The problems are complicated more once the birds start to spin and become weaker from the basic action of rolling. So many learn to get down as fast as they can or risk being chased longer the longer they remain in the air. This is a learning curve for most but they will learn or be eaten, many learn that trees and bushes can be safer place then flying. I guess the term is survival of the fittest, smarts is part of this. Now when the birds are low enough I try to call them in so they don't stay circling very long and due to the landing tower they can evade them once they land as well. So part of flying and surviving birds is having your lofts set up properly to help prevent this.

There are things you can do to further assist your birds to survival and this can be as simple as putting up erectable large fish nets (black or brown is the best color) in specific parts of your yard to prevent sneak attacks or as complicated as using a quad copter to deter the BOP and some with falcon issues have even been using megaphones preloaded with falcon and various hawk voices to slow them down a bit. Many of these megaphones now have an option of uploading or plugging you MP3 player into, which makes it very handy to use hawk sounds that can be obtained and downloaded from websites like; http://www.bioacoustica.org, http://www.allaboutbirds.org or you can even purchase CD's of falcons and various birds of prey that can be uploaded to your MP3 player.

The concept is not to prevent them from catching your birds but to make the predators have to hesitate when he hears the sound of another predators in his area. If you are really clever maybe you could even rig up a quad copter that omitted a falcon sound from it while in the air?

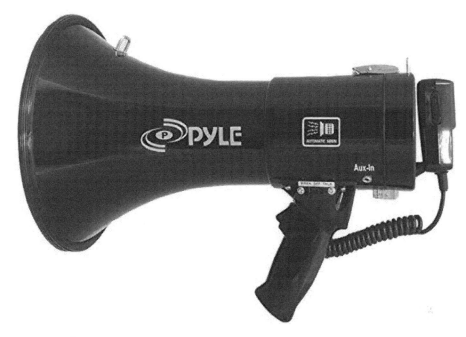

Common megaphone that can be found online

It is also not out of the question to just simply train your birds to fly into the night to avoid the falcons and various day time predators but in some locations you might be simply trading one predators for another one when you take in to account the various nocturnal predators. Many will not have an issue with owls but some might.

In order to train birds to fly into total darkness you have to start getting them used to it in good weather at either very early morning flights when the sun is not totally up or flying them closer to darkness when the predators are not around, this is up to you.

Notice the picture of my landing tower and see the various lights mounted to it. These lights are used to illuminate the roof and surrounding areas new my kit boxes. My loft roof is white so these lights really make it "glow" with these 10 watt LED flood lights. Your birds will have no problem identifying your loft from even high up in low light. You could also get creative as well by using orange road cones with lights inside them as a glow and identify your location to them from the air.

I find to make this lighting system work properly you will need lights inside your kit boxes and at least 3 other lights outside the kit box. You want to illuminate the roof, the front of the boxes as well as the ground around your lofts. These lights will make your birds comfortable about landing in darkness. You will need to train them to do this and this process starts from flying around 2 hours before dark and then gradually get them closer and closer to dark until they get used to it. I find this also is good sudden low cloud cover that can cause them to get lost also.

The one issue I found was that, might be an issue for young birds, flying at night is having them develop in to the roll while you are flying at night. I discovered that some that are coming into the roll tend to roll deeper than they would normally roll in good lighting conditions and I had a couple that actually rolled into neighbors trees and were out all night several times so I stopped flying them. I think if you have birds that are already rolling good and fly like this you will have no issues so long as your birds are stable. I think with the ground being dark some will have a problems with depth perception. However I have found that over time the birds that are adults and fully matured they tend to gain mental control of this aspect as a reflex action.

If you have any questions in regards to this article and missing details that it pertains to please feel free to email me at davesrollerpigeons@gmail.com

Dominic Carton and WC Judge Joe Emberton in Ireland - 2013 World Cup Finals, mocking their friend Sid Love from overseas

The Bird Flu and BOP's

I think many out there can recall the first time you heard of the "Bird Flu" over in Asia. This scared everyone and you would see pictures of some in that area starting to walk around wearing medical masks to help prevent them from getting this so called "Bird Flu". The original Bird Flu or Avian Flu came to our attentions back around 2005 and is the H5N1 strain. This strain did actually claim some human lives but it was nowhere near the magnitude that it was made out to be. In fact it's mostly deadly to the chicken, turkey and other specific birds that can contract it. The good thing for us roller flyers is that is cannot be contracted or spread by pigeons.

There have been more than 25 varieties of the Avian Flu discovered and like many other viruses out there they continue to mutate and this is what we are seeing here.

Well some of you might be wondering why I am so concerned with the new strain of the Bird Flu? Well it might just be Mother Natures' own way of population control, read below for more on this.

Most of the people that have contracted the Bird Flu were handling sick or dead bird when they were exposed and the vast majority of the human cases have not been fatal. Just like the more common flu viruses in humans most that get it don't die from it unless their immune system is compromised in some form or another. We see most that have health issues getting the flu are with the elderly and this plays true with the Bird Flu also.

I remember the panic and the first cases in my county here and the various birds that were exposed to it. In my area it was with the jay birds and crows mostly. It really knocked down their populations when it first hit this area about 4-5 years after I first heard about the bird flu. Like anything else as the severity of the cases are discovered to be not a huge concern to the human population people stop noticing it in the news.

However being a pigeon breeder for most of my life I find myself digging up stuff about it all the time and especially since the new strain hit here in the US last fall that is the H5N2 strain.

It was isolated in the North East last fall and winter and this month (July 2015) it was discovered in Missouri and Arkansas. The migratory ducks are the culprit that is spreading this new strain and it is thru contact of the bird poop. We know that birds poop a lot more than you might expect and it is really going to be impossible to keep the new strain from spreading all over the US in the coming years. The natural migratory routes for our water fowl is to fly from the North to the South and this even mean down to places like Mexico and South America even. So it's just a matter of time now before it's everywhere. I would expect we will see it showing up here in California within 15-18 months from now.

As noted above there are real concerns with any type of Bird Flu here in the US as well as other countries due to the effect of commercial chicken and turkey farmers. This new H5N2 strain as I noted above might just be the answer to many of the roller flyers prayers. Why is this you might say?

The fact is the new H5N2 is especially lethal to the various birds of prey out their namely the Peregrine Falcon. Because the duck is the most likely culprit to spread this virus and also a very key food source to the Peregrine Falcon, also known as the Duck Falcon, it's just a matter of time before their population is decimated by this virus. I am sure this could be the coming relief that many of the pigeon breeders in general might be looking for. They have also noted that the Cooper Hawk is also affected by this strain of the Bird Flu, however it is suspected that the spread in the western states will take longer due to the higher temperatures we see out here on the west coast in the summer months, like other viruses the UV light will kill the Bird Flu as well.

We may not feel the presence of this strain for several more years but it is coming I can assure you. Keep your eyes posted in the upcoming year for more updates on this topic.
http://birds.about.com/od/birdhealth/a/avian_flu.htm

http://www.motherjones.com/tom-philpott/2015/04/avian-flu-bites-us-poultry-industry

http://www.agweb.com/article/new-bird-flu-strain-has-poultry-farmers-scrambling-NAAassociated-press/

http://raptorresource.blogspot.com/2015/05/can-bald-eagles-get-avian-influenza.html

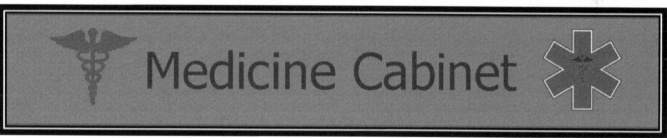

PARATHYPHOID (Salmonella)
By
Dave Henderson

Many have heard of this in the term of Salmonella as people can contract it as well from the food they eat that has been exposed to the bacteria and not prepared properly. It will commonly be called "food poisoning" us as humans. In recent years there has been a lot of Salmonella outbreaks from beef patties to even spinach from farms.

So it is important to realize that you can get it from your pigeons if you are not careful. It is not highly certain but certainly possible as it is zoonosis, can pass between different species.

This illness is perhaps the most common illness found in our domesticated pigeons. This is a negative gram bacteria not unlike other bacteria that can be also gram positive as with Cocci. These bacteria basically live at a specific PH level that makes them thrive, if you change the PH levels even in the birds it will kill the bacteria. You can either raise it or lower the PH to kill it with acids and bases. We can use these substances to spray in our lofts to kill the bad bacteria that is passed through our pigeons' poop or via our water fountains. Bleach in a spray bottle is a very common way of sterilizing our lofts. Bleach is probably the most common thing that we use for this sort of thing and even chlorine bleach in the water will kill bacteria in their intestines before they poop and can spread it. Bacteria should not be confused with viruses and single celled organisms like protozoa (or internal parasites).

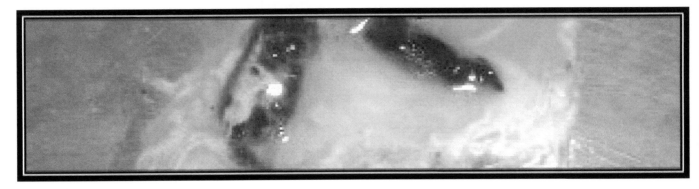

Common watery poop seen with Parathypoid

Our pigeons carry many bacteria in them and under certain circumstances these bacteria can attack and even kill our pigeons if their immune system have been weakened. Most pigeons with a healthy immune system will be able to fight off bacteria. Long term stress to our pigeons can compromise their immune systems. Examples of stress is anything from shipping birds thru the mail to moving a bird from one loft to another and in many cases this will not cause an outbreak of Parathyphoid but it can if the birds are young or their immune systems has been weakened (as in some older birds) as in the case of breeding and feeding babies over extended periods of time.

This illness can affect every facet of a pigeons' life and at any time of year as well, however we see it mostly during the breeding season (warmer weather) or towards the end of the breeding season when birds are in a weakened state (especially in cock birds) and are feeling the stress of feeding multiple rounds of babies in the season.

Parathyphoid can also cause eggs not to hatch, the bacteria will penetrate the egg shell and grow inside it. The eggs will appear to be developing like normal and getting dark, however they die in the shell several days before they are scheduled to hatch. Many times the eggs will be dark but the matter in the egg will be lose if you shake the egg. The bacteria is passed thru the egg from the hens' reproductive tract.

Common symptoms are as follow;

Loss of weight (feels boney in the hand) Lack of appetite and appears to be fluffed up and obviously sick They also appear to have lack luster in their eyes Sudden death Green slimy droppings, lots of whitish water in the crop swelling in the legs and wing joints limping or partial paralysis Twisting of the neck unable to fly (uncommon, twisting of the neck is a sign of PMV mostly) Infertile eggs

Ways to prevent Parathyphoid or the spread of it;

I find the prevention can be handled with floor bedding that will absorb all moisture including poop which will keep the spreading of it down. However your best bet is to pull a bird showing any symptoms so as to prevent further spread of this illness that can also be air borne and passed thru drinking water. ACV (apple cider vinegar) in the water can help with this too but overcrowded lofts will need tending to.

It is also suggested to clean/sanitize or replace nest bowls after each round of babies and to give Apple Cider Vinegar in the water or even normal chlorine bleach in the drinking water and let's not forget the common probiotics and even giving minerals, amino acids and other supplements into the water periodically and help maintain proper health in our pigeons. I like to use supplements in the water at least 3-4 days a month at various times of the month.

I have found that if you put one of the above on average of once per week throughout the breeding season and to also keep the floor in your loft dry it will greatly decrease the ability of this bacteria to become active in your loft. Prevention is the best approach. Having dirt floors will be nearly impossible to counter these issues especially if the dirt is moist. Powdered lye on the floor can also kill active bacteria and can be obtained at most pharmacies.

I would suggest that you don't breed your birds all year long like some will do these days, it's really very stressful and will keep them in a weakened state. I find that a 4-5 month long breeding season is ideal and if you would like to breed more birds from your stock pairs to simply introduce foster pairs into your loft to take a big burden off your prized stock birds and prevent stress. You can also break up pairs after 3 months give them 4-5 week break and then repair for another 3 months, these breaks greatly help.

If you really want to learn more about bacteria and other illnesses in your own birds I would give you the suggestion of purchases a good quality microscope and start educating yourself of what to look for so that you are able to better evaluate and treat your birds. A class at your local junior college might really help you with this.

I would suggest looking at places like amazon and you will need a microscope that is from 40x to about 720x (minimum). Viruses can only be viewed using an electronic microscope however and when viruses are active there is often a secondary infection like Parathyphoid at work due to the stress this virus plays on the immune system. Unfortunately there is nothing that can be done to kill viruses, the immune system will have to fight it off and work it's course but treating for the secondary infections can help sustain the bird at times. Like the saying goes when you get a virus it has to run its course before it can be treated once it turns bacterial, what works for people is true with animals.

Common medicines to treat Parathyphoid;

The most common medicine to treat this is Baytril or Enrofloxacin. This can only be treated for 4 days before it will give you birds a yeast infection and in that case you will have to give antifungal meds to stop the yeast infection when done treating. You can get injectable and pills in this medicine.

Here are other popular meds you could use;

Oropharma Amoxicure (MICRONIZED AMOXICILLIN)

Baytril 10% drops by Magistral Formula

Gufarma Enrotron 10% injection

DAC Furadoxine powder

MedPet Trimethoprim/Sulfa powder (this stuff knocks it down very fast)

It is important that you do the least amount of medicating that you can. The bacteria has a way to build up resistance to drugs so it is also advised that you don't use the same meds twice, but instead rotate different meds should you find yourself treating for Parathyphoid once per season or more. I see a lot of places advertising antibiotics to be used to "prevent" illnesses, and it is my strict view that this should not be a practice we do. Whenever possible I would suggest you simply cull a bird that has an illness unless it happens to be a prized breeder or something. Over use of antibiotics will actually make your birds immune systems weaker and at times will need to be treated with meds just to prevent getting sick and this is not where you want to be.

These various type of medications listed above can be located at several sites but I have taken these products from http://uspigeons.mercasystems.com a site I like to use in my area here. I can get stuff almost overnight at times from them they are so close. They also specialize in only medications.

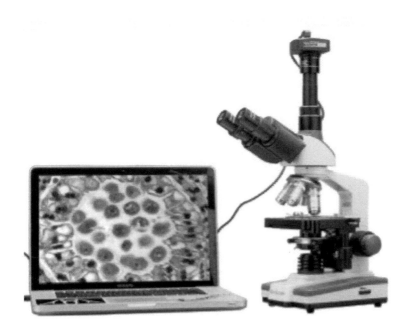

A top end model like this will allow you to take photos of the bacteria and email for advice at various supply houses or even vets for sounds advice what is going on. Entry level models are also available that will get the job done.

Here is a short list of online pigeon supply houses I have used over the years to obtain medications for my own birds. It is always best to have at least a couple of items on hand should outbreaks occur.

Jedds Pigeon Supplies at Jedds.com in Anaheim, CA (714) 630-5921

New England Pigeon Supples at nepigeonsupplies.com in Preston, CT (860) 889-0078

Foy's Pigeon Supplies at foyspigeonsupplies.com in Beaver Falls, PA (724) 843-6889

Global Pigeon Supplies at globalpigeonsupplies.com in Savannah, GA (800) 562-2295

Chas Siegel Pigeon Supplies at siegelpigeons.com in Jeanerette, LA 1-800-437-4436

Pigeon Products International at www.pigeonsproducts.com in Spokane, WA 1-509-919-9516

You will find many others out there but these are the mainstream ones that I have used, if you call them please tell them you heard about them in Spinner Magazine.

http://www.poultryhealthcentre.com/index.php/pigeons/16-pigeon-paratyphoid#Treatment

http://www.pigeonracingpigeon.com/menu/pigeon-disease-the-eight-most-common-health-problems-inpigeons

Untitled Roller Pigeon Documentary

Coming in 2016

Created by Milena Pastreich
www.milenapastreich.com

**2019 and this Documentary is still not out

Dominic Peters S. Africa   Hannes Rossouw S. Africa

MODOC BIRMINGHAM ROLLER CLUB
CALIFORNIA

Adin, California

Home of the Duren's
Danny - Debra - Danny Jr - Eric - Steven - Elizabeth

beeman503@gmail.com - (530) 299-4253

My Start in Pigeons
By
Dan Duren Sr.

I first got started raising pigeons from my stepdad when I was 13 years old. Jeff Moore gave me the pigeon bug and I have loved pigeons ever since.

I first started raising West of England Tumblers and I did very well with them for years and then I joined the Army in 1993 after graduating from high school. I literally graduated one day and was on a plane headed for Oklahoma the next. I went to Fort Sills and had gotten into field artillery, but enough with that.

I have been blessed to have my wife, Debra that I have been with since 9th grade. She has supported me through everything I have done over the years and we have 4 wonderful kids.

My family really does love pigeons. My wife Debra likes the Egyptian Swifts, my oldest Danny Jr. enjoys the Pigmy Pouters, my middle son, Eric, likes the rollers and Komorner Tumblers and my youngest son, Steven, the rollers and Pomeranian Pouters. Then of course there is my daughter Elizabeth, age 6, she just enjoys all the birds and is currently really having a lot of fun watching the rollers fly. I think over time once everything is done, lofts and such, we will have a "pigeon ranch" here in Adin, California.

New construction of our loft, still in under construction

Well as for me I am the true competitor and am looking at my rollers with this in mind. My goal is to win the World Cup fly multiple times but we have to start somewhere and work up to this I know.

When I lived in Fresno, back in 2003, I belonged to the racing pigeon club there and this was my first year flying them. This first season for me I won all the speed averages; short, middle and long distance. I also won the California State Hall of Fame with Hapyco 503. I won a stormy day race by 1 hour with a granddaughter of DeSenna and took 2nd place in the money race that year.

Like many things life changes and we switch gears on priorities and I ended up starting up a honey bee business and Colony Collapse ended that for me.

I now have moved to the Modoc National Forest up near Alturas, California with my two boys; Eric and Steven and we are now setting our sights on the World Cup. I know it's going to take a lot of hard work and dedication, but I think I can and will be able to do anything as a family once we set out minds to it. Family is very important to me and with the support of my family anything can be achieved.

Some of our rollers messing around on the loft roof Getting back into pigeons has been a real god send this time for me and I would like to personally thank Robert Rives and Dave Henderson for assisting us with the birds we are currently flying. I am a happy camper at the moment and I will continue to work with the birds until I get them where they need to be. I am focused and am willing to do what it takes to be successful with this. I am in this for the long haul and with the support I have the sky is the limit here.

One of my favorite rollers

I look forward to 2016 being a very prolific season for me and hope they skies are BOP free!!! Here at the Modoc High Mountain Spinners I wish all of you, Peace, Honor, Respect and love.

P.S for those on Facebook, please keep your eyes open for my video posts at; HBRC ROLLER CLUB WORLDWIDE, SPINNER MAGAZINE, THE HOUSE OF THE TRUE SPINNERS, AND OUR FACEBOOK PAGE, THE MODOC PIGEON CLUB.

Best of luck to all reading this in the coming season.   Please email me with inquiries at beeman503@gmail.com

2015 World Cup Finals Top 10 Scores

Place	Name	Region	Kit Size	Weather Conditions	Breaks Scored	Raw	Quality	Depth	Bonus Factor	Score
1	Theodore Mann	Northwest, USA	20	7:45am, 68 degrees, clear and sunny	7,6,6,10,7,6,6,5,7,5,17,14,6,5,7,7,14,5,5,16	265	1.5	1.6	2.4	636
2	Robbie Mc Nally	Republic of Ireland	20	9pm, 62 degrees, overcast and rain	8,9,5,6,5,6,8,6,7,5,6,8,5,5,9,14,9,5	140	1.6	1.5	2.4	336
3	Alan Milne	Sunderland, UK	20	8:30pm, 68 degrees, clear, calm	5,5,5,5,9,6,5,6,7,6,5,5,8,7,9,8,5,9,5,7,7	134	1.5	1.5	2.25	301.5
4	Mark Coady	Republic of Ireland	20	8:15pm, 62 degrees, very windy	7,14,5,10,12,6,5,11,9,5,6,5	142	1.4	1.4	1.96	278.32
5	Colin Bailey	Middlesbrough, UK	20	9pm, 72 degrees, overcast, calm	5,8,6,6,7,5,6,5,9,7,5,9,5,6,6,5,5,11,9,6,7	149	1.4	1.3	1.82	271.18
6	Arnold Jackson	Southern California North, USA	20	8am, 76 degrees	6,5,5,6,14,6,8,11,9,7,11,10,8,8	160	1.3	1.3	1.69	270.4
7	Andy Dawson	Middlesbrough, UK	20	8pm, 72 degrees, overcast, calm	5,6,5,14,6,5,5,5,12,8,5,7,6,5,6,5,5,5,5,6	152	1.3	1.3	1.69	256.88
8	Marcel Steegh	Holland, Netherlands	20	9:30am, 66 degrees, clear, slight breeze	5,8,14,6,5,5,6,11,6,5,5,5,6,7	119	1.5	1.4	2.1	249.9
9	Bob Hord	North Central, USA	20	7:50am, 80 degrees, cloudy	5,8,8,6,10,10,5, 14,8,6,7,5,5,5	136	1.3	1.3	1.69	229.8
10	Vukasin Pejcic	Serbia	20	6pm, 22 degrees, overcast, windy	9,7,11,7,9,6,6,14,5,5,7	111	1.4	1.4	1.96	217.56

 *Thinking Outside*
The Box

Investigating Oddities
Genetic Defects
By
Dave Henderson

It was around 2000 that I first discovered something interesting with some of my birds. I had never really had the opportunity to investigate issues like this myself due mostly to the financial obligation to investigating via autopsy and it might be this sort of thing is more common then I know. I will discuss what I know and heard in this short article. This might provoke you to future investigate issues with your birds.

I had enjoyed sending off birds to various futurity events in the country during the 1990's and most of these events were extinct by the early 2000's. It was not so much the competition that stopped these events but the bacteria and illnesses associated to these events when you take in birds from all over the country, you also bring in many bacteria and even viruses into one loft which can almost be like a bomb waiting to go off so to speak.

Several guys I became acquainted with purchased my birds from these events and would then continue flying them for themselves. Several would fly them for another 6 months to a year before they would want to breed from them to see how good they really were. Others I talked with would just have birds from me and find things similarly.

I had got a call from one of these guys that was flying a bird of mine and it was consistently ripping off 30-50 footers. Then one day it ripped off a slightly deeper spin than usual, going over 60 feet or so and was slow to return to the kit. The next time it ripped off a similar spin the bird kind of folded up and came whirling down to the ground. He could tell the bird was either dead at this point or unconscious.

After retrieving the bird it showed no signs of why it died. He had a friend that was a licensed vet and asked him if he would not mind looking at his bird to figure out how it died. Upon further investigating it was determined that the pigeon had had a heart attack and died. He contacted me after finding this out. He asked me if I had ever noticed this before and I could not really say one way or another but I do at times loose birds that I have no idea what happened to them. I usually would just chalk it up to the BOP in my area or maybe it accidentally bumped into a tree and or structure and killed itself.

It wasn't 3 months later that I got a call from another individual that also had a bird do the very same thing this one did while rolling. He told me he had also known of a vet close to him that would do an autopsy of the pigeon and also determined it to be a heart attack. I told him of a recent phone call I had gotten telling of a similar event not long ago. These birds were coincidentally 1st cousins and linked directly to one of my foundation hens #0076 which was part of my sister line.

Less than a year later I get yet another call from an individual that had purchased a kit of birds from me and he explained that he had a breeder that was less than 3 years old just drop dead with no apparent reason. It showed no sickness or signs of even being sick and would also be driven to discover why this bird had died on him. He was afraid it was an illness that might start causing more of his birds to die so he took it to a vet to dissect as well. In this pigeon it was also determined that it died of a heart attack. I look up the back ground of this pigeon and again notice the direct link going back to #0076 and was a half-brother to one of the others that died.

By this point I had already sent #0076 to my good friend in Hawaii, Rodman Pasco. I called Rodman I explained to him that there may be a genetic heart defect in birds that are off of #0076 and asked him to look for it. I am uncertain if Rodman ever discovered this issue with the birds he bred from #0076 of not. He was very pleased with her young and would go on to win the NBRC National Fly with birds from this hen.

After learning this news about the possible genetic heart attack issue in birds that came down from #0076 I decided to start moving out the birds this related to this direct line for fear that it would further perpetuate itself. By 2002 I had all but rid my loft of birds directly off #0076 but did have a few grand kids to her. Looking back on things I do recall signs of this in some of the birds. Some would be seen flying erratically and when they would land they would be breathing heavy and almost seem to be dizzy or something. After about 10 minutes these birds would be ok and on their way. This could have also been some sort of heart issue with these very young birds. I wish I would have documented it more accurately to see if I could discover more about this in my family. It is not a common occurrence but does happen I would say from time to time.

I had not thought of this episode for many years until recently, 2014, my friend Brian in Pennsylvania and I were talking on the phone. Brian has a lot of birds down from my family of birds from several sources. He was telling me of how and where he obtained his birds from my line and was interested in more birds directly from me. He would also tell me how he bred them.

We were talking about common genetic defects in my own family, the few that we get, and out of the blue Brian asked me if I had ever noticed that a lot of my birds would die before they reach the age of 6 years old. I said no I had not noticed this in mine. Then I had a flash back about the birds coming down from #0076 hen from 14 years earlier.

I went on to tell him the entire story and he said that it now makes sense. I think I also mentioned that I had located the birds in my records that I sent to our friend Scott Rice, which some of his birds came from. I discovered that I actually gave a bird to Scott that that was a son of #0076 and also the dad of one of the birds that died of a heart attack listed above in this article. He mentioned he was not sure on the pedigrees behind the birds from Scott as Scott had lost all his breeding records in a flood of his home years earlier but that they were Henderson birds. I knew right away that the particular bird that Brian was working with was a direct descendant from this son of #0076, no doubt about it. The other issue was he feared that his best cock might also die as well so he began tightly inbreeding him in a way to preserve his genetics. This of course could have increased this negative trait in his own birds.

If you have the means investigate oddities with your birds (sudden deaths or even illness) I would encourage you to try and get to the bottom of why a bird died if it's a mystery. I know in terms of illness I plan to educate myself with bacteria and viruses and plan to purchase a microscope to aid in this. I know that some might not see this heart issue as a major problem so long as they are getting top rate spinners but if they eventually get to where they are only living for 2-3 years on average what can you gain by it? This would almost be like you raising a family of pigeons that would die if you did not treat them once a month for canker or some other common ailment knowing that you have created genetically weak pigeons that could not survive on their own for long.

I know I might have just jumped the gun on this issue and that chances are not all the kids from #0076 would be passing on this trait and I knew it was not the case but if it's was some recessive "lethal" gene so to speak and if I got the right 2 birds together this could slip by for maybe generations. I feel horrible that Brian had to deal with this and is still dealing with this. I suppose the more ethical thing would have been to just cull all these birds for good but there were so many out there and this was not really a viable option. One of the good things that happens to most is they don't keep birds "pure' and by crossing them they are probably also irradiating this issue on its own.

I hope that you are able to gain some insight in this short article and can monitor issues with your own pigeons should be, sickness, rolling down or some other issues related to your specific family of pigeons that you can figure out how to deal with it and move forward. Worst case scenario, you cull everything and start over fresh.

Dr. Spintight

Question and Answer Column

This section of Spinner Magazine will be seen in every issue. If you have a question you like to submit to Spinner Magazine's to be answered for this column please send your questions to; davesrollerpigeons@gmail.com

Question: I have a problem getting my birds to develop in to the roll. I have had my birds for several years now and even picked some from the air but I can't seem to get them to spin. Are there any things I can do that will get them to roll like I would like them too?

Answer: Good question. What I normally find is that the majority of the issues stem from the fancier that is flying them, however at times it can obviously be genetic and or simply just not a pairing that works. In your case you sound like its' all birds across the board or you would not have asked.

My first question to you would be, are you flying them enough and feeding them the right amount of feed?

I find that many guys can complain about this sort of thing but in the end it comes down to not flying them enough and or the combination of over feeding them. I know you did not mention if your birds were trained properly and land and go in within only a few minutes once they land from a flight.

I would only again have to assume that you are maybe even just letting them out and then going to work or in the house if you are not aware of these things. It is important that you watch the birds while they fly so you can observe what is going on. Not just to let them out and then leave and allow them to trap on their own etc...

When I bring up flying and feeding this might seem very trivial but you would not believe how often this happens where the birds just don't do what they were doing when I bought them or were told they would do. Most if you ask them will say they have a conflict with work and that they just can only fly the birds 3-4 days a week consistently and at the same time due to the extra rest they are also being overfed even just slightly which can also lead to habits you will have issues with to include birds wanting to pair up.

So this is generally speaking not an easy question to answer without asking more questions.

On development of the birds. Let's say the guy you got these birds from told you they develop in to good spinners at 3-4 months of age but your birds are 7-8 months old. I would assume the fanciers you got them from flies his birds at least once per day and this could be part of the issue for you, just not enough air time yet. Your birds may also not be flying long enough to build up endurance either? I think it's important that your birds fly for no less than 45 minutes and no more than 1 ½ hours. If they are only flying for 20 minutes or less you can blame yourself for this problem!

Now all is not lost and if you are only flying 3 days a week on average you should start to see the roll anytime unless the birds are so relaxed and over fed that they have no real ambition to fly and come down right away once you leave. Problem birds are not uncommon especially horny cock birds that have gotten themselves a mate. They can be unmanageable but in reality you are again to blame for this problem. Regular exercise will keep them more disciplined and tired. Birds that are in proper condition will not have a real sex drive like stock birds. They might dancing around a bit but if they wait too long to go into the loft they will not get any food and this is the trick. So if you are just tossing in feed and then leaving for work etc. then it is also possible that some are being way over fed and others are not getting enough, again a management issue.

It's very important to watch the birds while they are flying and keep track of them when they land. I know this is time consuming but it's is necessary if you want to fly good kits of rollers. If you can't do these minimum thing then you are not putting in the necessary time with the birds to progress them to a good level of performance. I would suggest that you try to make more time for the birds and or simply keep less birds so you can spend more quality time with the ones you have. It's easy to waste good pigeons with poor management skills but it takes a lot of discipline to create a good kit and good family of rollers.

Now all is not lost and if you are only flying 3 days a week on average you should start to see the roll anytime unless the birds are so relaxed and over fed that they have no real ambition to fly and come down right away once you leave. Problem birds are not uncommon especially horny cock birds that have gotten themselves a mate. They can be unmanageable but in reality you are again to blame for this problem.   Regular exercise will keep them more disciplined and tired. Birds that are in proper condition will not have a real sex drive like stock birds. They might dancing around a bit but if they wait too long to go into the loft they will not get any food and this is the trick. So if you are just tossing in feed and then leaving for work etc. then it is also possible that some are being way over fed and others are not getting enough, again a management issue.

It's very important to watch the birds while they are flying and keep track of them when they land. I know this is time consuming but it's is necessary if you want to fly good kits of rollers.   If you can't do these minimum thing then you are not putting in the necessary time with the birds to progress them to a good level of performance. I would suggest that you try to make more time for the birds and or simply keep less birds so you can spend more quality time with the ones you have. It's easy to waste good pigeons with poor management skills but it takes a lot of discipline to create a good kit and good family of rollers.

I hope that I helped you realize what your issue might be. If you have any more questions please feel free to contact me again

Joe Martinez of North Carolina

My Pigeon Loft

for all your pigeon and dove needs

Jesse Moua
559-313-2365
www.mypigeonloft.com
mypigeonloft@hotmail.com

Guest Writer

The Irish Way
By
Dominic Carton
Waterford City, Ireland

Dave has kindly asked me to write something for Spinner Magazine and I thought it would be a great time to share how I do things here in Ireland, Waterford City to be more precise. I live in the South Eastern part of my country. Here where I am from, the Irish flyers have a genuine interest in building great kits of rollers. As I say this is the Way of the Irish.

Most of the lofts in this part of the World are very similar in design. We keep them pretty enclosed mostly due to the inclement weather conditions here. We do get 4 seasons here, but you just never know from day to day what season will show up on any given day.

The first and maybe the most important facet of this hobby as I see it, is the design of the loft and how we house our rollers. Fresh air is very important on a regular basis and this means dry damp free conditions with good air flow. It does not matter at the cost to erect such lofts, but there are basic principles, brought on by our inclement weather we must adhere to, to be successful with the rollers here. The ventilation in these lofts also needs to be properly designed so that birds get good clean air. Damp lofts with stall air will harbor ill health to yours rollers so things need to be built correctly.

My current loft at this time was at one time a larger racing pigeon loft. It had a 2 foot crawl space underneath with steel floor grills in the floor at one time. So now this loft is basically 2 feet shorter than it was at one time. This loft consists of 4 kit boxes and breeding being done in a smaller adjoining loft. My kit boxes are timber made on 3 sides with a lathed door on each one. The doors are made with 1x2 white timber and are the slide in variety, which are very easy to remove and replace at will. These kit boxes are single stacked and have wire floors in them which allows for the birds droppings to drop 2 plus feet to the concrete floor of the loft where I can scrap and sweep out every forth night.

Here is Dominic's loft

Once I clean my loft floor I dust it with a fresh argil lime brushed back on to the floor. These same kit boxes have wire ceilings with 12 inches of space in the front and 18 inches of space at the back of the kit boxes, between the kit boxes and the main roof of the loft. I think it is this space that allows for proper circulation of air inside my loft. The stale air is expelled thru near roof vents and fresh air pushed in from vents at the floor level. I have a 2 foot wide corridor in front of the kit boxes with a seat at one end of this corridor. My seat might possibly be the second most important thing in my loft. This is how I am able to relax in my loft and practice my management methods.

So here you have a clear lay out of my loft. This is best suited for my birds and my methods. You must remember though if you are constructing a new loft you need to build it with the welfare of the birds in mind and not your own vanity. If you have a choice it would also be suggested that you face this loft to the south as it will get much more direct sun light facing this direction.

It is also important to have your loft with a front facing slope so that at all times you are aware of anything that is on top of your loft. It is also possible that you can put up a 2 foot tall fish net border around 3 sides of your roof to protect your birds from a pesky Sparrow hawk that tend to bother most of us these days. This net serves as a pretty good cat deterrent also. I find these nets offer a large degree of safety to me and my birds.

As stated again my loft is set up and designed with an environment that is healthy and safe for my rollers. This is my priority here and it should be for you too.

Some of Dom's kit birds

My birds are always in their kit boxes until the doors slide out and they are able to get out and fly. When the birds land and are walked back into the loft I feed them on the ground in front of the kit boxes. By feeding the birds on the floor in the open I am able to observe them eat to make sure all birds get their fair share. I find I am able to identify loft of would be problematic kit birds by their erratic eating habits, more on this topic later.

I also use solid plastic "V" perches in all my kit boxes, 24 perches per kit box. The reasoning behind this is that every time I enter the loft I observe the droppings at a glance and then am able to scrap these perches every day so I can get to know where the birds sitting on the same perch. Being able to see the dropping daily can tell me a lot of things in respect to the health of the birds too.

I like the "V" perches because there is limited space on them, just enough for 1 bird. There is no place to fight or squabble and if there is such a fight it lasts for a very short time as it forces one or both of the birds to fall from the perch. Other perches can cater to birds wanting to pair up in the kit boxes but "V" perches do not.

Also being made from plastic are easy to clean and less likely to hold any harmful bacteria that wooden perches can absorb. I know there are many other types of perches that can be used successfully but as I stated earlier in this article this is just my way of doing things and my own reasons for using them.

There you have it. This is my type of lofts. For information in regards to the rollers within this loft and the breeding and feeding of them I will deal with these topics in future article.

In The Spotlight

Interviews in the hobby

Meet Hannes Rossouw of South Africa

I feel pretty excited that Hannes has allowed me this interview of him and his roller world from South Africa. It really didn't even dawn on me that South Africa was so rich in Birmingham Roller history until recently. They have always been a huge market for the competitions over the years but being here in the US you just don't think about some of the other countries at times that are very much involved and flying some incredible pigeons. I personally had not competed in the World Cup since 2004 (before this year) and I lot has changed since then.

I came back into the rollers in 2013 and was like many others participating in online chat forums when I heard many talking about these South Africa birds that are here in the United States but had no idea what they were or who they came from. I was getting one name in the mix, Ron Swart. Ron was from Kennewick, Washington and had imported these birds back in 2010. In a very short time Ron did some very impressive things with them.

I did a little digging and found out that Hannes Rossouw was the man who imported these birds into the United States to Ron. I saw his profile on Roller World, a very popular online media site similar to facebook, and Hannes had some pictures of his birds posted. I immediately noticed the similarity of the heads of his birds with some of my very own birds and was suddenly curious if they were somehow related to OD Harris birds. I contacted Hannes via facebook and discovered they were indeed ½ OD Harris and ½ Ken White birds.

Here is the interview of Hannes and I hope you will enjoy it. Thanks so much for sharing with the Spinner Magazine readers.

Here is Hannes shown with World Cup legend Heine Bijker of Holland

Name, age, where do you live; describe your location in SA

My name is Hannes Rossouw, 44 years old, living in Vanderbijlpark, I am approximately a 1 hour south of Johannesburg, South Africa.

When did you first start raising the Birmingham Roller?

I started raising Birmingham rollers as a kid back in 1985, this year will mark my 30th year having rollers.

Who have you looked to for advice and guidance over the years?

In the early years I joined a local club and really knew nothing about rollers. I asked around for help to see if I could learn more about my rollers with ideas and good advice. I was very lucky to have a few of the older timers in my club help me out.

Later years I started experimenting with various feeding methods and breeding, I learned by trial and error. Before I knew it, the old timers that had helped me early on were asking me for advice and help.

How long were you flying in competition in SA before SA joined the World Cup?

My 1st competition fly was in 1986, South Africa join the World Cup in 1999 for the 1st time, so for 13 years I flew competition before that.

Here is Hannes shown with 2015 World Cup judge John Wanless

How was kit competition ran in SA before the World Cup and how is competition ran now? Do they have like an All SA champion fly there?

In the old day we only had local clubs in this area. In 1998 the South African Roller Federation [SABRF] came into the scene with the goal to unite all the local clubs and to improve our sport here in South Africa. The SABRF is like a national club, the World Cup Regional Directors from each regionare the committee members of the SABRF. Twice a year rollers shows are held here in South Africa as well as the SABRF National Fly with 3 classes in September, October. We have the Open Fly, Yearling Fly and a Young Bird Fly.

I have seen some old articles that talked about competition in SA going back to the early 1970's, are there any roller guys from that era that are still flying today in SA? Or were there any when you first started competing yourself?

Competitions here in South Africa have a long history and it goes back many years. The very first competitions were for depth only, later they used a sheep counter and counted all the rolls from a 12 bird kit within a 15 minute time frame.

Many of those early roller men lived when I started in the roller and we all learned a great deal from them. As the times changed we joined the World Cup, now we are all breeding for different traits then they did back then.

I have seen some pictures of flying roller events held there in SA and I notice a lot of the lofts there tend to have barb wire on their fences. Why is this type of security needed where you live? Are pigeons commonly stolen in that region?

Security can be a problem over here, you need to protect yourself and your property with high fences and gates. This is just the way it is and we have all learned to live with these situations.

Pigeon theft is really not very common over here, it has happened in the past but it is not something we hear about very often.

Here is Hannes' main loft

How did you get started in your current family of the BR and how many pigeons are behind this family you have? Do you have a partner behind the scenes that you work with in conjunction with your breeding program?

I started off with just 3 pigeons in my program back in the mid 1990's, 2 cock birds and a single hen. These birds had the qualities I was looking for, feather quality, body type, speed in roll and incredible stability.

I was working on my own for many years here and later on I shared some of my bloodline with some other club mates to help them. I needed to share my birds just in case something happened; disease or some sort of disaster. I think sharing your family is really the only way to preserve them.

Who or whom would you say has contributed the most to the current competitions going on in SA today?

I would have to say there is really a few that have really contributed towards competition flying here in South Africa, Gerrit Celliers, Johnnie Conradie and Irvin Kay just to mention a few. If it wasn't for these men, South Africa would not be where it is today.

How did the Anglo Fly come into play I see these days and what rules does it fly by?

The Anglo cup is a competition between South Africa and England that we fly every 2 years. This is not an individual competition like the World Cup. This is a team event between our two counties. You enter the prelim fly and judge goes around and picks the best 15 teams from each country that will then go on to compete in the finals fly. In the final fly we use a two judge system where two judges travel to both counties to judge the final fly. One judge will count the breaks and the 2nd judge looks for quality and the best individual bird in the competition. The rules are a mix between World Cup rules and All England fly rules.

England and South Africa flyers both agreed to the rules and it has worked well for many years now. The 1st fly was back in 2006. John Wanless and I judged the finals in 2010. It was an awesome experience for me.

Here is a great shot of my area here in South Africa

How many stock birds do you breed from on average each season? How many babies do you produce on average?

I don't like to use too many stock birds, I normally use 8 to 10 pair. I like to breed 50 birds per year for myself and then I normally will breed a round or two for some that are looking for a start in rollers.   I really enjoy helping other fanciers with good birds. I find this very rewarding when they are able to fly good birds knowing I helped them to achieve specific goals with the birds.

I have heard your family of birds come down from some birds from OD Harris and Ken White? Where did these sources come from, and how long were these birds in SA before you got them?

This is correct, my family does come down from some Ollie Harris and Ken White. I got to meet Ken 3 times many years ago on his regular visits to South Africa. The hen I started with came from Gerrit Celliers who imported these birds from Ken in 1967. The Ollie Harris side came from the late Gert Duplessis who imported birds directly from Ollie Harris in the early 1970's. These families of birds where in South Africa long before I started with rollers.

#80 2012 nice bird from Hannes' family

What is the best Bird you have every flown? Describe it

The best roller I ever bred and flown was JAR218/01, he was a red check self cock bird. He was amazing to watch and would spin 3 to 4 times a minute good style and with lightning speed. I had never seen a bird like this in my life! He inspired me to breed a family around him. Most of the birds currently in my loft have his blood in their back ground.

What has been your best stock birds in your family?

JAR 218/01 was for many years my main stock bird and was a very good producer. I was able to pair him to many hens over the years. I even was able to use him in a bull system. He has bred me many outstanding rollers, later on had many of his sons and daughters in stock. I even some of his sire to develop them in to their own lines.

What kind of schedule do you have to fly your rollers? Many of us are working "stiffs" and are limited to how many birds we can keep and train due to working and or family constraints.

I can only manage two kits per day. I can fly 1 kit in the morning and another kit after work in the afternoon. Once my young bird teams come in to the roll, I begin to fly them every other day. I never fly the two teams together as one big kit, I try to keep these team together for a few months so they are able to develop as a team. Later on I can take these two teams and create one great team. I find that keeping and breeding too many rollers that you can be easily handled is simply just a waste of resources.

How did you get acquainted to Ron Swart of Washington State here in the US? Did Ron have some ties to SA? I know he got birds from you but just curious of how this came to be considering that SA joined the World Cup venue just when Ron had imported them, so there must be some ties to SA that most don't know about.

When I was judging the World Cup in 2009 I got a phone call from Ron Swart while I was in West Texas. I never met him before and never met him face to face. On the phone he told me he is a former South African citizen and was now living here in the US for the past 10 years. He said to me that he had rollers back around 20 years ago in South Africa from Ollie Harris and Ken White but he had switched over to racing pigeons the last 10 years he lived in South Africa. He asked me for my number and said he would call me again after the final fly had completed and he did.

A Foundation cock for Hannes

Foundation Hen for Hannes

He called me 2 to 3 time per week and we soon would became good friends over the phone. He asked if I could send him some birds to the US and I told him no problem. I send him 14 birds free of charge, he only paid for the import duties and quarantine costs on both sides.

I had heard some rumors that the birds I sent over were somehow his old family of birds, this is not true as these birds were the family of birds I created back in the mid 1990's. Another story I heard was that we were somehow related, this is also not true.

South Africa joined the World Cup venue in 1999. From the very beginning South Africa had many flyers in the top 10 and this was many years before I even sent birds to Ron Swart.

I recently saw a ban of Racing Pigeons there in South Africa. Do you think this ban going to eventually affect the BR and competition in SA do you think?

The ban on racing pigeons never got off the ground and a court order stopped it in its tracks. The pigeon industry is going on like it always has. I don't think it will ever effect the Birmingham Roller competitions here in South Africa, the ban will only effects birds in transport.

What advice would you give to any new flyers out there wanting to fly in competition?

Go out and see as many competition kits as you can before getting any birds yourself. You need to get your mind set on the right type of family you want to fly and the qualities they possess. It is important to get acquainted with the fanciers you are interested in getting birds from and visit them multiple times. Once you feel comfortable ask this fancier if he can breed you a round of babies, and don't fly them. When they are ready to breed, put them together and swap the pairs around for several years and keep good breeding records on them.

I would say if you do what you need to do within about 2 years you will be on your feet and flying in competition, I never said winning! You need to have long term plans to be successful in roller flying.

Sparks, Jody, Hannes and Graham Dexter

Here's a great shot of the late Morris Hole with Hannes

ANGLO CUP RESULTS 2014 SA

	COMPETITORS	BRAKES	RAW	KITTING	QUALITY	FINAL SCORE
1	HANNES ROSSOUW	5/6/5/6/5/5/66/6/6/6/7/6/5	80	30	80	190
2	POEN SAHABODIEN	5/10/5/5/7/66//5/6/5/8/7/6/8/6/7/7/5/6/6	136	0	40	176
3	EWALD BOTHA	5/5/6/5/6/8/5/7/7/8/7/6/5/7/6/7/5/5/5	113	0	60	173
4	CLINT MIOCH	5/8/8/8/7/5/9/7/5	62	30	70	162
5	KENNY SNYDERS	5/8/5/7/5/6	36	0	90	126
6	PAUL ERASMUS	7//7	14	30	60	104
7	EDGAR ROSCOE	6/7/5/7/5/5/8	43	0	60	103
8	WIMPIE FOURIE	5/5/6/5/6//5/5/6	43	0	60	103
9	MARK SACKS	5/5/6/5/5/8/6	46	0	50	96
10	DIRK VAN NIEKERK	5/5/7/5/6/5/6/5/7/6	57	0	30	87
11	TOMMY LAUBSCHER	5	5	30	50	85
12	FRIK DE BEER	6/6/7/6/6/5/5	41	0	40	81
13	HERMAN VAN ZYL	5/5/5/5/5	25	0	40	65
14	JAMES TEMPLE	5//5	10	0	30	40
15	LOUIS BARNARD	5	5	0	0	5

NZBRC; The New Zealand Birmingham Roller Club

We started the NZBRC around about 5 years ago, by myself and Kerry Swasbrook helped form the club to promote the hobby and connect the local kiwis with the world as well as gain momentum in the competition side of flying performance based rollers here in New Zealand

From the 1970s through to the early 1990s, there was three main blood lines (Monte Neible Canada) (Skidmore UK) (Scottish line McDonalds)that were imported into the country via Australia before the government set the ban on bird imports in 1996.

The NZBRC grew and went online via social media the guys came out and started connecting with the world and found that the NZBRC was formed and joined in our mission to promote fly and breed these birds competitively and one day our aim is the World Cup.

These 3 blood lines were kept around the country, some keeping them pure and preserving this good blood, and others started crossing them with show roller here in New Zealand ruining them. Finding good rollers in this country for most of the younger guys had proven very difficult as all in this hobby want it to take off so that we can build great programs. I must give credit to Fred Parret for preserving some of these rollers for what they do best rolling and kitting.

I thought coming from South Africa were I lived, before moving to New Zealand, that I had seen the best of the best in the air and never thought I would see good roller again. It was frustrating that finding some quality birds, that was, until I took a 4 hour drive to Fred Parret's loft. After seeing Fred's birds in action I would have to say that they are very much on the same level as many I saw while living in South Africa. These birds were fast with good style and perfect kitting. They were also very frequent displaying loads of breaking and birds falling from the sky. Fred kept these lines pure and has created his own family of birds over the 30 years he has had them. Fred kept both the Neible and Skidmore lines that were imported. We have all dedicated Fred's efforts by calling his birds by his name. These birds are some of the best around in the air and will be able to compete on a World stage with ease.

Another thing to keep in mind is that here in New Zealand there are very few birds of prey, and none are real threats to eat our pigeons at this point. Not one person here in Auckland, New Zealand has ever lost a bird to a hawk or falcon. I think this fact will give us a huge advantage in breeding and being able to fly better rollers in the future of our hobby. Being able to breed as many birds as we want and not losing any means the birds will get to prove themselves in the air fully and show their full potential before they make it into breeding loft.

If not for some good club members here in New Zealand all might have been lost, but thanks to dedicated club members like; Kerry Swasbrook, Warren Kennedy, Fred Parret and Barry Cox just to name a few we are all headed in a good direction. We know have a good communication between flyers here who want to fly good performing kits and push towards local competitions and even joining the World Cup one day.

Guys like Warren Kennedy have been gained a lot of knowledge in a short time and he has put together some really good kits and has been helping a lot of the new members with birds. It is with his efforts that we are getting ready for local competition around New Zealand. Today we total 28 members and are gaining every month. It will not be long before we are fully able to compete all around New Zealand and then apply for the World Cup. As I have said even if we join and come in dead last the experience gained will have long lasting positive results here.

We still have allot to learn and a long way to go we understand this and will be persistent. We have been helped with our quest and will try keep in contact with as many fliers around the US and the UK via social media. It is thru these great media outlets that will be able to gain the knowledge to take our birds to the next level

I will say this to our members and comrades, that one day we will back at this article and say well we never knew we would be where we are today and that others around the World will know what a force New Zealand has become in the World Cup. We have big dreams for a small country and let's hope that someday we all have a World Cup judge in our back yard.

I want to thank Anthony for taking the time to promote is club and country in NZ. We all know that there are roller flyers in nearly every part of the world today and New Zealand is no different, the internet makes the World we have today feel so small and that we have friends at every facet of modern life today. I have heard that NZ is a very beautiful country and it's quite apparent if anyone reading this has ever watched "The Lord of the Ring's".

A very disheartening part of being a roller breeder in NZ today is that the country has banned importations of live birds and pigeons to their country going back to 1996.

I want to again thank Anthony for taking to the time to share a little about the rollers there in NZ. I wish you all the very best in the future and you can always get good sound advice from a great bunch of roller flyers that read Spinner Magazine.

Name, age, where do you live and how long; describe your location where you live

Anthony Kotze. I Live in Auckland. We have great weather in the summer months with long days sun sets at around 9:30 pm. In the winter months we have a lot of fine rain and get to fly all year round with out to many issues really.

How long have you been breeding and flying rollers? Where get your start?

I been flying and breeding rollers off and on for the last 16 years. I started flying in South Africa as a kid I found a roller in a local park and this pigeon had a personalized leg band on it. I called up the owner of this bird and he came to fetch it. He invited me to come see what the birds do in the air and from then on I was hooked. I have been currently back breeding and flying rollers for the last 6 years now here in New Zealand

Can you tell us more about the Birmingham Rollers that reside in New Zealand?

We have been able to get 3 imported blood lines here in NZ to my knowledge they are as listed below.

1. Jim Skidmore line from the UK

2. Monte Neible line Canada

3. Dr Mc Donald line from Scotland

I understand that importations are no longer allowed there from other countries? Why and when did this happen?

Bird imports were banned in 1996. New Zealand has a very unique population of rare and endangered birds and our country is free of a number of major bird and poultry diseases so they made the decision to stop all importations of live birds here. There is a ban in place until the Import Health Standard (HIS) can better evaluate the risks. The IHS is currently looking at this ban and there is talk that they could raise this ban within the next 2 years or so which is very exciting for us roller breeders. This blood line has been moving about here for a very long time now and many would like the opportunity to bring in some fresh bloodlines to work with.

Is there talk that one day the World Cup bring in New Zealand as a new area?

We are in talks currently with the world cup committee to one day be part of the World Cup. We first have to have to get the number of participants up here. We need to come up with the minimum number of flyers to be eligible first. There is a good move for this and things are looking up, but we will keeping doing the best we can until this day comes.

What kind of pigeon seed is available in New Zealand? What do most fanciers feed their pigeons there?

We have all the standard stuff available here. I feed my Breeders chicken layer pallets and my fliers get wheat with a small amount of milo

Has there been any visits to New Zealand by any prominent flyers since you have been flying rollers?

We had a good friend come over from California named Don Clark last year. He came out and spent the day at my lofts we had a lot to chat about. It was very nice to get someone from outside of New Zealand give us some honest feedback on our birds. He said one day we will be a force in world cup rankings if we are able to get into the World Cup. We have an advantage of no birds of prey here and this could really help us in this very prestigious event.   Don also said that we just need time to better develop our birds are very close to World Cup standards now.

Pics of NZ members and Fred Parret's line below

Spinner Magazine Worldwide
Volume 3   January 2016

Bird bred and owned by Eric Laidler of Denmark

BACk to the PAST

Interview with Ollie Harris

Interview Compliments of my friend Arif Mumtaz

George Mason and OD Harris (MRPC archives)

This interview was first published in 1989 in the PRA bulletin. The PRA is no longer around but this interview possess some good information. OD Harris did a few video interviews and this transcript was taken from one of his video interviews by Bill McRae in 1986. Bill McRae did a series of video interviews after relocating to the UK. The video is actually very difficult to understand what they are saying with the slang that use there, especially for none UK readers but this version really made it enjoyable for everyone. There is really some tidbits of important historical data in this interview and for those who really enjoy this sort of thing will really enjoy this interview. It's really one of the hidden gems out there from a UK roller legend.

Mr. Ollie. D. Harris Birmingham England

Feb. 28, 1986.

Interviewer: William Crosby McRae

Place: The home of Mr. Harris

McRae: How long have you kept Rollers? How many years?

Harris: Well, I've been with these rollers now since 1916.

McRae: Did your family keep them then?

Harris: Yea! I've been with them right the way through, and my father had em, and his grandfather. I was more or less brought up with them, and I've stuck to them ever since.

McRae: Did you ever have breaks from them? Like the war?

Harris: Only one break I had, that was six years away, but me father, he looked after them until I came back from the war.

McRae: Did you obtain your pigeons from your father? And if so where did he get them?

Harris: Only one or two of me fathers pigeons, those were blues. By all accounts his father used to go with Richards father up Kings Swinford on pony and trap and pick these pigeons out.

McRae: So he knew the great Bill Richards father!

Harris: Yea, well they lived down Ladywood together. Pensom come from Ladywood as well, down Monument Road, they all came from Ladywood mainly, then they all went over the Harborne.

McRae: You must feel pretty lucky to have grown up amongst real rollermen?

Harris: Well! They was all roller blokes around Harborne! As far as I can remember there must have been twenty odd members in Harborne - Horborne alone!

McRae: Were they members of the Harborne Club then? When did that start?

Harris: Most of them were members of the H.R.C. yes, and I can remember it when I was a kid, and they had M.R.S. (Midland Roller Society) as well, which Ken Payne took over. When he packed up a chap from Yardlywood took over from him…but of course in that society they reverted to the (tumblers) Red Badges, the Magpies and the Black Badges - competition short workers.

McRae: When did you first come in contact with Bill Pensom; How far away did he live?

Harris: Well, when he came from Ladywood, he went to live up Tennal Road in some little cottages, and then he moved from there to Vicarage Road, and from there he moved to Victoria Road - two houses down from us see - and seeing all these rollers around Harborne - which I don't think he'd seen before this - he seemed to get "the bug!" and he went all the way! He was everywhere after them! And I think a lot of Harborne blokes let him have pigeons and then a bit later he stretched his wings and went down the Black Country, Quinton, and all around there, and that's where he met Skidmore, Bellfield, and all those other blokes.

McRae: What was the difference between Bellfields stock and the Richards birds? Did you see them when you were growing up? How often? (I was rather excited, hence run on sentences!)

Harris: I saw them pretty regularly when I used to go up with Bill (Pensom). Skidmore was the first chap he took me to - in Blackheath, from there he took me to Bellfields, and he's got a wonderful place. Right on top of a sand pit or knoll. I've told you before today you could see his pigeons roll down in the knoll! It was a sight you could never forget!

McRae: What were they like in type - the Bellfield stuff?

Harris: Well, they were more cobby than other peoples, and more deep in the keel at the front. They were lighter coloured birds, bellnecks, mottles, and a few light blues, oddsides and what not. Where as Skidmores were all a mixed up lot. Richards' were more less all selfs.

McRae: On the Richards birds what colours did he have?

Harris: Well, Richards were red chequers, blues, black chequers, red selfs with white center tails, and a few chequer badges out of them. A few red cheq badges and saddles - not many.

McRae: Eye color?

Harris: More or less all pearl. A really lovely pearl eye.

McRae: What were these Bill Richards birds like on the ground?

Harris: Well you look at one you've seen the lot! All the same type! They were beautiful pigeons!

McRae: I was told by Bill Pensom they were nice small compact pigeons.

Harris: Oh! they were - very, very nice!

McRae: What were they like in the air? You once told me you used to watch Bill Richards kits from school.

Harris: (Laughs) Oh yea, we used to go to Station Road school which was at the back of Richards backyard and we used to watch his pigeons fly through the back window. I've never seen pigeons like them at all! They used to roll that fast. It was really like they were rolling up again. And I think they were the fastest rollers that have ever been known.

McRae: How deep were they?

Harris: No, No, they weren't too deep, say about 7-8 yards, that's as deep as they were. They had to drop on the roof to drop and there were very few casualties with his birds - they were that sound.

McRae: How many did he keep?

Harris: Not many birds, about 30-40. Not many more. He's never sell a pigeon. The only bloke that ever got any - I've told you, was Austin Fellow, a mate of his from Upton-on-Severn. That's the only bloke he let have any pigeons.

McRae: So the only Richards birds around were "catched" pigeons?

Harris: Oh yes, he lossed some and people caught them. Yes.

McRae: So did you get a hold of a few?

Harris: Yes, I had a few off Tommy Richards, (Bills brother) who got them back from Austin Fellows - after Billy Richards died. When old Billy died Tommy let Bill Pensom and Ken Payne have most of them. But old Tommy picked out what he thought was best before they had them.

McRae: Were fanciers such as Bellfield, Skidmore, Richards etc. pals did they see each other?

Harris: Well they all knew each other, yea.

McRae: Did they see eachothers pigeons?

Harris: They did. They used to visit each other occasionally.

McRae: Did Bill Pensom go and see Richards then?

Harris: Well, he did but Richards was always cautious of letting anybody up his backyard. I remember when I went to see him as a kid, and he looked at me a bit quizzically, and I said "Have you got any pigeons for sale Mr. Richards?" he looked at me and squinted with that one eye - he had a squit, - and he said "you aint got enough for tail feather! (laughs) But I did visit him regularly afterwards, he would never sell. You could never get a pigeon from him. But I used to go and look at em. He'd got some in the coal house, more or less his stock pigeons, and these little two pens with his youngsters.

McRae: So when you started. Who did you try to acquire pigeons from? There must have been a few other good fanciers too.

Harris: A part from these blue (badges) of me fathers, I did have 2 off Billy Armshaw, he lived on Northfield Road, on the back of the allotments. Well, I too had a flying place back of the allotments, not far from where Bill Pensom went to live, next to old Joe Thompsons. Of course I've told you I caught that red necked hen and the dun badge cock.

McRae: Yeh! Tell me that story about that white, red necked hen, I know Herb Sparkes has an old photo of her.

Harris: Well… It was flying about for days. At the time I was a kid at school. Everyone was after her. Joe Edwards from Northfield Road, and Horace Wright were trying to catch it! And I walked out of the house one morning, (I was supposed to be going to school) and I saw this pigeon fly over from one place to another and roll, so I got my pigeons out, very cautiously, and got this red necked hen down! And around come Joe Edwards who said "have you caught that red necked hen?" I said "ah" I got it Joe. He said "ah, ooh! ah! I've been after that for days!" but any rate I had it mated it to a black saddle cock than Steve Stanly bred, and bred one good youngster from it - I only got the one - and it was a champion. Bill Pensom come around once and said "I'll have that, and bought about five, and what he did with them - I don't know!

McRae: You've told me that Bill Pensom once kept a number of whites, and these days we rarely see any whites - let alone great ones.

Harris: Yes, they come down from a white cock Albert Wyers let him have, and one of Bellfields, and I think he had one off Ben Homer. He mated these pigeons together and bred some real good self whites.

McRae: They were as anything in the air?

Harris: They were good rollers. The best whites I've ever seen in me life. I used to watch those birds up every day, for weeks and weeks and one day I looked and the pigeons never come up, so I went round to Bill and I said "where's those whites Bill?" And he said "They've gone, I've sold them" (Mr. Harris shakes his head and laughs) But those were good pigeons.

McRae: Weren't you near Elija Tomkins? He lived in Horborne.

Harris: Ah! Elija Tomkins! Well, he was dead when I went round, but Joe Tomkins (his brother) we saw, and I had two pigeons off him, a black chequer hen, and like a black chequer mottle cock, that what I had off old Tomkins. I bred some good pigeons off those.

McRae: He must have been getting good birds everywhere!

Harris: Well, he had a lot from Harborne, there was only Bertie Goode and myself that was left with em. He never cleared us out. Horace Wrights went to Bill, Joe Edwards, Harry Prestons, Bill Armshaws, Joe Thompson, a bloke named Walker, a bloke named Perry, Jimmy Broadfield, Oh! they all went to Bill, he cleared the lot out. But what he done with them I don't know. There were certainly pigeons that Bill sent over the America - particularly those first lots that were very good. Some of those come down from that chap from Stourbridge - Albert Wyers, the one he had the white cock off. A light red chequer bald hen from him went over.

McRae: Ah! that's it. Wasn't she pearl eyed one? There's a photo.

Harris: Yes.

McRae: So that's that pigeon!

Harris: That come from Albert Wyers, that did. Of course Bill sent the good odd wing cock too.

McRae: Did you see that red chequer bald hen in the air?

Harris: No, never saw her, the only time I saw her was when Bill had got her in breeding in the stock loft on the allotments. She was a beautiful hen! That was definitely from Albert Wyers.

McRae: And that red necked hen was a "catched pigeon"?

Harris: She was a catched pigeon yes but she was a marvelous roller!

McRae: Did you ever see any of the youngsters off 463-1613, the red odd wing cock and dun hen? I know Bill sent those two to America in 1936.

Harris: Well, he bred that red odd wing cock off the old spangled cock and an old black badge hen. If I remember right? He was a red white wing with a few white feathers in his secondaries wasn't he? (sorry Ollie, I don't go back that far!) And he was a bit flat on the top of his head. He couldn't roll, he was a good roller.

McRae: The dun hen, 1613, didn't Bert breed that?

Harris: Bertie Goode bred the dun self hen. He lost it, that chap from Borl Street caught it, a chap above Bertie Goode bought it, then Herbert Hitchcock caught the hen, let this other chap from Ball Street have it, where Bill picked it up from there! But he picked it up when the old chap Bob Harrison was on his last legs - he picked up the dun hen and a black self hen before Bob's son killed the lot. His son killed the lot after that! But that dun hen was a real good stock pigeon. She bred some good uns.

McRae: A lot of people in England and America got pigeons from that pair - they were responsible for a lot of good pigeons.

Harris: Yea. Well, in 1937 Jim Skidmore gave me a black mottled hen - off a young one off 463-1613, a dark chequer white winged hen that Bill let Jim have. He'd mated this chequer white wing hen up to a spangled cock which was off half Skidmores and half Richards. This youngster - the mottle hen - was a real rattler.

McRae: Which were the best pigeons you've ever seen?

Harris: Well…a part from the birds of Richards, Joe Edwards had a spangled dun tailed hen, which may have gone to America, I am not sure. Also he had a white black necked cock - another terrific roller! (all Edwards birds went to Bill) I bred a blue - oddity hen in 1951. Unfortunately I let Ron Adams have it and he lost it.

McRae: You mentioned a black badge hen you bred in 37.

Harris: Bill got that. That was off one of Joe Edwards, a rosewing cock, and Albert Wyers little chequer white winged hen. She was another terrific roller she was! Bill also had that, and what became of it I don't know. (We both had a fit of laughter here - we shared lots actually!) He had some real good pigeons from Harborne and some real good pigeons from Bellfield and Skidmore - and Richards, I do know that.

McRae: A lot of these Black cheqs we've got now, (referring mostly to the stock Sparkes, Guthormsen, myself and others have in North America) Bill sort of finished up with - a lot of those - the black cheq bronze, go back to the 463-1613 and a black self hen I believe Alf Roper caught, but I think Skidmore bred it.

Harris: Skidmore bred that hen off a black self cock, and a chequer badge hen. Roper was a bloke who'd drive all over the country to buy a kit for one pigeon, and that black hen was in one of those kits, and when Portman was going around he happened to pick that hen up from Roper. Portman paired it to a cheq beard mixed tailed cock and bred 4 good youngsters. One went to America at the finish (ome sired 514's father - McRae) Barrett had one, Bertie Goode had one, chap up Quinton had one, I think Skidmore had one didn't he? Black badge cock?

McRae: I don't know.

Harris: That black badge cock ended up with Ken Payne, and then Bob Brown barrowed that cock off him, and Bob never give it to him back! He kept the cock! Bob bred some real good ones from that pigeon.

McRae: You've talked about a red chequer badge cock Bill sent over in 51?

Harris: I think it was 51. Sent him to Ken Payne. He sent him a few birds over - 4 or 6 pairs - and every pigeon could roll! Every pigeon was a good un. But the one that was best was a dark rimmy tailed red cheq badge cock. Of course they mucked him about - never mated him up to anything to suit him, really mucked him round - but I've seen him in the air - ah he's a good un! He was a good bird. Outstanding. Joe Thompson saw him, as did Harry Preston (who bred the father to Bills famous old red spangled cock) He was marvelous roller. Marvelous.

McRae: What became of the red chequer badge cock?

Harris: He let Wilf Portman have it. Portman lost it. Put a reward out, got it back, let Adam Jones have it from Blackheath, he lost it. Another bloke caught it and kept it in the bedroom! (hidden) Ron Goodby. He had it up in the bedroom. That's the last we seen of that pigeon! It's no wonder we never get our lost pigeon back!

Harris and McRae: Keel over with laughter.

McRae: A few pairs of your birds were sent to Guthormsons, Kiser, and Borges about 5 years ago in Canada and California. Is there any pattern you follow in matings. Your birds have a lot of "roll" and I also think they make excellent outcrosses.

Harris: All those these pigeons are bred close, and I've kept them as pure as I can, I always make sure I use a good cock, a good sound cock, if it's paired up to a hen that can roll 2 or 4 or 10 yards

- the cocks for me have always seemed to dominate that roll, that's what I look for, a good sound stock - cock.

McRae: Are there any colours you've found more successful?

Harris: All colours are good. There's only the yellows that they seem to condemn. But I have seen some good yellows - that chap up Quinton, "Leggy" they called him - a farmer - he'd got some good yellows. But unfortunately they got killd off by drinking the slop out of the cow manure!

McRae: Has fit!

Harris: They started drinking slop - and that's it, they died!

McRae: I've never seen any yellows out of your pigeons or out of Bill (Pensoms) do they ever come out?

Harris: No. No. No.

McRae: I never did…

Harris: No, never.

McRae: Most of your strain come into the roll fairly early - say six months. Have you ever had any good ones come late?

Harris: Yes. For one that silver hen (blue grizzle) I had off a pair of Jim Skidmores - a black badge cock that couldn't get off the pen for tumbling - he was mostly frightened to fly - and the black mottle hen I mentioned earlier I had off Jim in 37. That silver hen took 3 years to turn out! But when she did she was terrific! But again unfortunately I lost her - and some of her youngsters.

McRae: Did you ever get anything off her? Did you lose all of them?

Harris: No. I've still got that breed now, some of that breed. The duns, blues and mealies (lavenders) and odd mottle one.

McRae: if you compare the fancy today with the pre-world war II days, how does the fancy birds and the birds compare?

Harris: Well, there seems to be more fanciers around - worldwide. But from what I've seen the quality does not seem the same! As was when I could remember - in the oldish days.

McRae: Where do you think it is gone wrong then?

Harris: Well really I don't know. Could it be the money matter? Could it be that money has stepped into it - commercialized it. Like everything else today. Like sport. Also when you have to fight for something you seem to do good with it.

McRae: I think people are more impatient too. It's an impatient age. Fanciers don't fly theirs birds out, stock on pedigree, and aren't putting the hours of study in. People like Skidmore and Bill Richards were probably more harsh on birds for the stock pen and culled hard - kept fewer stock birds than most do today.

Harris: That's right. And if they'd got a "Humpty-Dumpty" pigeon as they called it, they'd soon neck it, or put it in a bucket of water. I've known Richards put a dozen in a bucket of water. He could tell em. Sometimes he could tell em in the nest even by looking at the heads!

McRae: Did you ever get to the bottom of how he mated up his pairs?

Harris: He seemed pretty well the same - good cocks all the time, and he never entertained a cross to them. Never. In the beginning I was told by his brother Tommy he got a couple from Whittingham - from Worchester, there was a little staley white wing hen from Bill Budd from Selley Oak and that's all I know. I don't know where he got the others!

McRae: It makes you wonder how long rollers have been around - where they come from....?

Harris: Well! I don't know! According to me father, his father was messing around with them in the eighteen something. They must have been around hundreds of years back.

McRae: Did you ever see that stuffed roller old Jack Taylor owned?

Harris: Oh, Jack Taylor! He was an old bloke! He was on his last legs when I seen him! But I've seen a couple of good stuffed rollers in Somerset, when I was in the forces I visited a house (public house - ie a pub) and the young lady there showed me these two pigeons in a glass case, a spangle and a blue oddside. They were typical rollers. It seemed they were a tidy age then! That was about 1941. Smallest pub in England - in a little village called Godmanston. Whether or not they're still there I don't know. Her husband was a prisoner of war.

McRae: Skidmore didn't feed his birds very well I'm told.

Harris: No, No, No, he fed them on the rough stuff. But Richards and Bellfield fed them on good stuff - tares and dari. They always carried a little tin of hemp seed with em - little tidbits, and when the pigeons had come down, they've give a little of this.

McRae: Sometimes you hear fanciers say Ken Payne didn't fly very good birds but you were a friend of his and should know what of his kits?

Harris: The only trouble with Ken was that he gave em too good of food. Therefore, they went a little bit seldom. He used to feed them un peas, tares, milo, dari, and canary seed, and of course the "ruddy" pigeons ended up flying like tipplers at the finish. But, they was all good bred pigeons. All good pigeons - I've seen em roll as youngsters, but he fed em that way. Portman had em in the end - and Bertie Goode. I still remember those birds Bill sent to Ken Payne! And every one was a good roller!

McRae: When Bill was over in England in 65 he took a number of pigeons from you - which you can talk about - and he also took a gorgeous black badge hen from Portman NBRC-6230-63 - actually a 61. There is a little controversy as to where that hen came from.

Harris: Well Bill thought it was one of mine. But it was a caught pigeon and we found out later it belonged to Barnsley. Barnsley of Blackheath. He lived right below Skidmore, and he'd got a lot of Skidmores pigeons. She was a good roller - she only come about six yards - but she was good, straight, sound, and stopped dead fast.

McRae: She did look like one of yours.

Harris: She did. She looked like the black badge I let Bill have in 65.

McRae: Was Bill over in 65 for 2 weeks?

Harris: No, a month.

McRae: Did he stop with you most of the time?

Harris: Mainly. He did spend some time with Portman and Barrett. But I told him "I can't stop away from work all this time! You'd better have the car and do with it as you want to! He used to come and pick me up when I closed the shop.

McRae: What birds did he take from you?

Harris: Well those birds I let him have in 65 - he just picked em out and that was it! There was mealy self splash cock, a red chequer badge cock, a mottle cock, which came down from Bellfields - there was a dun saddle cock, a mealy badge cock 1673 - I think Kiser got him at the end. There's a blue badge - bald hen (1605), a black badge, a black saddle hen - I think he took eight. The black badge and the black saddle were the best in the roll. The black badge had pearl eyes, her brother (1673) had yellow. He had all these as youngsters. I'd been flying black badge and he'd seen it roll and said "Oh" I must take that! And the mealy splash self cock (lavender) he saw roll.

McRae: Aside from the fact he liked your pigeons in the sky, do you think there was any other reasons he took them?

Harris: Well, he saw em up, seen em roll, and he took a liking to the colour as well. He said his pigeons were nearly all dark pigeons. He thought these would make a good cross with them.

McRae: Can any difficulties arrive from dark chequers continually together?

Harris: They go seldom. I found out they really go seldom. But if you cross em out again, they seem to come right again.

McRae: What would happen with mating whites together? I've rarely seen anyone do it even. They used to.

Harris: Well I think if you continually bred whites on whites and reds together they might deteriorate in time. You've got to cross a darker colour into them and then cross em back again. Like to the grandparents.

McRae: With your pigeons it seems any combination of pairs will produce almost any colour offspring. You must be deliberately mixing them.

Harris: Yes, old Skidmore said "If I got a pair of pigeons that keep breeding the same colour each time, I know there is something wrong!" He said "I like em to knock out a few different colours"

McRae: Your own pigeons tend to be small and of very good type. You must have concentrated on that.

Harris: Well, they've a good type of pigeon - and they've got good bodies on them. When you handle them the keel seems to vanish below the vent bone. They always should seem a bit deeper in the front - not too flat, cause you can lose that many pigeons with these flat keels. They don't roll so nice and neat as the one's with deeper keels. They are likely to wobble - like a raft on the water. Aren't they! A flat raft goes any which way.

McRae: You've said your general goals and ideals have stayed fairly steady. Who did you learn the most from?

Harris: Skidmore was one and watching Billy Richards perform. Horace Wright and Joe Edwards. They were the main blokes. I used to concentrate on - the old timers. You watched their movements and seen how they mated their pigeons up. The way they studied the beak settings, the head, and eyes, and the body. Most of these good pigeons look as if you've been shoving their tail into the body. Not long cast, a shortish tail. More robust at the chest, power at the butts, plenty of power. You learn by watching.

McRae: Smallish and very powerfully athletic.

Harris: Now Pensom. I was with him all the time when I was a kid and watched his performance, but I could never be completely sure what exactly he was trying to do (laughs).

McRae: He was always writing, but he still never really got himself across. I can't totally explain it, and I spent years with him too.

Harris: I know he did a good thing by writing and putting these pigeons on the market, making them popular. He did a good thing there I think. The amount of blokes that've got rollers now is vast isn't it! Worldwide! And it's only due to Pensom.

McRae: I bet the fanciers of sixty years ago would never have imagined it.

Harris: No! No! Before when people had those pigeons they only did it as their hobby - serious - but still only for their personal pleasure. But, he could see something more in it - something bigger and he commercialized it. It was a good thing in one way and a bad thing in another.

McRae: The old families were kept as pure as practical, with performance as the judge. It seems to me one of the problems is that fanciers with the blood of say…Bills' birds seem ready to cross with all sorts of strange blood. What do you think of that? They crossed yours too.

Harris: They don't seem to know they're all about! They don't seem to know the background of these pigeons do they? Or the roll. If I wanted a fresh pigeon to add to mine, I'd want to know the background of it. It's the same as these pigeons your having from America now (refers to my July 86 importation from Herb Sparkes and my resident study) they've come from some of those that Bill sent over there. I can more or less tell by looking at your pigeons what the background is. Those are the rollers I'd like to cross into mine, to see the results. I wouldn't try any other blokes pigeons. You've got to know what you're doing and their a bloody headache at times! (laughs) Oh dear! My Mrs. says if I'd put my mind to something else but pigeons I'd be a millionaire today.

McRae: Didn't Bill Pensom have a job working as a bus driver as a carpenter over here?

Harris: First of all he went to work at Simsons, the shed people as a carpenter, and his old man did as well. When he chucked that up he went on the busses. He was on busses until he went to America.

McRae: The story goes that when Bill was driving, if he saw a kit of pigeons up, he'd stop the bus. Is that true?

Harris: Yea, that's true! And many's the time he'd spot me on the road, stop, and chat away about pigeons for five minutes! You could see the people on the bus getting aggitated! Then he'd say "Well, so long, I'll see you tonight" and roll off! When he went up to Quinton driving the number 9. He'd park the bus at the termanus, with the passengers waiting, and go see the old fancier Harry Thatcher, have a chat and tea - spent quite a time with him! He used to roll back to the bus and that was it! (I nearly passed out laughing here!) If he saw a kit of pigeons up, he'd stop! He'd stop the bus and get off to have a look. When he started with these rollers seriously, in the early twenties, his mind seemed to go all one way. They got under his skin. In his blood. Everything was put aside bar rollers. Course he had racers. Also, tipplers and modenas. But the main one was the roller. He always stuck to the roller. He had some good tipplers from Sheffield once, when he lived next door but one from us, he sent away to Bob Storey for em, Bill bred these youngsters off em, started training em, and he used to say "Blimey, those flew all day today" (sometimes they did). Anyhow, my father happened to come home one night a bit early and saw these tipplers on the passage, above our lane, and so he said to Bill "How the tipplers doing Bill?" and Bill said "alright, their flying a hell of a long time!" and my father said "oh yeah? They're upon the passage sun bathing!" any rate that upset Bill! And he gave em some wine in their drinking water, he loosed them up the next day and they were gone! Never seen again! They just went barmy!

McRae: Have you ever put anything in your rollers drinking water?

Harris: Not dope. But I generally give them a bit of iron sulphate in their water (a pinch) which tittles em up. I give em Epsom salts, skip a day, then pinch of iron sulphate. They should perform after that. Should liven em up.

McRae: Bill once told me that as a kid an old man used to pay him to pee on crushed brick - then the old man used to feed this stuff to his pigeons.

Harris: They used to, ah. Some of these old tumbler blokes used to piddle on bread, then give it to em. They reckoned that made em work. But that was a funny trick! I'd never do that! I'd never do that to me worst pigeons!

Mrs. Harris: (Enters after shopping trip) Hello! What have you two been up to?

Harris: We've been on the tape, talking pigeons all morning!

Mrs. Harris: Well that's nothing new! Stop and have a cup of tea.

Harris / McRae: Right!

I want to thank Camilo (Milo) for doing such a great job on this article. It's very thought provoking and will tell you what needs to happen to progress your pigeons to the next level. Great insights. I am very thankful that Milo has sent in some great information to the readers.

Cause and Effect Breeding Practice
By
Camillo Paci

I truly enjoy hearing how others plan their breeding seasons. It isn't so much what I agree on with the other fanciers that I find interesting, but the differences we have in our practices that always has me thinking. Raising a decent family of rollers isn't a terribly difficult task. In fact, I've seen some fanciers apply haphazard strategy to breeding their pairs, yes still succeed in putting up some fairly good kits. This approach may work for a while, but moving a family forward requires more close attention in my opinion.

The veteran fliers that amaze us with their kit performances and score cards time and time again, possess an intimate knowledge of their family of birds, and a great understanding of what makes them tick. More importantly, they also understand the art of pairing their rollers and how to choose the best matings that will make the best performers based on basic genotype. It starts there but comes full circle every season. Since phenotype is the set of observable characteristics of an individual resulting from the interaction of its genotype with the environment, those observations we make regarding phenotype, directly influence our selection process for the following season. Neither stage is more important than the other, for it is simply a never ending process which moves the breeding program forward. In fact, there cannot be one without the other. If one wishes to create and maintain a top-shelf family of birds, close attention must be paid to all aspects of this process.

Before going into my own personal breeding practices I think it is important at first to disclose the concept that not everything that is written about the breed has value for everyone. There is so much subjectivity in rollers that what could be considered a focal point for one individual, might be of little value to another. I recently participated in a spirited discussion regarding type. It is something I factor into all of my breeding plans because my best performers share the same build, while many I have spoken to claim the practice to be nothing more than an aesthetic preference, and put very little value on it. I know we have all seen some offtype birds that roll as well as the well-balanced birds, so I leave this category off my priority list as far as advice goes. There are categories however that I think apply to all families of birds, and all programs. Those are the ones I will try to describe here.

Some general breeding practices as a whole that encompass things such as character, mental stability, rolling impulse, and other performance traits are in fact universal, but I believe that some are NOT. There are many unproven theories and commonly accepted ideas that are not based on facts. Many of them are based on the untested observations of a few. They are partially true at times, but do not encompass all of the details. For example, to say that one cannot breed dark check to dark check continually without compromising frequency is partially true, when breeding the incorrect dark checks together. Nobody ever talks about "what kind" of dark checks are being used. What are the character traits of these dark checks? Are they hard feather, or softer? Were they flighty, or where they calm when handled? What was their mental predisposition to handling the rolling impulse during development? How long were they flown? The lack of such detail in these generalized statements essentially nullifies it as truth. So, broad-brush statements can often be confusing and even misleading. There is so much more to selecting a balanced mating than one single factor, especially based on one such as color or pattern.

In the movie Hannibal, Dr. Hannibal Lector makes a comment about rollers. I'm sure many of you reading this have seen this particular scene. Although it's a cool tribute to the roller guys out there, it is a perfect example of those broad-brushed statements we often read about on breeding practices. "Do you know what a roller pigeon is, Barney? They climb high and fast, then roll over and fall just as fast toward the earth. There are shallow rollers and deep rollers. You can't breed two deep rollers, or the young will roll all the way down, hit, and die. Officer Starling is a deep roller, Barney."

After the "cool-factor" wore off when I first watched this scene, I gave it some thought. Certainly the writer of the film heard or read this breeding theory somewhere, or perhaps threw in the dialogue without doing the appropriate research. Breeding two deep rollers together does not give you rolldowns. It is possible, but unlikely based solely upon their depth. Now breeding two unstable deep rollers, most likely with either or both possessing control issues, could and most likely will result in birds rolling down to their deaths. There is also the implication that one should breed shorter rollers to deeper rollers to achieve some sort of mid-depth roller, or maybe a more stable roller. I believe you would just get rollers of various depths. That has been my experience. Now obviously I know this is a movie, but this is the kind of misinformation that I have read or heard about most of my life. So the details as far as how we pair our birds should not be generalized in this manner, especially when trying to educate new fanciers. In my formative years with pigeons, I was quick to regurgitate advice that I assumed was roller gospel. It was through years of trial and error, that I found many of the things I was told or had read simply were not true. I often find myself reading the old publications, and marvel at the contradictions I see, including by many of the greats. The "truths" however, being the practices and concepts I have observed that remain constant from loft to loft, and have stood the test of time, are the ones I try to practice in my own loft.

We can all disagree on many things, but there must be some common ground as what constitutes a truth within the breed. I think we can all agree breeding roll downs together will give you more roll downs. So what factors are the most important when pairing our birds to achieve the results we are looking for? Since the desired results we are looking for in our performers directly influences the birds we select for matings, we should pay close attention to those attributes that create the performers we desire. These are mine, and I believe them to be useful to all roller fanciers.

There are 3 main categories I use when pairing up birds. Everything other than these three categories, as important as they may also be, are much smaller considerations in comparison to the main areas of focus. All three categories overlap in some way or another also, but they can be separated for the sake of observation and discussion. I don't go off a check list obviously, but I constantly monitor and observe birds within a kit to see how they fare in these categories. I take careful notes on the birds of interest, both positive and negative, and am sure to log them into my books. These records are very important, because even after years of forgotten documentation, I can go back to them if I need to. After each flying season I also write a few paragraphs documenting the best matings of the season, and which kit birds were the stand outs and why. I rarely write up a pedigree unless asked. That's not to say they don't have their place.

For new fanciers, or guys trying something new, it's good to know the lineage of the family. In most cases it will "soften" up an old jaded fancier when he sees a new fancier taking interest. As for the value of the pedigree, there is not much. Pedigrees do not have notations on them that are detailed enough to describe key birds and their important stages of development. I have also found fanciers will "mentally" assume siblings on a pedigree have the exact same value individually. Nothing could be further from the truth.

When I'm asked to print up a pedigree, I do so willingly, but I don't see any good they will do another fancier knowing anything past the attributes of the parents. That's when valuable information turns into a marketing tool for others. William H. Pensom said "Pedigree is an important asset in any loft but its uses are restricted to recording how anything is bred and regarding them as anything else can be fatal, for there is no reason to suppose that any two birds that are identical in pedigree, they are equal in merit. They are not, and never could be, and neither will two birds produce the same quality." This is GOLD. I value my notes much more then my pedigrees.

The first, and most important category I consider is mental stability. This category encompasses a lot of the attributes a bird will exhibit while flying in a kit. A mentally weak pigeon will show flaws all through its development. Some in different ways than others, but I have found that problem birds show themselves early on in development. I have observed that the birds that develop very early, go through such an exhausting developmental process that it seems they never truly come to enjoy it. Many of them don't even moult out correctly. When flown past their second full moult, we can see many of these weak minded birds fall apart. Mentally weak birds are uneasy with the development process, and not only resist the roll but can be afraid of it. We can often see these birds flipping at the most inopportune moments such as simply returning after a fly, or upon release, usually bumping the kit box roof. They can also be seen trapping last, or staring vacantly into the kit box door as if frozen, even when they are famished. Some birds even develop bad habits like a clip, or quick switch to stop the roll. Birds that cut the kit, steering them to turn instead of roll, are serious problems in so much that they can corrupt perfectly good birds.

I believe that how a bird finishes the roll is indicative of its mental awareness. Birds that come out of the roll crooked or in the complete opposite direction than when they started, are struggling as well. I have seen the type that free-fall at the finish of the roll, appearing to be disoriented or tired. This in my opinion is also a major flaw in the bird's stability. Many believe these descriptions to be genetic, in that whatever specific flaw it has, will be passed on in the same manner. I do not. For example, breeding a wing switcher may not necessarily breed more switchers. I think a switcher has a problem coping with the roll itself, and can manifest its weak character in any of the flaws I have described.

No list of faults would be complete without mentioning the notorious back-flipper. Besides the non-kitter, the back flipper is quite possibly the worst offender. This type seems to be so overwhelmed with that rolling impulse that it can barely keep up with the kit. It will flip continuously behind the group, never really establishing a good position within the kit, and in the most extreme cases, it can show a total disinterest in kitting entirely. Nothing good can come from a bird like this, and should never be considered for breeding stock. This type of roller could possibly iron out its instability, but the mere fact that it went through such a stage, is enough of an indicator that something isn't quite right with it. These are all mechanisms to avoid rolling, showing the inability to cope with its very basic development, which simply results from the fear of it's genetic impulse. I believe this fear is so great, that it surpasses its natural instincts such as breeding or even socialization. They never seem to establish a strong connection with the handler. These birds always seem "off" when observing them.

So now that we know what not to breed from, what makes a mentally stable roller? A stable bird seems to have a sense of where it is at all times. It flies comfortably within the group and goes through a much more stable development transition into the full rolling. A truly stable bird will come to vary its depth as well. Birds like this will seldom bump, and upon close observation, will be the heart of a good kit. When exiting the roll it finishes strong and snappy, and the bird will dart back to the group seeming to not even be phased by the tremendous feat. It's usually the first out the door, and never has problems coming back. A mentally stable roller in my opinion appears to enjoy rolling. A mentally stable roller in my opinion appears to enjoy everything really. These are birds that can be flown well after their second season of flying, and if they develop into an exceptional spinner, they will remain consistent until they are pulled for stock.

Character and expression are quite important for me in the selection process. At the most basic level, I don't like stupid birds. I've always been at a loss for explaining to others what character and expression are in rollers. It's almost something you feel coming from the bird. Good character birds have brilliant eyes, express confidence, are quite calm, and have an alertness about them. When a bird of high character is placed in a show cage for observation, it appears to be doing the same to the observer. It is not fearful and does not have a confused or vacant look about it, in fact, it appears confident and almost curious. Selecting birds with such qualities makes for better breeders. They make for better parents and keep the family strong, especially in highly inbred families that could potentially open themselves up to inbred depression, and other weaknesses. Part of this package is also temperament.

Although temperament could be considered a category all in itself, it's visibly tied to character so much that I consider it one in the same. Wild birds should be avoided. A roller with poor temperament can be spotted very easily. When placed in the show cage, they may appear to have the attributes we look for, but when we reach in to the cage to handle the bird, it seems the bird fears for it's very life, grunting angrily and banging itself up on the wires in the process. These birds have a seemingly unbridled energy, and while it may serve them well when executing a high velocity spin, this behavior comes with many pitfalls. Besides having rollers that are frightened all the time, they are harder to train. They are distrustful, and so flighty they can really throw a wrench in the training process. They also have a tendency to fly high and strong, so for what we are trying to do, that is a flaw. I believe that they also scare at the first sign of anything, even a group of sparrows, so unless you want the team flying off into the night, it's best to avoid this type if possible. Birds that don't seem to mind being handled are the better choice. Calmer birds have a much more relaxed wing beat, and that type of chemistry is crucial for concert performances.

The final, and notably the most visible category is rolling impulse and resistance. Rolling is not a depth-based concept. I do not even take depth into consideration when pairing my birds. If anything I breed the deepest birds possible. I certainly wouldn't want to lose that attribute. As I mentioned earlier, depth does not cause instability. Instability can occur at any depth. Rolling to me falls on a spectrum. I consider that spectrum to be one of the roll resistance. On one side of the spectrum there is the non-roller, while on the other end we have the true roll-down. The birds we find on the non-roller end, have a greater control over the rolling impulse, while the birds we find on the opposite end have a far less ability to control the impulse to roll. The seldom birds have the ability to resist it, while the opposite seem to be fighting off the urge to turn. I call these two types roll-resistant, and roll-side rollers. Breeding two birds too close to the roll-resist side will get you seldom rollers. Breeding too close to the opposite end will get your closer to roll, but increase your chances of producing mental instability. It is a careful balance. Flying the birds and evaluating them for as long as possible in the air will put into our minds the value of the individual, but most importantly, at least for myself, will tell us where the bird falls on this spectrum. The more balanced our matings are, the closer we can get to the exceptional pigeons. This is not to say we can breed one with the complete opposite. The spectrum merely defines the type of performance an individual displayed. It's a "worst to worst" spectrum if that makes sense. I believe that when one can identify the "sweet spot" on their unique spectrum, then the differences will vary slightly from right to left. This is the art of selection in my opinion. This is what we as breeders do. We are controlling this recessive anomaly, and all the while trying to keep the birds stable. This is where the most important decisions are made to move a program forward.

Another important part of this spectrum principle is having enough birds to select from to make balanced matings possible. Obviously when first starting out, one can only breed what one has. Over time, with enough high quality rollers being stocked, it becomes easier to hit the elusive sweet spot with matings. Again, Its never perfect, it just brings birds that fall closer together on a desired range on the spectrum. No particular individual bird will totally share its spot on the spectrum with another in terms of total package, in any program, which is why we will always have a moving target when breeding. That target however may not necessarily be the same target for another breeder, after all, the end product is subjective. I have found when handlers earn a particular reputation for their family of birds, be it negative or positive, it is because the birds in the stock loft available for breeding all share that attribute so closely. It really comes down to selection. If someones family is what most would consider to be "too hot" or even "too stiff" then they're most likely filling the loft with birds of one particular type. Having a slightly wider breeding pool is good so that adjustments can be made. Some fanciers have a zero tolerance when selecting, while personally, I am more forgiving when putting away birds for stock. I think selecting for one particular type of roller can put the breeders into a corner, having to look for an outcross of some kind because they have lost one of even more desirable attributes.

So here's the kicker. None of what I have mentioned is perfect or can guarantee a specific outcome, because oddly, even once we have identified a pair with exceptional mental stability, excellent character, and great rolling abilities, there is no guarantee that when paired together they will create their likeness. It's more like a moving target, with so many genetic variables, that we are lucky to hit the bull's eye with our pairings. There is also the variance from one young bird to the other. As I mentioned, no two birds will be identical. We are simply increasing our chances of getting the same, or rather decreasing the chances of creating undesirable performance with more balanced matings. Genetically speaking, there is just too much stuff floating around, that is not being expressed for us to make perfect choices based on what we can see. Even so, I think these practices get us closer to the mark we desire.

These areas of focus have helped me tremendously in my own program, so much that I feel confident sharing them with others. I have found that you only get out of your program what you put into it. Also, don't rely too much on what the Roller world considers to be the norm. Test the theories that are so commonly accepted, yet don't make sense to you in your own mind. There is still so much to be learned about our birds. So pay close attention and keep excellent records, because everything you pair up, will decide what happens in the sky. Then what happens in the sky, will decide what you put in the stock pen.

Meet Eric Laidler of Denmark

It is my great pleasure to introduce you to Eric Laidler of Denmark. Eric won the World Cup Fly in 2010 and then went on to judge the World Cup Finals in 2011. Shortly after his own World Cup region in Denmark fell apart due to lack of participation and they are no longer active in the World Cup. I met Eric online about 2 ½ years ago and it has been a real blessing to associate with him. He is very positive about the hobby and very energetic to keep the hobby going as well even considering his situation and the World Cup. He also has an extensive library of roller literature. I hope you enjoy and are able to gain some good insight from a very humble and great guy in this wonderful sport/hobby we have, that is TRULY Worldwide.

Water color rendition of Eric and his grandson Alex

Here is Eric with his grandson Alex feeding the rollers

Name, age, where do you live; describe your location in Denmark and include your location to the ocean and weather climate

Hej, my name is Eric Laidler, I´m 66 retired and live in Hvide Sande which is a small fishing village in Denmark. Hvide Sande is situated in the middle of a narrow strip of land on the west coast of Denmark. On one side (east) is Ringkobing fjord and to the west is the North Sea. Being close to the sea and fjord, means there is often an onshore breeze coming off the sea and in the winter the atmosphere is often very damp, the sea mist can also be a problem for flying rollers also. I´ve lost many a bird due to the mist (like fog) just rolling in under them, even though we do get a lot of wind here, we do get some good flying days.

How long have you been working with your current family of rollers and what various families of birds or bloodlines are behind them? Did you ever import birds to Denmark or did you just start with birds that were already there?

Once I had settled down here in Denmark, I decided to get back into pigeons. What I wanted was to get some tumblers or rollers but no one knew what I was talking about, they had never heard of pigeons that could tumble or roll, anyway I got a tip to visit a fancier who kept bantams, I wasn´t really expecting much but I went along. When I got there I could see he also kept a few Danish

Tumblers, which are show birds but most importantly, to me anyway, he had a copy of the "Raceduen" this is the Danish Fancy Pigeon magazine and in it was an article about the Birmingham Roller, at last now I had something in Danish to show people what I was talking about. I saw some ad`s in the back with Rollers for sale, so I was able to buy some, they were mainly Yellows, Rec Reds and Black Grizzles. I flew them for a couple of years but they were hopeless, I had started to subscribe to Pigeons & Pigeon World again and Eamon Dillon who was the secretary of the AERC would often put the fly results in along with some articles. I got Eamon's address and wrote him, asking if he knew anyone with some birds to sell. Not long after I got a letter back from Eamon telling me that his birds came from Ollie Harris and that he would send me 5 pair as a gift. This was early in the 1982 season and went and picked up the 5 pairs at the airport. There was a lot going on at that time, what with a new club and fanciers wanting birds, I ended up depleting most of my stock. In 1986 I decided to go to England to get more birds, Eamon in the meantime had gotten out of Rollers but I had heard about a fancier named Morris Hole, mainly thru the Pigeons and Pigeon World and what Eamon had told me.

I contacted Morris and made arrangements to visit with him and was able to obtain 2 piars. Morris`s birds all go back to Bob Brown, through his good pal Norman Chapman. I had no plan as such about what to do with the 2 families, the only difference between the two families was their size as I could see. The birds from Morris a bit smaller, the first year I bred them separate and bred 10 youngsters from each pair and they were all Reds, either Mealy or Red Cheq. This is when I discovered that these two cocks from Morris were homozygote for Ash Red. It was a bit overwhelming to see al them Reds in my kits, so the following season I crossed them together, putting Blue to Red. I put good rollers to good rollers and if the pairs produced great and if not then the birds either went back into the kit or in many cases I gave them to others fanciers looking for rollers. The resulting progeny from these crosses is the basis of my current family of birds even today.

A pair from Morris Pole in 1986

I know that you were originally from the UK, how long have you been in the UK before relocating to Denmark?

I was born and brought up in North Shields (near Newcastle) in the North East of England, the area was known for its Ship Building, Coal Mining and heavy Engineering as a whole. I served an apprenticeship as a Marine Plumber and on completing my apprenticeship, I went to work on Oil Refineries and Power Stations in England and Australia. I had just returned home from working in a ship yard in Germany, when I bumped into a lad who lived in the same street as me and I had went to school with, he had a small fishing boat and he asked me if I wanted a job, so I said I would give it a try. I ended up fishing for the next few years. I later joined another boat and the skipper of the boat I was on decided to buy an even bigger boat and I ended up working on that boat for 3 months here in Denmark,.

I worked for quite a while there before I met my wife and the rest is history, as they say. I have now lived here in Denmark the past 36 years.

I know we have talked a lot over the last year or two about the history of the Birmingham Roller and the origin of the BR. What is your personal view of this and what time frame might you suspect is the Origin?

I don´t doubt that there have been tumblers and rollers around for hundreds of years but I don´t believe that there have been as many crosses with other breeds as some fanciers like to make out. I would like to start off by saying anyone who claims the Birmingham Roller came about by crossing with the West of England's with a Tippler does not know what they are talking about and they are totally ignorant of the history of all three breeds. Just for the record, the first "WEST" club was formed in Bristol in 1907 and Bristol is in the west of England, hence the name West of England Tumblers. The Tippler is thought to have its Sheffield origins in "Maclesfield" in 1843, again it was the Coal Miners in and around Sheffield that made the Tipplers, the term "Tippler" is a North Country expression, when the birds threw themselves backwards they "tippled" hence the name Tipplers, it´s also said that "Maclesfield" Tipplers were unknown in the Midlands until 1875. The Oriental Roller has also been named but I´ve never seen it mentioned in any books I´ve read, the Dutch Tumbler yes but not the Oriental. I read somewhere that it was Wendel Levi that claimed all the diving and performing pigeons originated from the Oriental Roller, whether or not that is true I don´t know nor do I think we will ever be certain, Pensom I believe was just agreeing with Levi, when he talked of the Oriental Roller. The Oriental Roller was first introduced into England in 1870 by H.P.Caridia a greek Merchant who had also brought in the Oriental Frill in 1864. I don´t doubt that the ability to roll came from an Oriental Roller hundreds of years ago but I do not believe for one moment that the Oriental Roller introduced into England in 1870 has anything to do with our Birmingham Rollers today, I don´t doubt, that some fancier will claim that they could have bred out the extra tail feathers and altered the flying style but there were already birds capable of rolling before 1870. When you read or see the old photos of the Flying Tumblers of yesteryear they are not so different to the birds today.

The following was written in 1849, The Pigeon Book by BP Brent

Variety 1-The Common European Tumbler.

"This variety is very plentiful in Germany, Holland and France and I believe it may be met with in most parts of the Continent. They are about the size of a Dove house Pigeon but of a rather different build and a more gentle and less wild expression, neither is the beak so much dove- shaped or depressed in the middle. They are good breeders and attentive nurses. They fly well and tumble much. I believe this is the breed that is now often sold in England as Rollers, so called from their excessive tumbling or rolling over so many times as they fly. In comparison with our finer bred English Tumblers, they are coarse, mousey or jowlter headed, as the fanciers term it, that is to say, the beak longer and the forehead less raised. They are clean footed, though some of the Dutch have small feathers on the feet. In plumage they are very varied, possessing all the known shades and colours of domestic pigeons. Some are whole coloured but the greater portion are black, blues or reds with white flights. Others also have white tails and often a small white splash under the beak. There are also mottles, grizzles, haggles, splashed and pied, as magpie, or white with dark heads and tails."

As you can see they were not all muffed, they were also clean legged.

As Dave mentioned in the first edition of the "Spinner Magazine" George Smith wrote about the "Flying Tumblers" the following is what Smith wrote;

"Many years ago birds did not fly as long as they do now, five hours was considered a very good fly. The reason, I account for it, is because a kit of Tumblers in those days used to Tumble more than they do at the present time, every circle they took they would all Tumble together and some of them would roll five or six yards - in fact, I have seen them roll down to the ground and kill themselves"

Obviously the birds being flown at that time were also capable of breeding birds that could roll. There is no doubts in my mind that birds being flown in those kits went on to form some of the other performing breeds we know today, the Wests, Tipplers, the Badges, the Maggies and the Birmingham Roller.

Pensom I think it was wrote the following;

"There used to be a group of fanciers in this part of the country (Birmingham) who knew a Roller from A to Z, and were always on the look – out for a good bird. Distance and money were no obstacle to them, and they would start off with a pony and trap on a Saturday afternoon for the Black Country and such places as Cradley Heath, Halesowen and Stourbridge etc, where even today are flown some of the best Rollers in the World. These old fanciers would regain their homes in the early hours of Monday morning, either with a sack with a number of birds inside or in the pockets of their swallow - tailed coats. They bought a quantity on the chance of obtaining one or perhaps two good birds, the others

being sold for shooting parties. Such Stalwarts in the Roller Fancy as the late T.Wicks, Dick Stokes, A.Fellows and H.Young were perhaps known to some readers and I believe were associated with many of these outings".

Well as you can see it's easy enough to see how the Birmingham Roller evolved into the Birmingham Roller.

What was the first good spinning/breaking kit you remember, and who owned this kit?

I had Rollers as a lad in England in the 60´s so I had an idea as to what a good Roller was, plus when I got back into Rollers in the 80´s, I was visiting fanciers in England on my trips back home. Although I had seen a lot of good Rollers, I hadn´t seen a good kit, there were no shortage of fanciers who could tell me but none of them could show me, they all just wanted me to purchase and try their birds but their birds were no better than what I already had. In 1986 on a visit back to England to see my family, I arranged to visit Bill Barrett for the weekend, as it happened the Severnside Roller Club in Bristol was having a fly that weekend, I think it was for holdovers, Bill, Bob Brown, Jay Lucarelli (Canada) and Eamon Dillon were all going, we didn´t really see much until we got to Arthur Chadwicks, Arthur released his kit and they came out quiet, until they reached a decent height, then they just exploded, they were fantastic, it was the first time I saw a kit break together and I´ll never forget them, that kit set the standard for me, needless to say Arthur´s kit went on to win the fly.

What do you think of the general overall quality of the BR today (2015) and how was it different when you first started with rollers? Did any of the old timers you ever sat down with give you any insight on this?

Well, I was just a young lad and I don´t remember that the birds were better back then, the kits I saw back then had more birds that just tumbled rather than roll, whether it was because they were of poor quality or mismanaged, I don´t know. I didn´t really get to know any old timers, I had met a lad at school, who had pigeons with his older brother, they had Rollers and show birds, the older brother had a pal who worked on the local farm who also kept Rollers and show birds, it was them that put me onto the "Pigeons & Pigeon World" magazine, it was here I learnt more about Rollers, in fact Pigeons as a whole.

What has been the best recent kit you have seen, and how does it compare to what you had seen earlier in your BR career? (If you have a list please list the top 5 or so and what years you saw these kits going back to say 1990)

Over the years I´ve seen a lot of good breaking kits, the only thing that separates them, would be the amount of really good quality birds in the kit "on the day" I don´t have a list and I cannot remember the order of years in which I saw the kits, one of the better kits has to be Ronnie Schoemakers kit in Holland, they broke as a team should and they had the quality of Roll to go with it, there were plenty of good quality Rollers in that kit, "on the day" they were a great kit of Rollers, I stayed at Henri Smits one weekend and he flew a good breaking kit for me then and of course Heine, his record speaks for itself, I judged the AERC fly in 2010 and Paul Green flew a good kit as can Ken and Trevor Weaver, Kevin McKinney again his record speaks for itself, Ceda in Serbia has also flew a good kit for me, I have never really talked much about the birds and kits here in Denmark, I have always said let the birds do the talking but over the years I've seen some great kits and birds at my good friends, Henning Pedersen (deceased) Jorgen Rosengreen and Ferid Catak, all these birds and kits have been seen and judged by fanciers around the world, not just me.

Eric's magic feed mixture

I know that you started or help to start the Euro Fly. Why how did this come about, and how is it going? (Increased interest or less than expected)

Yes, I started the Euro Fly, as I was travelling around I was meeting small groups of fanciers in countries that wanted to compete in an international competition but they couldn't meet the criteria set down by the World Cup. Because of the World Cup, the RDs were in place, so it was just a question of getting in touch with them to find out if they were interested in starting a new International Fly and they were, so a committee was formed and the World Cup rules adopted and the rest is history as they say. The first fly was in 2009 with 8 countries, Denmark, England, Serbia, Holland, Germany, N.Ireland, R.Ireland and Sweden but Sweden had to drop out because of lack of support and have not rejoined, so we were 7. In 2011 we welcomed Bosnia, Croatia and Slovenia which made it 10 countries. In 2013 Croatia split into Croatia East and Croatia West. This year (2015) we welcomed Hungary, so I would say its going well, we'll see what happens in 2017.

If you could just name 1 person of interest that has influenced you the most over the years with the BR, who would this person be and why?

If I can only name one person, then I cannot name anyone. From my travels around England I knew what a good roller was but I have to thank, Eamon Dillon and Morris Hole for the birds they gave me, they formed the basis for my family of birds today, also Arthur Chadwick for flying a kit of rollers that could actual break as a team, Bill Barrett and Morris Hole for giving me other ideas on feed and feeding. I get the impression off some fanciers, mainly novices that they expect to be able to go to a fanciers loft on any given day and see it all, it do´s not work like that, if they see a little here and a little there, they have to learn how to put two and two together, that is how I learnt.

If you could sit down and talk with up to 3, living or deceased, roller flyers and pick their brains, who would they be and what would you want to ask them?

I´m interested in the history of the Birmingham Roller, so I suppose it would be the likes of T.Wicks, Dick Stokes, A fellows and Harry Young. I would want to know what the state of the fancy was like at that period of time. While I´m interested in the history of the BR, I don´t want to dwell on it too much and at the end of the day we have to move forward. It is what happens in the future that matters. I believe the Birmingham Roller is still evolving, these birds are capable of doing a lot more than they can now, those fanciers that want to stop the clock in the past and preserve the BR as it was with some of the greats like OD Harris, Jim Skidmore and Pensom then these fanciers are more collectors or feel that the BR has already reached its full potential50+ years ago. I am afraid that I don't share that same belief.

How many stock birds do you breed from on average each season? How many babies do you produce on average? Do you use foster parents?

Over the years I have bred from between 5 and 10 pairs on average. Most of this depends on how many I survived from the previous years. I breed from 30-60 birds usually. The first year I got the birds from Morris, I did foster some but that was the only time. I do on occasions move eggs from to other pairs, but otherwise I just let the birds do their thing.

What is your ideal kit of spinners? (Describe what they do or should do) Have you seen anything close to the ideal in your mind and who was flying this kit? How has your ideas on this changed over the years.

Well the kit I have in mind is the same kit I saw many years ago at Arthur Chadwicks. This kit has always been my standard and my ideas have not changed over the years. What is it I want to see? We'll I´ll put it this way, first off we have to assume that we have some decent weather, when I come home, I want to relax and enjoy my pigeons. I like enjoy watching them fly so they must stay at a good height, anywhere from 100 to 500 feet will suffice. There is no enjoyment in watching a kit pin out or fly out of range. I also want to see some good rolling, after all that's why I have the Birmingham Roller. I generally like my birds to fly for approximately 1½ hours so I want to see them rolling the entire time they are up. I do not enjoy watching birds that are only active for the first 10 minutes and then fly like homers, this is no interest to me. Even when the kit is active they have to maintain good kitting habits. I get no enjoyment watching out birds or birds that fly and roll as individuals. The icing on the cake, so to speak, come when that activity comes with the kit breaking as a team, those spontaneous, explosive breaks with good quality and depth. This is what I like to see. Does it happen every day, No…

What is the best Bird you have every flown? Describe it

Well, I cannot say that I´ve only had one bird that stood out above all others, there are several good birds that come to mind, the ones I didn´t lose have all played a role in building my family of birds over the years. When I say "lose", I am not talking about birds that rolled down or bumped, but good stable birds which were lost in the sea mist here that can come in very unexpectedly. I would describe my birds as being medium sized, some might be a little larger or smaller but not too big or too small. I don´t like deep keeled birds either, they always seem to be the first to cause some problems. As long as the birds have a balanced look about them. I don't read a whole lot on a specific type so long as the birds is balanced.

What has been your best stock birds in your own family? (Attach pic if possible)

Although my family of birds are crossed, I have always thought of the Bronze Cheqs (Balds & Badges) Blacks & Grizzles as being the Eamon Dillon side of the family and the Red Cheqs (Balds & Badges) as being the Morris Hole side of the family but of course they are mixed. Both sides of this family I am working with have produced me good stock pigeons. I keep good records on my birds, so I can trace all my birds back to the original birds. Unfortunately, I don´t have photos of all these birds or the photos that I do have are not good enough to publish. Here are some of the birds that have played a role in my family of birds.

What would you say are the most important qualities in selecting a good solid stock bird? (Please rank these qualities by their importance)

What is important is that the fancier is selecting for all the necessary qualities. It has to be a good strong flyer and great kit bird, it must be capable of doing a good clean stable roll, regardless of speed or depth of roll. It really doesn't matter if one selects for H style Rollers or A style rollers, which ever you desire to see, they are both good enough to breed from in my opinion.

How was your trip around the World when you judged the World Cup in 2011? What was your gained knowledge after doing it?

Well needless to say it was fantastic it was fantastic, and to see the various rollers around the world and meet the fanciers in this sport was incredible to say the least. Where else can you go and meet people you have never talked to and they will invite you into their homes and back yards, like that. The World Cup has been going for 25 years now and Denmark was part of it for the first 22 years. We flew in 19 of these events and with our one kit each year we managed to place in the top ten 12 times, including winning it twice. This is really something we are very proud of.

I didn´t gain anything from it as such, what I learned was, is that us as fanciers have a long ways to go and there are many good birds out there, but good kits are still few and far between. As I´ve said in an earlier question, I believe the Birmingham Roller is still evolving and until there are more excellent rollers breaking as a team should evolving that break well together I will keep believing this.

Eric Laidler, Morris Hole and WC Legend Heine Bijker

What advice would you give to any would be roller flyer that is open minded out there wanting to fly in better rollers?

First off they need to have patience and then need to learn that there are no short cuts in this hobby/sport. They cannot do it by sitting in their armchairs, or sitting or talking or writing your way to the top. It can only be done in your back yard underneath your kit.

Many come in to this sport/hobby and think after only a couple of years they can win everything but when they discover it is not that easy many will give up and drop out. They need to gain knowledge and learn about what a Birmingham Roller really is and maintain the ability to keep wanting to learn more about them. One of the biggest issues for new flyers seems to be, getting good quality birds and by that I do not mean young birds or trying to establish a family of roller from unflown young birds. This is not the way to go about it correctly. You need to start with yearlings or old birds and if you can get 2-3 pairs and use feeders this will be a good start for you. You need to fly them and cull hard. It takes years to build up to a quality family of birds and continue to improve them is a never ending. It is a process that goes on year in and year out for most. Even though you can encounter many opinions about how to do the rollers correctly, they need to remain firm with their birds in their own back yards, this is what matters at the end of the day.

Danish Flying Breed Club (DFK)
(Danske Flyvedue Klub)

This flying club was for in January of 1983 in Odense (birth place of Hans Christian Anderson)

This club quickly grew to over 100 members and has maintained that membership over the years. In 2004 we formed the Danish Birmingham Roller Club (DBRC under the DFK group). Unfortunately our membership has diminshed and only have 3 memers remaining; Edin Kazarcannin, Steen Christiansen and Eric Laidler

The Danish Birmingham Roller Club is down to 3 members, not the Danish Flying Breeds Club

Dr. Spintight

Question and Answer Column

This section of Spinner Magazine will be seen in every issue. If you have a question you like to submit to Spinner Magazine's to be answered for this column please send your questions to; davesrollerpigeons@gmail.com

Question: Hi I am wondering what is the best way to test and evaluate my stock pairs? I don't want to keep too many pigeons around and I am finding myself just getting way too many.

Dr Spinight: Hi thank you for taking the time to send me your question. This is a very interesting question and one we have to look at nearly every year. Keeping too many pigeons is really easy to do and if we want to be able to evaluate our current pairs as best we can we need to keep on top of this stuff. The more breeders you accumulate the longer it will take to properly evaluate them.

Well first off I feel that most should be breeding as many as they can handle and manage well. Having too many young birds to fly and evaluate is worse than having too many stock pairs/birds.

The real issues arise when we are just not able to fly and keep track of the kit birds we have with ease. Having too many birds to manage properly will work against you. You will get frustrated much more often which leads to prematurely culling birds just to make things easy on you.

I know that we need to keep the birds we all like best, no reason to keep birds you don't like. There are many good performing families out there and there has to be one that suits you. These should be birds that are performing for you with your management skills. Some birds are easy to manage others not so easy…

You never mentioned how many birds/pairs you are working with, but I would try to keep your numbers to 12 pairs or less, and 8 pairs is a good number for most fanciers that don't have a lot of predators. I know that many find various ways to work around the predator migrations and the residential BOP. So a lot of this plays into that scenario.

The fewer pairs you can breed from and fly the young from the faster you can properly evaluate your stock birds and progress your family/gene pool. I would try to breed at least 8 babies from each pair, so gauge that number on how many kit birds you can handle efficiently. So if you have 12 pairs that is breeding 95-100 babies if you have 8 pairs that's 60-70 babies. I can't really answer the question effectively without asking more questions…?

Another issue that can greatly affect a fancier is how the birds develop.

Some guys might have birds spinning at 3 months 15-30 foot range and some others aren't even flipping until they are nearly a year old. If the birds you have are late to develop then you have to deal with this also.

It takes your average roller 5-7 months to start spinning/rolling with enough speed to get you excited about it. This could be 4 to 6 months of flying pretty much daily for this period of time. If you can't fly your rollers daily then your birds might even develop at a much slower rate even. The feeding is also important as well and not feeding too much or too little. So there are a lot of ways to look at this equation in order move forward in a timely manner with current stock birds. I would say that you should be flying the birds daily at daily up until they start their adult molt.

For example: Here where I am I generally get my last round of babies are June hatch because I have to lock them down generally in November. So this will give the majority of them a chance to at least be doing even a little rolling before I have to start flying them less or go into lock down. Many times if you birds that are able to get good flying habits before this lock down period will have a great chance to get back out flying come March the following year.

Young birds that have not even completed their baby molt by November will be very much wasted, at least the vast majority of them will be.

If you are surviving 5 babies out of 8 and 3-4 of these become good rollers then you have a pretty good pair. If another pair survived NO birds before the lock down then these might be bad pairs? Especially if you have no accounting of these birds and why they vanished. I find that good birds have a knack for surviving also, they are somehow smart enough to evade the BOP longer then you average pigeon.   If you breed 8 and survive them all but only 1 of the 8 is a good spinner then you have a hard decision to make also.

The way I gauge my own is I give them 3 seasons at the most to show me something. This will also be with 3 different mates. If I don't get a descent number of good spinners in those 3 seasons to get my attention then theses will generally go bye bye or at the very least go back out to fly again. The majority of them, especially cocks, will find another home however, as I find it can be tedious at times to retrain some of these birds. It is generally much harder to re-tame cock birds that have already been breeding for several seasons but hens tend to come back most of the time.

So I hope you are getting a little insight from this answer. It might not give you your answer immediately but it will at least give you a way to get there.

Again a major thing is to work with birds you like, birds that respond well to your training methods and that are able to develop the way you want them to develop. The longer it takes a bird to develop the spin the more birds you find having to keep around each season.

Please feel free to contact me if you have further questions.

South Africa Import Pair #108 and #184 (Ron Swart)

In The Spotlight

Interviews in the hobby

Meet Ken Billings of Idaho

I want to give big thank you to my friend Camilo Paci for getting this amazing interview for Spinner Magazine of a Legend in the sport and Northern California Native, Ken Billings.

I have always referred to Ken over the years as Kenny having first met Kenny in 1984 while he was living in the region of Medesto, California. I have some fond memories over the years on various pigeon excursions in those days having both grown up also here in Northern California, many of these had to do with beer and pigeons... I never really knew much about their pigeons in Medesto and was not well versed on the "Pensom" pigeons they were all talking about back in them days but I always had fun times when I was there. I am lucky to have Milo that has first-hand accounts of things and was willing to do this interview for us, having better knowledge of the background on this fantastic quality family of pigeons that Ken has developed over the years.

Kenny has always seemed to be a level above most roller guys, even very experienced flyers and breeders, and I think it is the way he thinks having grown up in a "hot bed" of roller activity and many fanciers nearby. He had the likes of Sam Williams, Jack Meyers, and Don Ouellette pushing him to do better.

I want to again thank Camilo for getting this amazing interview hope you all can gain a lot of insight in this one.

Nestled in the beautiful hills of Kuna, Idaho, not far from the Snake River Birds of Prey Sanctuary lives one of the most accomplished roller men, and my mentor, Ken Billings. Accompanied by my close friend Shane Anderson and my Father, we arrived in Kuna to see an impressive roller compound with some kit action and great company. Ken let out his "A" team it was nothing less than extraordinary, as you would expect from breeder/competitor like Ken is. Although this explosive display of acrobatics was interrupted by an onslaught of Peregrine attacks, and followed up by a series of owl attacks. After which we retreated into the cozy home of a Master Flyer who spoke candidly to us about the history with the birds, and how he sees things in association to our hobby.

Shane Anderson, Ken Billings and Milo Paci at Ken's in Idaho

What is your name, age and where do you currently fly from?

Ken Billings, age 53 and I now live in Melba, Idaho.

Describe your location

Country setting

When did you leave Modesto?

I left in 1996.

Who have you looked to for advice and guidance over the years? How did you start off with your birds?

Jack Meyers and Sam Williams I would say. Jack would really be the only mentor really, and that's because he was the first guy I met that was organized in flying pigeons. With all the people in this hobby, you get pieces … A little from this guy, and a little from that guy etc… Then something you hear that just makes sense, you know? As far as some guy that came up and I molded myself after, I don't think there are any of those.

I got into inbreeding because of my dad, and his chickens. I was reading my old mans' book about breeding the Kelso chickens. He was supposed to be the winning-est cocker in the World, and it made sense to me. He talked about how he kept this line of chickens for 50 years, and then he inbred, inbred, inbred.... He would go to a pit, and find an outstanding individual in the pit, an outstanding athlete, a bird that just tore up another and would take that home and cross that over onto his truly inbred stock. He became the winning-est cocker of all time doing this. Even today, after 90 years, they still, people still talk about his birds. Anyway, I read this book by him, and that probably had the most influence on the way I breed more than anything else I do. So today, I still do a lot of that.

I have my foundation stock I got back in '84, '85 and '86 from the guys with the Sparks pigeons. I'm still breeding those today, and I still do the outstanding athlete thing too.

What were the most memorable experiences over the years with the birds and in competitions?

None of that stuff...I think that most impressive things to me were...The first time I saw a good spinner, the first time I saw a good kit... I remember the first time I saw a good kit and it was at Jack Meyers. I was laying on a dying board, and it was like raining pigeons man, I was like...I don't know...I was hooked. I had never seen anything like that, you know? Because I had birds from Elmer Smith and Ace Hogart. Birds like that...I can still see 'OL Ace putting his fingers together saying, "Those are choice Birmingham Rollers right there Mr. Billiings, you'll never find better than those." I saw Jack's and they just blew me away. Now that was memorable. Winning flies and stuff like that goes by so fast, you know? It just burns through, and that stuff doesn't do anything for me, but the friendships and the people I've known for the past 40-50 years... Now those are memorable things. There are pigeons that stick out in my mind, but those come and go also.

Many roller fanciers are unaware of the tragic loss of 1998, when a deranged teen broke into your breeders loft and brutally killed over 12 pairs of your best stock birds, including their young. Without going into much detail of this devastating event, how did this loss of 285, her off spring, and many other top shelf breeders affect you personally, and what impact did this have on your program today?

This event set me back 20-30 years. Simple. I still think about where I would be at today had I not lost those 12 pair that that kid killed. Yan, without a doubt. It set me back, it set me back... (Silence)

What were the key birds you focused on while rebuilding your program and why?

They were just sons and daughters to the ones I lost. I picked them, well, because the birds before them, were the best I have ever had. So instead of having 25 years of selecting the best, and having proven producers, I had to just take what I was left with. That's a hard road to tow...It's just like starting over. Trying to find the prepotent pigeons again.

NBRC-02-531 owned by C Paci bred by Ken Billings

How would you describe your percentages? So on average, out of 20 bred, how many are what you would consider to be "good" or stockable pigeons?

If I breed 20 pigeons I get 20 rollers. I have always said, "You cull for the roll." The problem with it is that, well, what makes a good pigeon? Just because it rolls well, doesn't make it a good pigeon. They can be too short, they can be too deep, or poor kitting birds, they could be seldom, or even too frequent…when you start going down the list, those things make good pigeons, well…It doesn't take very long to figure out, there aren't too many good pigeons.

There are many birds I could single out, but my best birds all go back to the IPB-86-21111 in some way or another. For those that aren't familiar, he is essentially an inbred TRC-68-272 bird.

And 50. Ya, the "Krenz" cock, or later known as the "Nazi" cock.

The bird is often referred to as the "Dog Trainer Cock".

One of Ken's passions since moving to Idaho-sturgeon fishing

What's the story there? How did you acquire the bird an when did you realize, considering his unimpressive build, he was so valuable and worth building upon?

Here's how it happened...So I went to what was called the Monday auction. We went to the Monday auction because Kiser and Borges, well basically Kiser, but Kiser and Borges would take their birds to the Monday auction. We could go down there to check things out and see if anything good came through. I met a kid there that worked for a dog trainer and he wanted some parlor rollers. He just bought some rollers, so anyway, I told him I had some parlors. So I took him over and I looked through a bunch of birds, and saw this bird with a blue band on it and I recognized it as being one of the Robert Krenz's birds. So I just traded for him and didn't think much about it at the time. He was, well the best way to explain that pigeon was, he was a "cigar". You could literally put your bird finger and your thumb together and you could slide him straight through. I had him for a year and a half, didn't breed him or anything, just had him in a box and didn't think anything about it, and finally one day, I don't know what for, I just threw him with a hen, and the babies were really good. I think put him with a good hen, and the babies were AMAZING. Still to this day, 30 years later, you know, that's one of the best pigeons I have ever had as far as production. He was just solid. So how it came about was, I tried to get ahold of Robert to find out what the pigeon was... Robert got ticked off. The story gets a little wrapped around here. You see, the parents came from Chan Grover, they were on loan from Chan to Krenz, and Krenz got them from Carry Mueller, while Krenz had them on loan, Ron Moden bought them from him. So anyway, they didn't respect the bird, they just took it down there. At first when I called him, he wouldn't tell me. And now today, if you call him up, he'll tell you he doesn't even remember the pigeon. Eventually I got the story that he had given it as a present and they must have flown it off... and then Kiser told me he took it to the dog trainer because it had poor feather quality but he didn't want to tell Robert because he didn't want to hurt his feelings.

You are also know for the "Hollywood", or the 285 line of birds. What can you tell us about CCRC-881090(Hollywood), or more importantly, can you elaborate on his mother, DJO-84-285?

I got probably 60 pigeons from Doug Ouellette over the years and I used 285. She was nothing special. She had a webbed toe, and she was a 35 foot average roller, and I had her full brother and I mated them together based on pedigree. I got Hollywood and he was exceptional in the air, exceptional speed. After the years what I found out about 285 was that she had a genetic anomaly that I think very few pigeons in the world have and that is... No matter how deep I inbred that hen... I went 10 generations starting with her on her full brother, then I bred her to her son, which was Hollywood and made the "Steel Cock". Then I took him, and the best sons of 10 generations, and bred them to her. That's what that kid killed. When I lost the birds those were the birds off those. Those pigeons, instead of getting weather or showing ANY kind of deterioration, either physically or their health, man, they just got stronger and better. So 285 was a freak to me. One of the most amazing producing pigeons I have ever seen. Still to this day, I look for the pigeons that can even come close to that deep inbreeding. I made up a name for it...It's not genetically sound, but the way I bred her, I just called it "direct-line-inbreeding", meaning I just inbred to her. Inbreeding to her, inbreeding to her, inbreeding to HER...Taking every good son and breeding it back to her. So I called it direct-line-inbreeding, but I really didn't know what else to call it because it wasn't inbreeding because you're breeding her to her grandsons, and to her great-great-great-great grandson, and it's still her son. They were kind of line bred before that. So she was a special pigeon.

Describe the best qualities of your birds, and some flaws.

Best qualities are the speed, depth, and just outstanding looking pigeons...The nice ones. I know people don't like dark checks, but to me, they are the prettiest dark checks I've ever seen in my life. So I just think they're awesome. To me, they are just black diamonds. Just a refined jewel. I just think they're awesome.

A pair of Ken's 272 blood

Now their bad traits? Their faults?

I think I missed it, I just try to handle it…They tend to want to fly high, and when you are really getting them on edge, you got to be careful or you will lose them. You know? Those are bad traits as well, at my age now I'm trying to fix that, I think I have missed when I was younger.

How do you handle that?

Well I went at it from three different directions… I went at it from of course, feeding, which I kind of picked up a thing from Dave Moseley that really worked. Then I went at it from breeding. Then I went at it from type. I found the type of pigeon that didn't tend to want to fly high, or as high, at least in my estimation. I noticed these pigeons that were a certain type than than the other pigeons I was breeding I noticed these pigeons had a different type than I was breeding. The pigeons that I love, are like balsa wood…Full, but they're just light inside. They feel like… I guess a good way to say it, they feel like an empty beer can. You got this bird that feels nice and full, but it weighs nothing. Those birds SMOKE. NO doubt about it, but those birds also can fly forever on nothing. You know? So it's a catch-22.

No. I can't. If I had to pick just one, I had a smokey blue bar off of 21111 and 285 that I thought nearly disappeared. He was a pencil line. That bird was awesome. But I bred a few of that pair that were that way. I've got that 557 cock right now you saw too. But over the years there have been so many nice pigeons. Seems like just when you lose a good one and you can't do without it, eventually one comes along and you think took another step maybe not forwards, but you're catching up. Seems like you're always three steps forward and four steps back in this hobby.

Describe some of your training methods, or maybe a secret or two for us.

I've told you before… I've got no secrets. I really don't have any secrets. There are no secrets. Hard work, and reading pigeons. Still to this day, shoot, I miss way more than I see…

What do you mean by "reading" pigeons?

Reading pigeons. You fly your kit, and the closer you get to a competition, you fly them, and you make adjustments. I've never found any system that you just "follow". Like feed them straight wheat, and throw in some peas, and safflour….And two days before or whatever, or rest them two days….I've just found nothing that works every time. So my system is this: Get better at reading my conditions, reading where my kit is at, watching individuals and seeing what they are doing, and see who's "off". Like I just had a bird that I pulled this last fly because of the way her feet looked.

Her feet?

Ya. If that pigeon was healthy, and feeling good, she's not going to be standing there with wet crap all over her feet. So I pulled her. Was it the right thing? I don't know. It's part of reading pigeons. Some pigeons look like they need a little more, some look like they need a little less. The bad thing is, your job, if you're still working, puts a damper on that. The more time you have with them, the better you're going to be at it. You should be with the pigeons. I used to have guys ask me all the time, "All those dark checks, how can you tell the difference between all those dark checks?" If you spend enough time with your pigeons, and one rolls, you know exactly who it is. It's that simple.

Hen, #613 x # 538 full b/s.
cock, 1290 x #1418 nest
mate to #1417

One of Ken's pairs

You have numerous flying accomplishment and accolades. Two National titles in the 11 bird, and a ranking as high as 2nd I in the World Cup. Can you tell us about these teams and the standouts?

Yah, the National team of 2004 I thought was as good as you can get them. Jon Farr has told me this a couple of times, saying that was the best team of pigeons he had ever seen, until he had seen Mark Ritter's recently. They were good. They were good enough that they scored 410 points, which still, I think is holding the record. The judge was apologizing to me, telling me that he just couldn't score them. He said, "I just couldn't give you all the points because I couldn't keep up. It was impossible". They were a good team.

What would you consider to be your greatest accomplishments in this hobby, and what goals have you set for yourself personally with regards to competition and moving forward?

My goal isn't like a lot of people. For many people, their goal is to win the World Cup, or to win the National titles. My goal, is to be the best pigeon flyer I can be, and to be that for however long I live. Whether I live to be 65, or 75, or 85 or even 95... Wherever I live, to still be competitive and still be one of the fly guys. Not to be one of the guys that find some reason not to fly, and bail. That's my goal. My goal, is to just be a pigeon man.

Ken's loft buddy helping on the roof of one of his sheds

What advice would you give to new flyers looking to get started or get into competition?

Probably the same thing that everybody else does... Don't just GET pigeons... Go around and find someone flying what you really like, and don't get any of them damn mongrels...

Old picture of Ken with Sam Williams

I just want to give a short introductiont to Deano Forster. Deano is of course a UK fancier and as you will soon read has been very successful in the last 10+ years there in the UK flying his family of pigeons. They have the speed and quality that many are after and I have heard incredible things about him and his birds, even from the 2014 World Cup Champion Keith Storey, that told me all of his birds came from Deano. As many know it's no easy task to win the World Cup and to repeat is even more impressive. Thanks for sharing with us Deano and I hope that you have a great 2016 season.

In The Spotlight

Interviews in the hobby

Meet Deano Forster of England

Deano in front of his main loft

Name, where do you live; describe your location in the UK

Dean (Deano) Forster and I live in the North Eastern side of England in a place named Middlesbrough

When did you first start raising the Birmingham Roller? As well as competing there? Give us a brief history of who Dean Forster is

I started raising and competition with Birmingham rollers in 1982. The birds I am currently working with come down from about a dozen or so birds I collected over the years. They come from no one in particular, just good pigeons that do what I need them to do.

I must be doing something right because I have won all the individuals in the AERC, Nationals, National Old birds and 2nd and 4th in the young birds Nationals. My teams have consistently put up the best quality points in these contests. Each time I have qualified for the World Cup, which is very difficult in the Middlesbrough area, I have gotten amongst the highest quality points given for the season. I am very proud of the quality of my birds even if I have never won this contest.

Who have you looked to for advice and guidance over the years?

Many years ago I got good advice from a man named Les Freeman and in more recent years Les Bezanze has been very helpful to me.

What club do you fly with? How many members in this club?

I fly with the All England Roller Club (AERC), the Cleveland County Roller Club (CCRC) and the Teesside Invitational Club. My local club consist of 24 member here in Middlesbrough.

Can you give me a brief history of the competition rollers there in the UK and how have they evolved since you have been breeding and flying rollers?

I have always concentrated on high quality rollers where in the England many are more interested in high frequency breaking birds to win competitions. These competition rollers are not my cup of tea. I have had birds since the 1980's and I think the birds for the most part have been very similar to what they are today in terms of quality.

Does your local club fly by the World Cup rules or do you use other rules? What are these rules if they are different?

Yes my local club does fly in the World Cup. Most clubs in England fly by our National Rules where we are given points for kitting and quality. I don't like the World Cup rules much and how the give bonus point for depth as it is very difficult to know just how deep our birds are rolling. The National rules allow for up to 10 points in quality per bird in your team. Example; 9 good quality spinners will earn you 90 points and this keeps things very simple.

A Few of Deano's stock cocks

What is the base of birds behind your family of rollers? When did you get these birds and how have they evolved since you first got them?

I got birds from many sources in the early days and there were no one in particular that I got the birds from that created the family I am currently using that I call my own. I must have used approximately a dozen birds in the development of my current family and the last time I did an outcross was approximately 4 years ago going back to some old blood related to Mick Proudman.

One of Deano's stock hen's

I talked to Keith Storey (2015 WC champ) and he confirmed that most of his pigeons come from your family, in fact he speaks very highly of you and your family of rollers. Do you have a partner behind the scenes that you work with in conjunction with your breeding program? I know many prominent flyers have flyers that work together.

No I have never worked with anyone with the birds. I work alone really. The only assistance I get at times is loaning out potential breeders to people to breed for me so I can test out more birds then I am capable of breeding at my own loft. This can assist me in finding future stock birds of worth to me.

How do you continue to progress with your family of birds? How do you breed them? What tend to be your best pairings and how much inbreeding do you do?

Some of my best mating's are Uncle/niece but I do a lot of closely related mating's similar to this in my loft. I don't out cross often but I am really not afraid of fetching birds from outside of my loft. I would really not hesitate if it were the right bird as I really don't believe in PURE strains. Adding in quality birds which I have seen fly and trust the judgments of the breeders that made them is part of this.

Some of Deano's mates… to include George Mason

How many stock birds do you breed from on average each season? How many babies do you produce on average?

I generally have 12 pairs of rollers and produce around 80 youngsters per season. I am mostly concerned with high quality rollers. I keep only 3 young bird teams and 2 old birds teams at the most. I do have problems with predators here so most of my stock birds are prisoners and will never leave my loft once stocked.

Can you tell us something about your' family of birds that many would not know? But might be interested to learn.

Most people know my birds here in England I really have no secrets.

What is the best Bird you have every flown? Describe it, when and where did this bird come from?

The best bird that comes to mind was a roller I had the would spin like a tennis ball and then snap right out of the roll as quickly as he started facing the kit every time. I bred this bird back in 1984.

These tennis ball rollers are very rare to see and I have bred very few of them over the years. I am especially fond of the solid ball spinning rollers.

What has been your best stock birds in your family?

I really have had some great success with my birds and have had plenty of good producing birds over the years. However the Stud Cock and the Red Wings have dominated in my breeding loft over the years, plus a blue hen from a lad named Mick Proudman that could no longer keep his birds.

What do you think the #1 key is to developing a successful family of rollers if you could just name 1 specific characteristic you must have?

If I could just name one specific trait that will help you develop good rollers that would be selecting for correct rolling ability. The quality of the roll is very important as it keeping your program small enough to manage properly.

What would you say is the average length of time a good spinner/breeder will stay in your loft productive? Other words how many years will you use a bird in your breeding program on average, please elaborate more on this if possible.

I give all my stock birds 2 chances as a breeder to earn its keep. If I am unable to find any good spinners from it after 2 seasons I will ditch it. If I have a good breeder it will stay in my loft for as many years as it's productive.

Some of Deano's 2015 young birds

What kind of schedule are you able to fly your rollers by? Many of us are working "stiffs" are limited to how many birds we can keep and train due to working and or family constraints.

I fly my birds' everyday weather permitting on my young birds. My old birds will only be flown an average of 3 times per week once they are fit and back in shape from the lock down that happens here between October and April.

I went thru the World Cup archives and over a few years of the finals I saw your kits scores and they jumped off the page at me. Some of the most incredible quality and depth combinations overall I would say. Can you tell us more about the specific kit from 2007 season? How long did it take you to develop this kit and what was it comprised of? Various sexes, ages etc.

This kit was a great team, but they were only together as a team for about 2 months. It was comprised of cocks and hens with an average age of 3 years old. These birds were from various kits and I simply missed them together, it does not take them long before they are working as a good team.

Now looking at these Q & D multipliers above, do you have stability issues in your family of rollers or do you have to fly them a specific way to develop them so you can prevent them from rolling down etc..? I personally find that you can roll down any pigeons if you fly them too much and do not give them adequate rest.

I get some birds that will bump at times on release, but I will never breed from a bird that becomes a roll down. I don't pay attention to depth much just correct rolling and I would guess that most tend to be 20 to 30 footers and all are of similar depths as this. It is difficult to really know just how deep they are really rolling. I lock my rollers up between October and April each year and once I get them back out flying again it will take several weeks to whip them back into shape. In this process I do get a few that will kill or injure themselves on the neighboring power lines here.

Can you tell us how you train and feed your young birds and also how this might vary from you're your "A" team. Do you use any special formulas for feeding or you fly the birds a specific way to get them to perform to their full potential?

I give my young birds wheat only and fly them once per day. The old birds get mostly wheat also but I will give them red dari (milo) as well.

What advice would you give to any new flyers out there wanting to fly in competition today and possibly get into the World Cup or other major competitions out there?

If I were to give a bit of advice I would say that you need to pay attention and OBSERVE your birds. You need to know the birds and how they act and fly. We as breeders are always learning more and more about these birds and we are never too old to learn new things.

Creating Your Ideal
By
Dave Henderson

The Ideal Birmingham Roller will not be the same at every loft, but many will share very similar qualities. Performance being this similar trait, at least this should be the goal for the pure performance fancier. Creating an outstanding family of pigeons is no accident, it takes many hours of observation of your birds in the loft and in the air to do this successfully.

I have seen literally thousands of high quality birds over the years and in the air many can roll or spin very similarly but on the ground they can look something completely different. This could be anything from their size, head shape, the birds stance, depth of the keel, leg length, webbed feet, tail width or length or even things not easily noticed like eye reflexes, pupil movement or even a eye flexing(bounce), tail reflexes and now even eye clusters can be a factor. There are literally many different types of birds that are capable to performing to a very high quality spin and yet many can look totally different to one another but still capable of a similar spin in the air.

It's about paying attention to the small details that many don't look at in regards to performance and even other management practices. Performance to me is more like a "whole package" thing and not just about their physical ability to spin or roll but how they act on the ground and in the kit while flying. It could be something as simple as how the eat and act inside to the kit box to where they fly in the kit, the position they stay at in the kit when flying and performing.

Sample eye cluster-what I call a foil cluster

To keep things simplified to me I like to lump all these characteristics altogether and call it "type". To me "type" is everything you look at in a specific bird to include the aerial performance. This is what I say when I see I bird is I like the "type", now granted this could be without ever seeing the bird in the air at times, but the term is used in this manner so to speak. This is having a solid idea of what you are looking for in a bird, both on the ground and in the air. These characteristics that are all present in our birds will allow you to rank the bird in your own loft, based on these various characteristics.

When you begin putting birds in your stock loft many that you like will start to show in the "type" you see in the loft. We are all just naturally a little biased so to speak and there is really nothing that can be done about this, but one thing is true that the birds must possess the same high quality tight spin across the board, no matter how deep they are. Deviating on this attribute will not ruin your loft but if you do it too often it can negatively affect your program if you are not paying attention. We have all deviated from our standards for various reasons and the saying is "you pay for the feed, so you can do whatever you wish with your birds", but if you really want to progress your birds you need to be disciplined in what you select to breed from.

Everyone has to start with less than overall desired birds and then hopefully over time progress them to be all that you are looking for within a reasonable amount of time. The thing about rollers is that you are continuing to learn the longer you keep them and because of this your opinions tend to change from when you first start until you would be considered a seasoned veteran. There is no magic number this you will learn what needed skills and gain the experience needed to be successful, but most of it is paying attention to detail and then knowing what you want and how to get there. This can take you maybe 10 or more years before you are maybe confident you are going in the right direction, depending on your specific program and how many birds you like to keep and breed from. The more birds you have the longer this process normally will take. Rollers tend to always be a "work in progress" which is what keeps us so interested in these birds.

I find it a needed thing to rank your pigeons that are in stock. It's not just ranking them but also grading them based on their personal attributes and the "type" they possess. I personally have a scale I use that rates my birds in 6 categories, two of these categories are not fixed and you will not fully know the score until the bird has been in your stock loft for several seasons. These categories are as follow; Velocity, Style, Kitting, Depth, Overal Impression and Breeding-Prepotency. So as you see Overall Impression and Breeding-Prepotency, cannot be fully evaluated until they have been in the stock loft for a few seasons at least, and paired with multiple mates.

The basic of my grading system is that birds must have a minimum standard in order to make the stock loft. The higher the grade the better but the depth ratio kind of throws off the equation a bit and can make a bird appear to have a higher score when in reality the depth is really not even a concern to me. Depth is more like a "bonus" category. Depth also does not have any minimum standard for the birds to make the loft like other categories. For example; I rate the birds in Velocity, Style and Kitting on a scale of 1 to 10, all birds must be at graded at least a "7" in these three categories to make the stock loft. I would prefer higher more like 9+ in order to make the stock loft but I have found several over the years where birds that rated only a "7" in these categories can end up being some of my best breeders. I have learned to pay attention to other characteristics of the birds and their "type" to better assist me in picking them over other birds that are also worthy of the stock loft. The other characteristics are things you learn as you mature as a breeder and it takes pure experience to see some of it.

Pensom states in his book "The Birmingham Roller Pigeon" that a breeder does not fully understand the birds in hand until you have approximately 30 years of experience under you belt. This experience is invaluable and as many will say to you it's the characteristics that you can see in the birds as an individual bird that are hard to describe that are the characteristics I am referring to. It's hard to put a label on "type" when it has many different characteristics involved in that single word.

There are other things at work too that I really don't want to mention like "pedigree" as again like Pensom feared of pedigrees is a reality out there and they are only as good as the guy that wrote it. Pedigrees are basic breeding records and are best utilized by the fancier that bred the family of birds and not to the unskilled fanciers. I have been told that Pensom did not even give out pedigrees on his birds for the fear that others would use this information and create fictitious documents of specific birds for profit, I must say that Pensom was right in saying this as this behavior goes on all the time, back in Pensoms' era and this era. Unless the birds came directly said source or family breeders, then you really can't trust it 100%. Here is what Pensom said about the pedigree phenomenom, "Pedigree is an important asset in any loft, but its uses are restricted to recording how anything is bred and to be regarded as anything more can be fatal, for there is no reason to suppose that any two birds are identical in pedigree, that they are equal in merit. They are not, and never could be, and neither will two birds produce the same quality."

I have on several occasions stocked up birds that were never flown due to specific reasons and many of us have done this, but it had everything to do with circumstances and the specific "type" of the bird in question I can assure you. Breeders get old and with the ever worsening predation problems these days you can easily lose many invaluable birds in no time at all and this can be a way to preserve specific bloodlines that could be in jeopardy of losing what we feel are key birds to our progression. These birds will be tested solely in the breeding pen with specific goals in mind when we do this, and it is no way a habitual thing for the ones that possess their own family of birds. At least it should not be anything that is done even annually. Birds should be flown out for at least 1 season and if possible 2 seasons. If you aim to fly competitive kits the longer you can fly birds the better, as longevity is the key I feel.

This sort of thing happens when specific "types" are seen in birds, specific key characteristics and for those that know what I am talking about can only say it's a fact. These are again very subtle characteristics and not easily seen by the normal fancier.

I am in no way advocating the stocking of birds on blind faith or stocking based on pedigrees etc... I am just saying that that there are specific circumstances of which this can be used on a trial and error basis, most are willing to take a gamble on a few birds like this, as in the worst case scenario it does not work out you cull the bird and forget you ever did it. We can't disregard that these are performance rollers we need to select birds that roll properly and if you don't fly them then you will quickly be putting your program in jeopardy if you are not very cautious of what you aim to achieve in doing such things. So be warned that this is not a practice that should be used, especially for the new fancier of this game.

As a manager of my own loft, progression is the name of the game. If I am not able to select the proper birds each year that will progress my program along in a positive direction then it will not be long before I am actually regressing, and for many out there they are somehow never able to progress their birds and thus end up changing birds often. Just like if you have a job and you are not able to progress to be a productive employee in this job you will probably not have that job long, even if you are self-employed!! Progression is also a term that will mean different things from loft to loft, all of which is based on your present situation as a breeders and or competitor. Progression is simply this; moving your family of birds in a positive direction over a period of time, meaning making them better over time. It's never being completely satisfied with your rollers and continuing to do your best to make them better and better, not being satisfied with the birds on hand. It's these ideals that will keep you having an open mind and continuing to learn more and more about the birds on hand and how to get the most out of them.

I think it's very important to set goals for you loft. Maybe a goal for each season individually, a 5 year goal and maybe even a 10 year goal. It's better if you write this down somewhere so that you will see it from time to time to remind you. This is a way for you to remind yourself about what is most important to you and there is nothing wrong with updating this list of goals as you move forward either as we continue to learn more about the birds on hand.

Our Ideal

I mean these are performance pigeons after all, so how much can they really be different? Something you must always remember is that what may constitute as an ideal bird or champion caliber bird at one loft might be a cull to another fancier. We might say, how could this be? I think the basic qualities of every roller should be the ability to fly in a kit and perform with the kit, but some don't think this is true with the birds that some say "Fly Happy" and do whatever they want to do while in flight, so long as the bird performs the roll flawlessly nothing else matters. However if you want a World Class Birmingham Roller with undeniable quality of spin then there are standards one must follow in the selection process in regards to your stock loft and what kind of birds you breed from.

After breeding and flying my own family of the Birmingham Roller for more than 20 years now I have been able to identify things that are generally consistent among good spinners, subtle physical characteristics. I have also developed a skill of being able to select good spinners in high percentage in my family right out of the nest. When I try to explain this to others the best that I can describe in what I am seeing is a head and eye combination with expression or "type". I can see this in some as young as 2 weeks old.

I emphasize that quality of spin should be very similar in all birds that are stocked and other qualities that would lower their score are; depth, expression or character and other minor qualities of the birds temperament or overall impression of this bird and my opinion of it. These qualities I list are also very subjective but I would suggest that you set standards for your own loft and stick to these standards, set them high but not unrealistically high. There are so many subjective qualities our birds can have that you have to be realistic and progressive at the same time with these qualities. Depth, behavior in the kit, desire to return to the kit after performing, consistent quality of spin when flown are all part of my rating system you will use at your own loft.

When you have been working with the same close net gene pool long enough all the birds tend to resemble each other in type, size and even color at times. The birds become part of you and what you like unconsciously. You are only selecting for the best performers but you also look at things that are very subtle physical characteristics you don't even really think about much. I think part of this is just "stock sense" or from experience with birds. I think it is important that you keep a variety of colors within your family of rollers. Color balancing, as some called it, deals with breeding birds of soft and hard colors together to keep them active for competition/enjoyment. There are ways of balancing the birds with specific characteristics and yet other attributes like pure performance tend to stay consistent. There has been many fanciers over the years that have bred dark families for long periods of time and they tend to get stiffer generation after generation and much of this has to do with selection of specific pigeons.

After seeing a high quality spinner and then matching these with others to balance them in the hopes of giving us a higher percentage of spinners moving forward and many times percentages are the best we can improve upon in our own stock lofts. We never know exactly what birds these will be until we find out by trial and error. We do this through breeding and selection of key birds to put back into your stock loft.

There is no compromise in our pigeons. What I mean by this is that you have to select every pigeon for stock at the same caliber of quality spin no matter what the depth is. Part of this is also knowing what a high quality spin looks like! I think a lot to this comes down to experience of the specific handler. Just because you would like deeper birds does not mean you sacrifice the quality of the spin to get it. When you start to compromise quality you will also start to compromise other facets of you stock loft and things start to fall apart pretty quickly after that. It's best to just stay focused on what you are striving for with no deviation. However don't be afraid to dabble a little with experiments just don't let it dominate your program or you will get lost for sure.

High quality spinners are in fact rare and this has always been the case but through selective breeding you can increase your odds greatly through line breeding and inbreeding techniques. You have to pay very close attention the subtle differences between our best birds and the average good birds. Make note of these differences and they could be something as insignificant as the design of the wing(s) or flights, small characteristics of the eye, body type and even head shape. We never know what these will be until we start to develop our own birds into a type gene pool of related birds. These characteristics can be unique from family to family even.

Within our own gene pool the best birds will stand out and it is this type that they will gradually over time dominate your loft. I like to use the saying that type will produce type. If you select for performance only the rest will take care of itself they say. However developing a family based on select individuals has guidelines to follow on their own. Part of this is seeing a type and selecting the birds that resemble good stock birds and breeding them back to them with a thought process of developing a tight genetic gene pool you can rely on.

There are usually several types within a family of rollers and you will get cocks that have a similar type as a hen or vis-versa. You also get the occasional mutation in type as well which can be something that could be a distance throw back or even a new flair.

You will need to keep good records on your birds. This means production records and performance records as well. Performance records I feel should follow the birds from first starting to flip or roll until you stock it and everything else in between. This includes selling, gifting, loosing, dying or whatever, and anything else that would make the birds no longer alive and flying at your loft. Among the good things should be when the birds first begins to spin (age), the quality of it at this time, the stability of it when learning to roll and so on and so forth. Too much data is better than not enough data.

#82-90, my foundation hen that quickly became the center of my loft by 1993

A stock hen 4 generations and 19 years away from #82 and very similar in type

#548-92 one of the best producing cocks I ever bred, carries rec red mottle

Here's one of my 2015 season stock cocks 4 generations and 17 years from #548

Why is this bird so good? Does it possess specific characteristics some of the others don't?   Are there any connections within your own family of birds that relates to what the bird looks and acts like on the ground and in the air. Pay attention and you will do well.

I cannot emphasize enough to keep strict to your standards and keep good notes on all aspects of your program from feeding to flying and everything that you may think is significant or not. It's about training yourself to pay attention to the small details.

If you have any specific questions or concerns please feel free to contact me.

Deisie Invitation Roller Club

L/R Roy Dalton and Eamon Keogh

A New Roller club in the South/East part of Ireland is now formed with the above name.
Elected officers for the 2-15-16 Year are Eamon Keogh President and Roy Dalton-Club Secretary, Mark Dody Treasurer and Dominic Carton as Club Chairman.
We have adopted World Cup Fly rules with no young bird competitions. There is also a Champion Individual fly that will be scored on a sliding scale of 1 to 5 and will be flown in a small kit of 4 others.
Panel judging will be used with 3 judges with the score being averaged.
For more information
Roy 087-9907957 or Eamon 051-376501

Guest Writer

My Way…
The Irish Way part 2
By
Dominic Carton Waterford City, Ireland

Now ITS TO BE HOPED we have the quarters all set up for your birds, it's now time to discuss the occupants that we wish to house in THEIR KIT BOXS. Many will concur that is not a bad way to start out by gathering birds here and there all in the learning process for a newbie just joining this sport.

Here is Dom's loft assistant Jack feeding some birds

You can spend time learning the game before you really settle in on the birds you will end up with down the road. You can now take the time to figure out how TO feed and fly them properly as there is so much to learn. Like I mentioned it's not so much important AS to what birds you have at this time in developing your management skills.   It is ever so important that you put in the time to learn how to handle the birds correctly and the birds are really second to this way of thinking at this point. It is important to keep an open mind and try to put things to work that you see and hear about as it's with these methods that become the backbone of thinking for you in the future.

Now later when we decide. We need to obtain a good line of birds to begin with and this just refers to the bloodline(s) and nothing else. You are best to obtain a fly report and study these reports. The internet is a fantastic tool for this and gives us an incredible communication tool; we are able to chat and even get advice on who has the birds you are looking for. On the flip side it can also be a tool for the fly warriors who are forever bestowing the alleged ability of their own prowess with the birds and hopefully most of you are able to see through this bullshit, sooner rather than later.

Some of Dom's breeders

I never show much interest in a fancier or his line of birds who has to brag up about his own line of birds. I am much more interested in fanciers that let their birds do the talking, and it's my hope that you are able to find a fancier like this to assist you with birds. Now that you have familiarized yourself with some of what is needed in this journey of a roller man, it's time to get out and see some kits. It is very important at this time to ask questions and pay attention. There is really no such thing as a stupid question, only a stupid answer. Now hopefully after getting out and seeing some kits you have been able to identify the type of roller that you wish to proceed with in your program. It's time to talk to the flyer(s) and don't expect them to be rapturous that you have decided that it's his birds you want to choose and work with, if the birds are of good quality and consistency. I can assure you he has had many other queries regarding his birds, and maybe like myself, he might have been burned by a few over the years as this type are out there. I like to reference these are "serial buyers" who at one time or another have brought in many good lines of birds. However without guided input to properly handle and care for the birds they will soon regress, and for those type flyers, it always seems to be the birds fault. This type of fanciers is an absolute curse to the rollers and any sport I would imagine. They are absolute fountains of knowledge as regards to any line of rollers, yet totally incapable of ever being able to fly a semi descent kit at any time. It doesn't even matter of which line they have tried. Luckily these fanciers are in the minority, and please readers don't ever allow yourself to slide into this category.

Some of Dom's young birds

Getting back to the family of birds you have chosen to start your family from. If I was looking to start back up in rollers today, my type of bird or line would be the majority of them being capable of balling up nice and tight from the beginning of the roll and with good speed and going straight down, and always striving to in time develop a kit of such birds, and this is where your selection process comes in to affect, always selecting only your best. We need to understand that it's a learning process at all times, none of us will ever have all the answers, but select hard, but fair, is as good a yardstick as any to measure your achievements...realizing the type of bird we require, and working hard at all the time, will eventually be its own reward, as for myself am of the opinion ,as stated above, none of us will never know enough it's a never ending journey as to just how far we can bring these complex little bird in its evolution... As to my line of thought, the ability of the birds are vitally important, but it's the ability and knowledge of the flyer. That puts the shine on them... It is especially beneficial when the entire kit is doing it with big numbers, because this is the aim of the genuine roller guys. Its real rollers hitting it hard, often and in big numbers but always rolling correctly. These are the type of birds we need to aim for, the depth of roll is your choice and subjective to where you live, whether it's a built up urban area or open space rural area.

It is important to let this flyer know how serious you are in acquiring his birds. I would suggest getting young birds if at all possible. These give you a chance to instill your own behavior rules on them, but with older birds this would be impossible and what you see if what you get.

Now that you have been able to see his kit more than once it's time to ask him for birds bred along the lines of the birds you saw in his kits. Hopefully are able to obtain brothers or sisters to the birds you saw in his kit and if these cost money it's no big deal, unless the price is pretty stiff. By no means is it wrong to pay for birds but avoid spending big money on birds, but you need to make up your own mind. To me spending big bucks on birds is a no-no, and at the time of writing this well-bred youngsters are available for in this area at 20/ 30 Euros per bird.

I would also avoid the fanciers that would first suggest you take them home and lock them up to become breeders as yearlings. To me this has to be possibly the worst advice any seasoned roller man would give to a

One of Dom's Best cock birds

Newbie and more on this later. You should pay approximately 20-30 Euros for un-flown young birds. If the seller is a genuine lad he will be much more concerned about the health and well beings of the birds he is selling. You need to also stay away from lad who sell a lot of birds, these fanciers that appear to have a roller factory going on and see all visitors with dollar signs ($$$$). This behavior is a common with the feather merchants.

Now that you have the squeaks and you paid the price which is suitable for you both now it's very important to open up the lines of communication with this flyer and keep them informed on how the birds are doing. If for any reason you have to get out of rollers be sure to contact this flyer and offer them back to them. Giving them first chance at any of the birds is a common courtesy. A genuine roller man he sees nothing worse than to see good birds go to waste or frittered away. You will be far better to offer them back to him so that he will help you later on should you need help. You never want to allow yourself to look like an unworthy fancier to others in the sport. Good behavior will always help you out down the road, it will be like good luck down the road, and it is just the right thing to do.

Your next step that is very essential for your choice birds is to, if not already done, get them vaccinated for PMV, like all viruses you can't really afford to have it hit your loft and possibly kill your most valuable birds. For the birds sake just get them inoculated. Now that you have secured your prized rollers for many years it's time for more homework.

Get your birds flying and when you are feeding them observe their mannerisms, especially when feeding. Make take note of their behavior. It is not advised that you ever fly your birds unless you are able to watch them for the entirety of the flight. There is no reason to fly them if you can't watch them in the air. These flights need to be educational for you as it's enjoyable for them. I find flying once per day will suffice and or every other day once they come into the roll. I have never really seen a point to flying young birds more than once per day. You should enjoy watching your rollers fly and if you don't then you are probably not doing this for the right reasons. My young birds get a small amount of protein rich grains until have mature both physically and mentally.

It is no interest to me to starve the birds to bring on or force them into rolling earlier. The birds must be strong and well fed until they mature and at that time they are fed mostly a high carb diet with a small amount of protein laden seeds on a weekly basis. Often too much protein can cause health problems, but for me the birds are basically going to enjoy their time for the year of their birth. I only pull birds that become compulsive non-kitters or birds that just are not with the program and real problem. If you are reading this thinking that I am giving some insight on how to get your birds to roll early I am afraid you are reading the wrong article. I have no interest in doing it anyway and getting them to roll at an early age.

Many rollers will roll if given time to do so. The vast majority take approximately 6 months to start showing some roll. I also have little or no interest in young bird's competitions, if I had my way I would outlaw them entirely…LOL. This is bound to get a reaction…LOL.

I just feel that too many youngsters are ruined in their first season by being rationed with proper feeding as regards to their maturity. They are flown ceaselessly in most kind of weather and all this when these youngsters are going through their first moult. Often being deprived of proper feeding plus a descent nutrients when they need it the most. I am possibly in a majority of one with this line of thought, but this article does say…It's my way… the Irish way. I have many of my youngsters develop and make very good old birds.

Have a lot at a winning kit of youngsters as yearlings or even 2 year olds if they are still around. I am of the opinion that most lads only want to know how to fly youngsters as there is a real scarcity of good kits of yearlings or older kits around these days. I take good care of my youngsters and I can get years of enjoyment out of them rolling. I keep them up to 7/8 years and I have no interest in 4 month wonders, but this is your choice dear readers. You must decide for yourself.

Birds are molting ALL YEAR ROUND, but it's with the BIG MOULT when the birds need to be fed carefully. More about the moult later in these pages. Well cared for birds all go through this process on a yearly basis.

It's with these youngsters, no doubt, that you will see the best of them and indeed the worst of them. It's up to you and what you do with them in this first year which will determine how well behaved they will be. It is important to instill good habits at a young age and these can stay with them forever, likewise bad habits that they might develop can be difficult to break as well. Always feed them 24 hours apart and they will do well. Do this later in the day and never early in the day. When they are young leave them out to sit on the loft with a miniscule of grain in their crops and teach them to enter the loft and use your method of feeding to get them in, shaking the feed can or whistling. I get them use to both these sounds before they ever venture outside the loft. At the risk of repeating myself yet again, observe and observe again especially at feeding time.

I also find if very important to not feed the birds immediately after they fly. Give them an hour to rest, especially if some of them have been working hard. If you don't allow the birds to rest the birds that need the most will not get what they need due to a lack of appetite from tiredness. So it's just a good habit to feed them at least 1 hour after they land. Don't be afraid to pull an extra tired bird out individually and feed it up separately at times either. Watch the birds as they eat and see what they are doing, you can see birds when they are acting out of sorts. Use this same feeding methods on your old bird team as well.

It's as youngsters that we are able to learn so much about our birds, by observing them as often as possible. This is why I have a seat in my loft so I can sit and watch them up close and personal. It is important to have all the birds working off the same mind set, so to speak, like a form of telepathy. Even when the kits are flying and working, seldom to they hit each other in a break. We need those type of birds, that hold their place in the kit and their presence is not a hindrance to any other bird rolling in the kit.

I have no doubt what so ever that if we can manage to get almost a full kit of the same type of birds with the proper mental attitude we will automatically see huge volumes of big breaks if we are breeding for proper rollers, that ball up tight with good speed and spin straight down in without hitting each other in a split second. We will need this type of bird in our programs. Mentally weak birds are inclined to be anywhere in the kits position when a break is made. One of two weak minded birds in a kit are capable of turning a pretty decent kit into a very mediocre one. It is us as handlers to weed out these weak birds and it all starts as soon as they are eating on their own.

As soon as my young birds are weaned to the kit boxes they learn to eat on a tray. I am always handling them for their first 8-10 days in the kit box, bullying them playfully and trying to earn their trust. I don't want to appear as a threat to them, and for me this is essential as I can't stand wild or scared type pigeons about my place. Consistently birds that are always hungry are the ones that don't develop quite right, for lots of reasons. Poor eaters, the ones that extend their wings for food, and ones that only seem to eat the smaller grains. There is a whole multitude of reason to be looking to out these type of birds, and as sure as night follows day... they will CAUSE YOU SOME BOTHER LATER ON…

If you are trying to build a good kit of rollers, they may indeed be good rollers…but good kit rollers is a different story and good rollers gives us about the same chance of winning the lotto…Never…

Now you should never see these kind of rollers in your old bird kit. The selection process you practice with young birds should take care of these and we can never stop observing the birds, they can't talk but they are still able to tell us a great deal about themselves. If we are able to recognize what is going on than we are on our way to learning more. Don't forget that we train them and we can determine their behavior for the rest of their lives. Under no circumstances should we allow them to develop bad habits. I apply the 3 strikes rule and after that its jelly regardless of what good habits it may be showing. If it is unable to behave like the rest using the same methods in a situation where space is limited then I have no place for it here.

When the young formative months are finished, they are what they are and are almost incapable of learning good habits, but they will remember bad habits they had learned and if allowed to develop in them. It is very important to let your birds know that you are not to be feared so you really need to handle them as much as possible. Never grab them or upset the rest of the birds when catching one of them. Don't let anyone else catch your birds either as they can sense the difference in strangers. Intermingle with them at all times, these methods are just like getting the environment of your loft structure correct and will pay you back 10 fold in the coming years.

As I pointed out you will be working with these birds for many years, at least I hope you are. The last thing you need around are birds that are distrustful of your presence. Fly them out at regular times in the first few months and how much you fly them is entirely on you and your schedule. I enjoy getting the birds out once per day and not forgetting that you are flying your old bird kit on some of them days also. The last thing I want to do is spend all my time flying birds and most of us have many other things that consume our time during the day. If I can fly my young birds 5 times a week for the first few months then I am doing well. I consider my time flying these birds an adventure for them. It will not be long before they come on to the roll and I drop their flying to 4 days a week, with always a 24 hour feeding gap between flights.

It's also important with young birds that you don't allow them lift. Try to keep their flying down low until they develop a habit of it. You need to be able to control the feed just enough that they are not hungry all the time and at the same time they will not lift. Many times there might be certain birds in the kit that are making them lift and you will need to identify these birds, these birds will need more attention, but I always give these protein in their feed until their bodies are matured. The "heavy" feed tends to keep them from lifting too high. Again getting the feed and quality right is paramount to how they fly and behave. When those balmy summer evenings come we all love to sit in the garden spending time with the birds.

Should the birds get into them hot rising air thermals I find it much easier to feed them in 12-14 hours before they fly and are fed their normal feed. I also give them some peas and do this three times in succession. While the birds may not perform very well with the 12 hour feed in them, this will normally keep them from lifting. Once these thermals are gone get them back to their 24 hour feeding plan.

The rest is down to themselves and I never bother them. I get them on a steady feed schedule and amounts of proteins needed. All living and growing creatures need protein and if they can't not get the proper amount of protein when they need it you will never be able to get them right later on in life and this is another reason I am not in favor of these young birds flies.

To me rollers are all about the finished article, adult birds who are right in their minds. If we handle the birds correctly they will eventually give us many years of pleasure as old birds.

arkansasrollerclub.com

Arizona Performing Roller Club

Jose Jimenez

623.209.9436

josejimenez155@msn.com

**1995 Redding Area Flyers: Daryl Rhoades, Fred Boyer, Illene Aadlad
Dave Henderson, Joe Urbon and John Leake**

**Classic Pic: Dave Henderson, Dan Swayne, Keith Caywood,
Carl Schoelkopf, Bill Schrieber and Ivan Hanchett at Bill's**

Printed in Poland
by Amazon Fulfillment
Poland Sp. z o.o., Wrocław

53010466R00119